ROBERT KEATS
BORDER GUIDE

Plaudits from Canada's Business and Financial Press

"Eases cross-border strain ...the questions are trickier than they look and not amenable to easy answers...The Border Guide is as good a place as any to start."

— Ellen Roseman, The Globe and Mail

"The Border Guide is a must for anyone who has ever considered investing, purchasing property, or seasonal residence in the United States."

— Canadian MoneySaver

"You can take it with you, to the United States!"

— The Toronto Star

"Blows away some popular misconceptions...discusses ways to live in the U.S. but still get maximum tax advantages from RRSPs in Canada."

— Saskatoon Star Phoenix

"The strategy works best for anyone with a large RRSP plus a substantial investment or pension income."

— The Montreal Gazette

"Provides an in-depth look at cross-border financial planning."

— The Simcoe Reformer

"Many higher income people at or near retirement age are seriously considering taking up residence elsewhere to avoid Canada's increasingly onerous tax burden."

— Gordon Pape, The MoneyLetter

"The Border Guide is a comprehensive cross-border financial tool."

— Alexandra Eadie, The Globe and Mail

"International financial consultant Robert Keats is the only financial planner in North America to hold both U.S. and Canadian professional designations"

— The Financial Post

ROBERT KEATS
BORDER GUIDE

A CANADIAN'S GUIDE TO INVESTMENT, IMMIGRATION TAX & RETIREMENT PLANNING IN THE UNITED STATES

The Ontario Motorist Publishing Company
Windsor, Ontario Canada

Edited by
Douglas O'Neil

ROBERT KEATS
BORDER GUIDE

Copyright © 1997
The Ontario Motorist Publishing Company

Written by:
Robert Keats

Published by:
The Ontario Motorist Publishing Company
1253 Ouellette Avenue
Windsor, Ontario, N8X 1J3, Canada
Printed in Canada

ISBN 1-895654-11-4 5th Revised Edition, 1997

website: www.ompc.com ~ e-mail: borderguide@ompc.com

TO ORDER CALL TOLL-FREE
1-800-933-OMPC (6672)

This book is dedicated to my late father
Gordon Keats, (1922-1992).
May he rest in peace with our heavenly Father.

The Border Guide

CONTENTS

Chapter 1
CROSSING THE BORDER

Chapter 2
THE VALUE OF A BUCK

Chapter 3
THE TAXMAN COMETH

Chapter 4
YOU STILL CAN'T TAKE IT WITH YOU

Chapter 5
DOCTOR IN THE HOUSE

Chapter 6
TAKE THE MONEY & RUN

Chapter 7
COMING TO AMERICA

Chapter 8
THE GRASS IS ALWAYS GREENER

Chapter 9
GIVE MY REGARDS TO WALL STREET

Chapter 10
TAKING CARE OF BUSINESS

Chapter 11
IN GOD WE TRUST

Appendix A

Appendix B

Appendix C

Appendix D

Appendix E

Appendix F

Appendix G

Appendix H

The Border Guide

ACKNOWLEDGEMENTS

No man is an island. This book with its five editions could not have been possible without the assistance of many people. I have been blessed with a lovely family; my wife Barbara and my children Sarah, Daniel, Carl and Rebekah, who have been my inspiration. My only regret in writing this book was the time I had to spend away from them all.

The research required to prepare any book of this scope is enormous, even under ideal circumstances. Taking highly technical topics such as immigration, tax planning and estate planning between Canada and the United States, and presenting them in a format that is both logical and readable, has been a particularly formidable task. I would like to acknowledge Tom Connelly, my partner of ten years for providing a great deal of the material for the chapters on investments and currency speculation.

Brent M. Gunderson LLP, a Phoenix immigration attorney reviewed all of the immigration issues presented in Chapter 7. I thank him for both his time and prudent counsel.

The vast majority of this book was conceived and written in a wonderful little cabin nestled among the tall pines of northern Arizona. I would like to thank Teresa Bertocchi, a long-time family friend, for the use of her cabin. I will never forget the fresh mountain air, the spectacular thunderstorms and the warmth of the fireplace. A special thanks to Robin Ingle and Ingle Health Insurance for providing me with much of the material included in Chapter 5.

I would also like to thank all of you who read the first four editions of this book, for your positive comments and enthusiastic support. My final and biggest thank you goes to all of our cross-border Canadian clients. Without their interest and encouragement, I would have never been in a position to write this book.

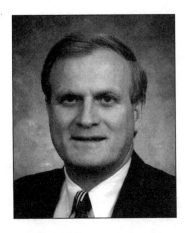

Robert Keats is an internationally known expert in cross-border financial planning. His views on how Canadians can better manage their financial affairs have been featured on numerous Canadian and U.S. TV and radio programs, *The Financial Post, The Globe and Mail, The L.A. Times, The Dow Jones Investment Advisor, Good Times* magazine and other international media. He is the publisher of *The Sunbelt Canadian* newsletter, and a financial columnist for *The Sun Times of Canada*, a Florida based newspaper for Canadians.

Besides writing and conducting workshops, Keats is also the founding partner of Keats, Connelly & Associates, in Phoenix, AZ., the only U.S. based fee-only firm to specialize in cross-border planning.

Keats began his financial planning career in 1976, after retiring as a Captain in the Canadian Armed Forces. A graduate of the University of Manitoba, he was one of the first U.S. planners to earn a Master of Science degree in Financial Planning from the College of Financial Planning in Denver, Colorado. He is currently the only person in North America to hold the highest financial planning certification available in both the U.S. and Canada. (CFP, M.S.F.P. and RFP) He currently resides in Phoenix, Arizona and his other interests include family, church and volunteer work.

The Border Guide

Canadians usually feel completely at home in the U.S., because our two nations' social and cultural institutions bear such a strong resemblance to one another. Many incorrectly assume that the laws governing investment, taxation, and immigration are the same as well. Unfortunately, this assumption can lead to some unpleasant surprises, particularly when conducting basic financial transactions, such as buying or selling American real estate. The Canada-U.S. Free Trade Agreement and more recently the North American Free Trade Agreement (NAFTA) have only served to fuel the fires of cross-border commerce. In addition many Canadians have migrated to the Sunbelt seeking temporary or permanent respite from harsh, Canadian winters.

The Border Guide was written for Canadians who are considering some form of permanent or seasonal residency in the United States. It will also prove useful for U.S. citizens living in Canada, or who are married to Canadian spouses. It will be of particular value to those of you who intend to invest, or do business in the U.S, even if your financial curiosity is limited to an occasional shopping trip or vacation. Whatever your interest, the information contained in these pages will help you to transact your cross-border business affairs, with competence, and with confidence. It is the only step-by-step guide for Canadians who want to understand and take advantage of American and Canadian tax, financial, and medical institutions. It will also show you how to avoid many of the common pitfalls of having assets, and spending extended periods of time in both countries.

In order to prevent this book from becoming the type of dry technical manual that is factually accurate, but functionally useless, we have presented our ideas in a non-technical fashion. Certain concepts have occasionally been simplified in the service of readability. Sound professional advice is also recommended for the application of any of the ideas or techniques detailed in this guide.

Crossing The Border

AN INTRODUCTION TO PERSONAL
CROSS-BORDER FINANCIAL PLANNING

1

T he economic and tax environment between the United States and Canada has grown in breadth and complexity over the past few years, and with it, the need for comprehensive personal cross-border financial planning. The intent of such planning is to capitalize on the most satisfactory mix of savings plans, insurance coverage, investment vehicles, tax strategies, retirement plans and estate planning techniques available in each country. Applied to your own specific needs and goals, these cross-border planning opportunities can reap great financial rewards for you and your heirs.

Cross-border financial planning encompasses all the basic individual financial planning requirements of both Canada and the United States, in the areas of net worth, cash flow, risk management, retirement goals, taxation, estate planning and investments. It analyses each area according to your particular situation, and then weighs option against option, completes timely currency conversions, factors in your immigration status, examines applicable tax treaty rules, and develops a road map for you to follow, to achieve your financial goals with maximum income, safety and tax savings.

One of the major difficulties inherent in cross-border financial planning is that the rules change depending on immigration status. For example, a winter visitor to the United States marrying a United States resident dramatically alters his or her financial planning options, and a new cross-border financial plan becomes necessary in order to take advantage of new opportunities and to avoid any mistakes. Figure 1.1 lists all the major immigration status options. All of the important planning issues for each respective status category are discussed in detail, in subsequent chapters of this book.

HOW LONG CAN YOU REMAIN IN THE U.S. AS A VISITOR?

Few things cause more confusion and controversy among winter visitors than how long they can legally remain in the United States without breaking any rules. The source of this confusion is primarily due to the fact, that there are at least four sets of rules governed by different government agencies that deal with residency. These residency rules sometimes conflict, and adherence to one set of rules does not automatically mean compliance with the others. The four sets of rules that tell you how much time you can legally spend in the United States are listed as follows:

1. The Immigration Rules. Canadian visitors to the United States may enter the country without any actual visa being issued. Technically, they fall into the B-2 visitor category (or B-1 for those entering for business purposes) allowing them to legally remain in the U.S. for up to six consecutive months. The B-1 business visitors can only conduct business on behalf of their Canadian employer and all compensation must come from the Canadian side of the border. Extensions to the six month

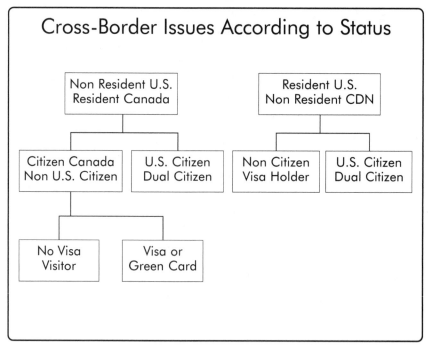

FIGURE 1.1

limit, primarily for medical reasons, may be granted by applying to the Immigration and Naturalization Service (INS). If you leave the United States and re-enter at any border crossing, including those between Mexico and the U.S., the six month clock starts over again each time you enter the United States. This does not mean you can legally keep leaving the U.S. and re-entering every six months perpetually because your intentions have changed from a casual visitor to resident. You will be stopped from re-entering the country, if it appears that you have taken up permanent residency, and may be asked to show proof you have not. Proof that you have not become a United States resident can be whatever the immigration official at the border decides, but will likely include one or more of such simple things as your last three months utility bills, a provincial drivers license, or a property tax notice. Chapter 7 provides further direction for those Canadian visitors who wish to legally become permanent residents of the United States.

2. The Income Tax Rules. Generally speaking, a person will be classified as a U.S. resident for tax purposes, if he or she is regularly present in the country for more than four months each year under the "substantial presence test" detailed in Chapter 3. Note that the number of days present in the U.S. need not be consecutive. An individual can be deemed a resident of the United States for tax purposes, although they may not have any right to remain in the country under the immigration rules. Thus, a person may become subject to income tax in the United States on their world income, without having the right to remain legally within its borders for more than six months as a visitor. Consequently, it is much easier to become a resident of the United States for tax purposes as noted in Chapter 3, than to become a permanent resident under immigration rules as explained in Chapter 7. It is also possible to be a resident for tax purposes, of both Canada and the United States, at the same time with the Canada/US Tax Treaty providing the tie breaker rules to settle this issue.

3. The Estate Tax Rules. What estate tax is, and how it applies to non-residents is covered in detail in Chapter 4 and in Chapter 8 for U.S. residents. Unlike income tax and immigration, there is no clear set of rules of residency for estate taxes. Residency is based on a series of facts and circumstances. Some of the factors that determine residency or "domicile" for estate tax purposes are: The relative size and nature of

your permanent homes in Canada and the United States, the amount of time spent in each country, your immigration status in the U.S., written declarations on such documents as wills or tax returns, the locations of your significant assets and important papers, personal, family and business connections. Generally, Canadians who clearly visit the United States, have no U.S. green cards and whose intent is to routinely return to Canada each year could not be considered to have given up domicile in Canada, and would not be subject to American estate tax on their world-wide assets. Court cases, where the IRS has challenged a Canadian winter visitor's estate, by attempting to tax world-wide assets of the deceased, have failed. The IRS was unsuccessful in those cases, because there must be a clear intent to give up one domicile for another. Visitors to the U.S. may still be subject to the non-resident estate tax on their U.S. located assets. This will be explained in greater detail in Chapter 4.

4. The Provincial Medicare Rules. These sets of rules are unique, because they act in direct opposition to the tax and immigration residency rules, by stipulating that you cannot be away from your home province for longer than a specified period of time. In 1991 Ontario, Quebec and Saskatchewan joined the remaining Canadian provinces by requiring that you must normally be present in the province for a minimum of six months a year, and have a permanent residence available to you there to remain eligible for provincial medicare. The amount of time included in the time out of province to potentially lose medicare from some provinces also includes time spent in other Canadian provinces, as well as outside the country. In most provinces, once you've lost provincial medicare, you will have to wait three months as a returning resident to reinstate your coverage.

We are often asked "How does a particular government department responsible for enforcing any of the above rules, know how much, and where you are spending your time?"

The fact of the matter is, they do not always necessarily need to know. Instead, they pass the burden of proof on to you, by asking you to declare, under penalty of perjury, that the facts you present regarding your travel itinerary are true. You should also be aware that we live in a computer age where information is easily stored and retrieved. This information is increasingly being shared by various government agencies and government owned corporations.

WHERE TO LIVE OR WINTER IN THE U.S.

The nature of cross-border financial planning will often be determined by which U.S. state you chose to reside or vacation in. This guide is not meant to provide you with a visitor's bureau style brochure about which Sunbelt state is the best, but examines some of the major tax implications of the three most popular Sunbelt states: Arizona, California and Florida. In Appendix B, we will provide tax rates and other technical data on these, and other popular states. From both a climatic and amenity standpoint, the reasons why Arizona, California and Florida are popular with Canadians can be summarized in a collection of comments from long time residents or visitors to one or more of the three states:

ARIZONA

- Offers the most sunshine of almost any populated area in North America. Expect clear skies nearly 85% of the time, and an annual rainfall of 6 inches (15cm). Winter daytime temperatures range from 65° to 85°F (18° to 30°C) in the Phoenix and Tucson areas.

- Great for people with arthritis because of the dry climate. Not so good for allergy sufferers, since something is always in bloom.

- Golfers paradise. There are more than 138 golf courses in the Phoenix area alone that are open 365 days a year.

- Geographically diverse state from the Grand Canyon to mountain high country to Sonoran desert. There is decent snow skiing in northern parts of the state during winter, and plenty of year-round water sports on the numerous man-made reservoirs and lakes.

- Arizona has embarked on a series of income tax reductions that may eventually eliminate state income taxes altogether. This will make it one of the least taxed states in the country and very desirable for a retirement haven from a tax perspective, much like Florida.

- The most frequently mentioned drawback about Arizona is that if you chose to stay in the Phoenix area during the summer, you can face average daily high temperatures of over 100°F (38°C). Popular retirement communities like Prescott in the central part of the state offer four distinct seasons (although snow is rare) and an ambience not unlike a small town in New England.

CALIFORNIA

- Plenty of sun and ocean. Temperatures vary considerably from the coast to the inland desert, with the coastal areas having less extreme temperature changes because of the moderating effect of the Pacific Ocean. The Palm Springs area has a climate almost identical to that of southern Arizona.

- Major man-made and natural tourist attractions abound, such as Disneyland, Hollywood and Big Sur.

- The ocean provides plenty of opportunity for sailing, fishing and whale watching.

- Geographically diverse state from the miles of spectacular coastlines to the mountains, farmland, vineyards and desert.

- The major drawback of this state is its population, which is more than all of Canada, causing gridlock on the freeways, and a great deal of pollution. Because Palm Springs lies next to a major fault, many Canadian visitors got shaken by the earthquakes in the spring of 1992 and winter of 1993. California also is noted for its high cost of living and relatively high taxes.

FLORIDA

- Very mild climate with a minimal range between winter to summer temperatures, 70° to 90°F (20° to 32°C) on average. Expect plenty of rain year round, and high humidity during summer.

- Provides two surprisingly different coasts, the Atlantic and the Gulf. Each has miles of beautiful beaches, islands and keys and all the year-round water sports that go with them.

- Like California, major man-made tourist attractions such as Disney World, Universal Studios and Cape Kennedy are located there.

- Florida has no personal income tax.

- It is easy to get to Florida by car from Ontario, Quebec and the Maritimes.

- This state offers the most services for Canadians. It has several radio and TV stations broadcasting Canadian news in both French and English. In addition, it has several major Canadian weekly newspapers.

- The major complaint about Florida seems to be that it is getting too crowded, particularly on the Atlantic coast, and its high humidity and hurricane season.

POPULAR CROSS-BORDER MISCONCEPTIONS

One of the primary purposes of this book is to dispel many of the popular misconceptions Canadians have about living, visiting and investing in the United States. Some of the more common misconceptions are:

- You lose money changing Canadian dollars to U.S. dollars!

  No, there is no loss exchanging one currency for another, other than the commissions you pay as a transaction cost. You don't make a profit changing U.S. dollars to Canadian dollars either. See Chapter 2 for a more complete explanation of this popular misconception.

- Canada has no estate or inheritance taxes!

  Wrong, Canada's deemed disposition tax on death on RRSPs or RRIFs and appreciated property can be as high as 54%. Many provinces also levy significant probate fees. For smaller estates Canadian estate taxes are frequently much higher than those in the U.S. See Chapters 4 and 8 for further details on this tax.

- The new 1995 amendment to the Canada — U.S. Tax Treaty eliminates the U.S. non-resident estate taxes.

  No, some Canadians are actually worse off under this new treaty and many are unaffected by the new rules. These rules are much more complex than the old rules so a new level of understanding is required to determine if you are any better off . See Chapter 4 for the real scoop.

- RRSP's can be left alone if you move to the U.S.!

  Leaving your RRSP's in Canada when you move to the U.S. can create many potentially costly tax problems, and you may miss opportunities to withdraw them at no, or very low tax rates. Chapter 8 will discuss how to remove your RRSP free from net income tax, once you have taken up residence in the U.S.

- You will earn lower rates of interest investing in the U.S.!

  For the first time in over 25 years U.S. banks are paying higher rates of interest on savings accounts and short term deposits. However, overall diversified investment portfolios earn about the same rate of return, for a similar level of risk in both Canada and the U.S. Chapters 6 and 9 provide further insight into this misconception.

- Wills are all you need for a complete estate plan!

  Wills are very necessary, but there are more effective estate planning vehicles like living trusts and living wills, that may provide for less estate settlement costs and better estate management. See Chapters 4 and 8 for a further explanation.

- Investing in the U.S. means you must file U.S. tax returns!

  No, there are a large number of investments that you can invest in the U.S. that are exempt from taxes and any filing or reporting requirements. Chapter 6 lists the investments that are exempt from U.S. taxes for non-residents.

- You can't be a citizen of Canada and the U.S. at the same time!

  Wrong, dual citizenship is possible, and has been for several years. Chapter 7 explains dual citizenship status.

- You lose your CPP and OAS by moving to the U.S.!

  No, you keep all these benefits, and in reality you will likely keep much more of your CPP and OAS after taxes once you have become a resident taxpayer of the United States. Chapter 8 provides the calculations to show you some of the tax savings available on CPP and OAS when a Canadian moves to the U.S.

- Medical insurance is too expensive in the U.S.!

  Some U.S. health insurance is expensive, however those under 65 can obtain very good coverage with high deductibles for less than $200 per month for up to a $1,000,000 limit of coverage. Those over 65 are usually eligible for U.S. Medicare, at no, or reasonable costs. Chapters 5 and 9 provide further details for those needing health insurance in the U.S.

- Investments in the U.S. are riskier than in Canada!

  No, the same rules of prudent investing apply in both countries. Because there are more investment choices in the U.S., there can be greater opportunity for an inappropriate investment to be chosen. This greater selection also allows prudent investors to find a larger number of safe investments in the U.S. at lower costs.

WHAT IS THE CANADA - U.S. TAX TREATY?

One of the most important documents for the protection of a Canadian's financial assets in the United States is the Canada — U.S. Tax Treaty. Most Canadians however, are completely unaware of its existence, and the benefits it provides them. Even though tax planning is an important part of cross-border planning, it is our experience that few financial advisors have ever cracked the cover of this treaty on behalf of their clients. They tend to focus instead, on the tax rules of their own, individual countries.

Canada and the United States signed their first full tax treaty in 1942, with subsequent amendments in 1950, 1956, 1966 , 1980, and 1994. The most recent amendment was written in 1994 & 1995, and took effect in 1996. It is undoubtedly, the most important tax treaty for both Canada and the United States. Millions of Canadians and Americans are affected by this agreement, and insofar as Canada and the United States continue as each other's major trading partner, its impact will only increase.

The Canada — U.S. Tax Treaty attempts to accomplish the same goals as any tax treaty: The prevention of tax measures that may discourage trade and investment, reaching a common ground on the taxation of non-residents to avoid double taxation on the same income, and to protect the domestic treasury. To a large extent the Canada — U.S. Tax Treaty has accomplished these goals. However, changes in domestic tax rules, in the area of non-resident estate tax in the United States, which took effect in 1988, prompted a new round of treaty negotiations that began in 1989, and concluded in 1994 with several technical corrections in 1995.

The two countries negotiated an estate tax article which was added to the existing treaty. For some people this will resolve the potentially high non-resident estate tax, and/or capital gains tax that Canadians face if they hold United States real estate and stocks. The U.S. non-resident estate tax and the effects of the new treaty will be covered in greater detail in Chapter 4.

Up until now, Canadian winter visitors have been able to use the Canada — U.S. Tax Treaty protection by default, without having to make any active filings or declarations. Current regulations now require that formal statements be filed with the Internal Revenue Service (IRS) forcing Canadians who spend four to six months in the U.S., to become more aware of the treaty, and how it can help them, if they do not wish to be taxed on

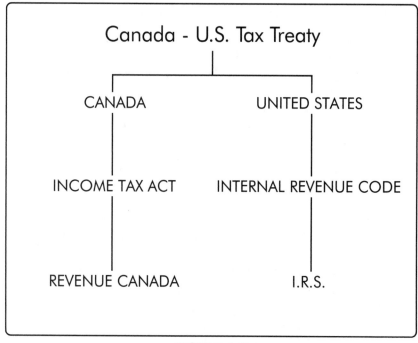

FIGURE 1.2

their world income in both the United States and Canada. Chapter 3 has been designed to show you who must file returns or statements in the United States, and under what circumstances these returns must be filed.

The Canada — U.S. Tax Treaty is one of the most important tools used in cross-border financial planning for two key reasons:

- The terms of the treaty take precedence over almost all the Canadian Income Tax Act (ITA) rules in Canada and the Internal Revenue Code (IRC) tax rules in the United States.

- The terms of the treaty seldom change. The Canada — U.S. Tax Treaty has been amended only five times in its 53 year history and can be relied on to a much greater degree for long term planning than either the Canadian Income Tax Act(ITA) or the American Internal Revenue Code(IRC). The ITA and IRC are subject to constant revision without notice, and impacted by the effects of annual budgets, bipartisan politics and election campaigns.

CROSS-BORDER Q&A

Many of the issues covered in the preceding chapter of this book have been touched upon in the author's weekly column *Cross-border Q&A*, which appears in *The Sun Times of Canada*, published in Tampa, Florida and circulated throughout the U.S. Sunbelt for Canadians living or wintering there. The majority of these questions have been posed by readers of the Sun Times and/or readers of the previous editions of *The Border Guide*. Most were looking for advice relating to their own specific problems or situations. At the end of this chapter, we have included some typical reader questions, along with our response, to illustrate and broaden the concepts presented in the preceding chapter.

RULES GOVERN U.S. RESIDENCE

I am a Canadian, female, 48 years old. I have been in Florida since September 1993 and intend staying here permanently if all problems can be solved. Unfortunately, I do not qualify for a green card. I do have a social security number. I intend to cross the border every six months to fulfil Canadian legal requirements. My health insurance terminates as of March 26, 1995, and most American health insurance companies require you be a permanent resident.

#1 Problem: Is health insurance possible to attain? If so, could you please recommend one?

#2 Problem: Am I considered a full-time resident?

#3 Problem: My car has Ontario plates and registration. Am I better returning my car to Canada and buying one here or can I change the plates and registration here? What does it entail?

#4 Problem: Do I need specific documents from Canada to obtain car insurance in Florida?

#5 Problem: I would like to buy a house in Florida with a friend. What must I do to insure my heirs have no problems?

I look forward to hearing from you shortly.

— *Susan G. Kissimmee, Florida*

Problem #1: This can be solved through the use of either a U.S. health insurance carrier who requires that you have only a U.S. address or using a non-U.S. insurance company such as Lloyd's of London or a Danish company called Danmark International Health Insurance.

Problem #2: This problem has a yes, a maybe and a precautionary answer depending on which perspective your are looking at. You would be a resident of the U.S. for tax purposes since you will be spending more than 183 days in the U.S. For insurance purposes the answer is a maybe, because each company has its own definition of what constitutes a resident. For immigration purposes you would likely be classed as an illegal alien resident since your intent is to live in the U.S. full time without a green card or visa. Simply leaving the country for a short time every six months to renew your visitor status does not mean you are escaping the need for a legal immigration status. When you leave the U.S. and attempt to re-enter as a visitor the U.S. immigration official can simply refuse you entry if he or she thinks your are living in the U.S. permanently without proper status. Because of all the things you are trying to do such as buying U.S. heath insurance, a car and a house you have all the makings of a resident, not a visitor, and would have to effectively mislead the immigration officials to gain entry as a visitor when you are in fact a resident. Purposely misleading an immigration official is considered more serious than being an illegal alien. You should speak to a good immigration attorney as soon as possible.

Problem #3: There is nothing preventing you from selling your car in Ontario and buying a new one registered in Florida. However there are numerous regulatory hoops you need to jump through in Florida to import a Canadian car into this jurisdiction.

Problem #4: This depends on which insurance company you talk to but most will require that you provide proof of a clean driving record and a valid Florida drivers license.

Problem #5: If you wish to keep your half of the house separate from your friend's in the event of your demise it would likely be best to register the property as Joint Owner as Tenants in Common. This will allow you to transfer by will, your share of the residence separately to each of your respective heirs. You should also have a valid Florida will. Before you go into a Tenants in Common situation you need to seek some professional advice so that you understand it fully and weigh it against other alternatives before you use it.

The Value of a Buck

Regular visitors who plan an annual winter migration to the Sunbelt, often exhibit symptoms of confusion, helplessness and insomnia, just prior to leaving the country. This highly contagious phenomenon is known as the *Exchange Rate Blues.* A general feeling of malaise develops when the soon to be departed snowbird begins calling banks or poring over the financial pages of the newspaper. This is done in an often futile attempt to pick the best possible moment to convert their hard earned Canadian dollars into American currency. Questions like "should I wait until _____ " (fill in the blank with an appropriate response such as: tomorrow, next week, until the Bank of Canada sets its rate, or the exchange rate goes up another cent, etc.) feverishly run though the mind of a traveller infected with the Exchange Rate Blues. Finally, the deal is struck and the currency exchanged, but the very next day the Exchange Rate Blues continue when new symptoms known as the "I should haves" appear. "I should have waited until _____ " (again fill in the blank with the appropriate response like "when the exchange rate improved" if dollar went up or if it went the other way, "I should have changed more.") It's funny that when the dollar is trading around 70 cents U.S. we'd give our right arm to exchange at 75 cents, but when the dollar reaches that level we still want to hold off for a better rate.

I have spoken to thousands of Canadians in the United States, and every one of them including myself has suffered from the Exchange Rate Blues at one time or another. The vast majority usually start feeling the symptoms around August.

ELIMINATING THE EXCHANGE RATE BLUES

Most people wouldn't dream of becoming currency speculators to earn money for their retirement because of the risks. However, going through the annual guessing game of which way the Canadian dollar is going, is precisely that; currency speculation. In fact, currency speculation is the root cause of the Exchange Rate Blues. The Exchange Rate Blues by the way, is very similar to the feeling novice commodity traders go through every time they make a trade.

How do you avoid currency speculation and cure the Exchange Rate Blues? The answer is very simple. Place enough income producing assets in U.S. dollar generating investments before retirement. These should produce sufficient income to safely cover expenses during your stays in the United States. This is simply a variant of the time-honoured tradition of not putting all of your eggs in one basket. You will be diversified against currency risk, and hedged against rapid fluctuations in either currency. You'll also save the commissions that financial institutions build into their exchange rates. These commissions are particularly high when small sums are exchanged. To determine the rate of commission, compare the rate listed in the financial sections of the newspaper, with that posted at your bank or at the airport on the same day. It can be as high as 3% or more.

HEDGING YOUR BETS

Almost every corporation conducting cross-border commerce practices some form of currency hedging. A Canadian airline for example, knows that next year, it needs to pay for that new Boeing 767 they just ordered. They need to generate more U.S. income from their assets, or purchase a currency futures contract locking in the current U.S. dollar rate; in effect an insurance policy that they will enjoy the current exchange rate or better, when the jet has to be paid for. Failure to hedge or reduce their currency risk exposure in this situation, might mean paying millions more, based solely on fluctuations in the Canadian dollar.

Canadians, who spend any part of their retirement south of the border, will require U.S. funds. If you are currently age 65, and want to maximize your time in the sunny south, you'll need at least $180,000 US, in today's dollars, to fund 15 years of six month stays at a spending level of just $2,000 U.S. per month. If you do not protect yourself, or hedge your currency risk like the Canadian airline, your retirement in the United States could end up costing you thousands of dollars more. Figure 2.1 shows the year end Canadian dollar values, as expressed in U.S. funds since 1975.

Figure 2.2 shows how the purchasing power of a Canadian winter visitor with $100,000 CDN invested since 1975 has fared, assuming that they earn an average 10% annual return in Canada, and then convert that interest into U.S. funds to finance their time in the Sunbelt. Figure 2.2 identifies this person as the Speculator. Compare this with the Planner, shown on the same chart, who converted their $100,000 CDN in one lump sum in 1975, and invested it at the same rate of interest in the United States, and then covered their U.S. expenses from the earned interest.

From Figure 2.2, you can see that the Planner, who decided not to speculate on the Canadian dollar, came out much farther ahead than the Speculator, who kept their $100,000 income earning investment in Canada, and then kept going through the Exchange Rate Blues. The Canadian who failed to hedge against the currency risks of the Canadian dollar, took a voluntary pay cut on their retirement investment income of over $44,345 or 22% including additional exchange commissions calculated in at 1.0% per year. In addition, the Speculator's original principal balance has been reduced from $100,000 U.S. to only $74,800 U.S., and they lost the opportunity cost of earning interest on the dollars they lost over the years. This lost opportunity cost adds another $120,082 to their losses, making a total loss of $164,427 in 22 years! Could this happen to you?

Dollar speculation for the five years prior to the fifth edition of the Border Guide has cost Canadians most or all of their winter vacations, since the dollar has fallen well over 20% during that time period. Speculating on the Canadian dollar can be profitable, if you happen to get lucky. If you want to have a secure retirement however, avoid the Exchange Rate Blues, and avoid becoming a currency speculator.

NO EXCHANGE LOSS IF YOU
CONVERT CANADIAN DOLLARS NOW

Investing a portion of your savings in the United States or in U.S. dollar securities in Canada is a sure-fire way to avoid the Exchange Rate Blues and protect yourself from currency risk. Whenever we recommend this strategy, nearly every client says "How can I exchange my dollars now, I'll take too big of a loss?" The real truth is there is no loss or gain at the time you convert Canadian dollars to U.S. dollars. Losses or gains occur prior to any conversion but only become visible or are realized when the actual conversion is made. To illustrate this point, Figure 2.3 shows that $1,000 CDN exchanged into foreign currency, would net you $748 in US dollars, $5,790 Hong Kong dollars, L1,196,800 Italian lira or 2.1oz. of gold. We'll assume that you paid no commissions and all exchanges transpire at the same time.

Would you consider it a gain because you changed $1,000 CDN to $5,790 Hong Kong dollars? Or, would you consider yourself a millionaire because your $1,000 CDN bought you over 1,196,800 Italian lira? Of course not. Why, should someone think they had lost any money because their $1,000 CDN bought them only $748 US?

Figure 2.3 also illustrates that it doesn't matter what currency you are using, or whether it is denominated in dollars, lire or something else. It takes the same relative amount of each currency to purchase the same tangible object such as the 2.1 oz. of gold used in this chart. Instead of gold you could substitute a months rental on a United States vacation property and the net result would be the same. To further illustrate that there is no loss or gain on currency exchange transactions, run through a full cycle of exchange from $1,000 CDN to L1,196,800 Italian lira to 2.1 oz. of gold, to $748 US back to $1,000 CDN. There is no loss at any time of the currency

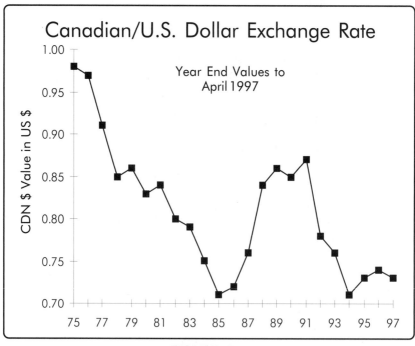

FIGURE 2.1

exchange. Losses or gains occur only if you repeated this full cycle of exchange, at some other point in time. The relative values of the four currencies and the gold will change, but guessing what those relative values will be is pure speculation and not for the risk adverse.

The only loss when exchanging Canadian dollars to U.S. funds is that which is perceived, not a real one. This misconception comes from Canada's proximity to the U.S. and the fact that both countries call their currency the dollar. At one time (approximately 25 years ago) one dollar Canadian was worth approximately one dollar US. But there is no law or agreement that says a Canadian dollar must be worth one American dollar. Just the same as there is no law that says one Canadian dollar must equal one Hong Kong dollar. The relationship between the Canadian dollar and the US dollar is market driven, based on world-wide demand, and is every bit as unrestrained as the relative values of the Canadian dollar and the Italian lira. Had the United States called their currency something different like *zlotnays*, this perception of loss would likely never have happened.

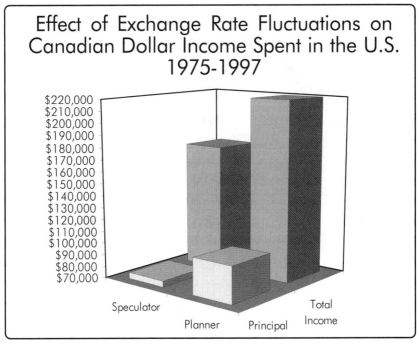

FIGURE 2.2

WHAT CAN YOU EXPECT IF YOU INVEST IN THE UNITED STATES?

Prior to 1996, interest rates on bank term deposits, GICs and government bonds in Canada have been higher than the same relative rates in the United States. Consequently, Canadians tend to avoid investing in the United States because they feel they can get better returns in Canada. Currently, if you follow prudent investment practices and take advantage of the higher U.S. rates in certain areas like bank deposits, you can actually improve your rate of return. The primary reason for higher Canadian interest rates in the past has been to compensate global investors for a perceived greater risk factor in Canadian currency investments. In an effort to stimulate the Canadian economy, the Bank of Canada has allowed rates to fall at the expense of a weaker Canadian dollar.

In today's global economy, investments need to be administered as if you were operating a business on a world-wide basis. Since Canada constitutes only 2% of the world's economy, you're not only taking a greater risk, but

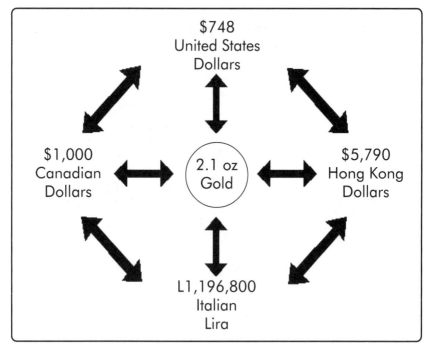

FIGURE 2.3

missing out on growth opportunities, if you don't invest outside of Canada. If the business of your investments is astutely managed, you'll earn the same level of profit or income at the same relative risk whether it's in the United States or Canada.

For example, compare a mutual fund in Canada to one in the United States with the same objectives, restrictions, management and fee structure, and over time, you will see that their returns will also be similar on a percentage basis. The only difference is that one generates Canadian funds, and the other generates U.S. funds.

As a result, you do not have to take any reduction in income and can maintain the same level of safety, by directing some or all of your investments to the United States. This effectively avoids speculation on the Canadian dollar, and will cure the Exchange Rate Blues.

AVOIDING U.S. INCOME TAX ON YOUR INVESTMENTS

Investing in the United States as a non-resident can be rewarding and worry free, if you follow the same investment principles you would use in Canada, and then stick with those investments which are exempt from both American income and estate tax. There is no substitute for diversification and good management, regardless of what your investment objectives are. Chapter 6 lists those investments which Canadians can use to produce a steady U.S. income, while avoiding the non-residents estate tax discussed in Chapter 4. The fact that these investments are exempt from tax and reporting requirements in the United States does not mean that you don't have to report the income to Revenue Canada. As a Canadian resident, you are subject to tax on your world income in Canada.

WHERE IS THE BEST PLACE TO EXCHANGE MONEY?

Most experienced travellers will tell you, the rate of currency exchange can vary dramatically, depending on the form of your Canadian dollars e.g. cash, cheque or travellers cheques, and the facility you are using to make the exchange, i.e. a bank, brokerage firm or airport. Whether you are in Canada or the U.S. will also be a factor in obtaining the best exchange rates. World currency markets dictate exchange rates based on numerous factors, but it is primarily commission rates , spreads and other related charges that vary between exchange rate vendors.

There is no exact formula that will guarantee you the best rate of exchange each time, but the basic guidelines listed below, have saved previous readers of *The Border Guide* hundreds and even thousands of dollars at a time in exchange commissions.

• Exchange large sums at one time, whenever possible.

• When exchanging at a bank ask for the "spot" rate. This is the special rate right from the market at that time. This service is generally only available when exchanging amounts of $5,000 or more.

• Avoid using Canadian cash for the exchange. Commission rates on cash can go over 5% particularly if you are outside of Canada. Cheques and travellers cheques generally attract the best rates. Personal cheques work fine only at a bank where you are known.

• Shop around at least three institutions and give each vendor the exact amount you want to exchange, and the form of Canadian dollars used in the exchange. Exchange rates vary widely from institution to institution and change constantly throughout the day. If you are going to use a bank, include both U.S. and Canadian banks in your survey. You may get some pleasant surprises if you do. There are now several U.S. banks and brokerage firms in Florida that exchange Canadian dollars at greatly reduced commission rates in order to attract new customers.

• Use foreign exchange brokers. Some even guarantee that they will beat the bank rate every time. We've found that some brokers exchange Canada - U.S. dollars at far better rates than any bank or brokerage firm. They also won't try to sell you something else you may not want or need. The good ones are easy to work with regardless of where you are, including the U.S., through their toll free numbers. See *Dealing With Foreign Exchange Brokers* in the next section of this Chapter.

• If you have a relationship with a brokerage firm you can generally exchange money there at no, or very low commissions. They are, of course, hoping you will invest the money through them and will often attempt to sell investments to you whether you are looking or not!

• If you're in a major gambling centre like Las Vegas, the Casinos tend to offer excellent rates of exchange. They may frown upon it however, if you do not stop to gamble with some of your newly acquired U.S. currency.

• Credit card companies may offer a preferred exchange rate when you use their card to purchase foreign goods. They also charge exorbitant interest rates, if you are not back in Canada, or have not made other arrangements to pay the bill when it's due. Some banks such as the Bank of Montreal, now issue U.S. dollar VISA cards, which means you pay your bill in U.S. funds. You can negotiate a better rate through an exchange broker at the time you make payment. Using a U.S. dollar charge card in conjunction with a currency exchange broker is a much better solution than being at the mercy of a Canadian dollar charge card for U.S. purchases. Taking that route means paying additional fees and getting hit with a poorer exchange rate on each transaction.

DEALING WITH FOREIGN EXCHANGE BROKERS

Foreign exchange brokers are a relatively new phenomena in Canada. They have been made possible by deregulation which took away the banks near monopoly on currency exchange. Banks do not really like this competition since currency exchange departments tend to be among their most profitable. So if you ask your local bank manager about dealing with these brokers, don't expect too many favourable comments.

Foreign exchange brokers have done much to eliminate the air of mystery and poor service associated with exchanging currency. They provide ordinary customers with the same level of service that banks usually reserve for very large clients and do it a much lower cost, even lower than special promotions and preferred rates for snowbirds. Brokers can give you real time dollar (or other currencies) exchange quotes from world currency markets at any time, and once you've established a working relationship, you can deal with them from anywhere in Canada or the U.S. using their toll free numbers. You could be in Florida, your Canadian dollars in a bank account in Moose Jaw, and the currency broker in Vancouver. Yet you can exchange any amount and have the U.S. cash wired to your Florida bank within the same or very next business day. One valuable service exchange brokers provide that banks do not, is allowing you to use standing orders. You can set the rate you want your money exchanged at, and when the exchange rate reaches your stated price your transaction is processed automatically. This standing order can be placed overnight or on weekends to be traded on the Tokyo Exchange. In certain circumstances you may wish to buy what is in effect, an insurance policy to hedge against a falling Canadian dollar, when your funds will not be available for a period of time because they are locked in a GIC, or you are waiting to close a house sale. A good currency broker can help you through the ins and out of this relatively complex transaction, to insure you understand how it works and the limitations of these hedging contracts.

The majority of foreign exchange companies in Canada are well capitalized and professionally managed. However, since this is a new financial industry and foreign exchange companies are not regulated like banks or stock brokerage firms, consumers planning to use them need to investigate who they are dealing with and what guidelines they should follow. The following guidelines will help Border Guide readers take good advantage of better exchange rates offered by foreign exchange brokers without being taken advantage of themselves:

- Know who you are dealing with by asking for referrals from other customers of the exchange brokers and their company. Ask for financial data on the company, get a banking report from the bank(s) the company uses to facilitate its transactions, determine how long the company has been in business and how many offices and employees they have.

- When dealing directly over the counter at a local foreign exchange broker, request that the broker have a U.S. dollar bank draft prepared in advance for you to exchange directly with your Canadian dollar draft or cheque in the applicable amounts.

- When dealing over the phone with a foreign exchange broker and where they are wiring U.S. funds to a third party such as a bank or brokerage firm, have the broker wire the U.S. funds in trust to the third party if possible, so you can confirm the funds have been released by the broker, before you pay the broker for the U.S. funds.

- Don't forget to use some of the exchange techniques we have discussed in the previous section of this Chapter, like exchanging large amounts at one time and getting more than one quote.

Two foreign exchange firms that my clients and I have successfully exchanged millions of Canadian dollars over the past few years are: Global Currency Corporation and Custom House Currency Exchange. Both firms are based in Victoria and both guarantee to beat the bank exchange rates. Global's toll free number, good anywhere in Canada or the U.S., is 1-800-655-0520 and Custom's is 1-800-661-3559. Global and Custom have numerous Canadian offices and Global now has U.S. offices in Arizona.

The Taxman Cometh

CROSS-BORDER TAX PLANNING

3

I n Chapter 1, we alluded to the fact that cross-border financial planning can be very beneficial for all those who undertake it diligently, and very costly to those who choose to ignore it. The key points, in terms of providing the best return on your investment of time and money, come in the areas of income tax and non-resident estate tax planning. This chapter will deal with the income tax issues, while Chapter 4 will delve into the non-resident estate tax.

Figure 1.1, in Chapter 1, lists the various cross-border issues according to your immigration status in the United States. Most of these issues deal with income tax. The first category that we will examine is the typical winter visitor, who spends less than six months a year in the U.S. and has no visa, or other immigration status in the United States.

TAXING NON-RESIDENT ALIENS

Non-residents, or non-resident aliens as the U.S. tax and immigration publications like to refer to them, are generally taxed on their U.S. source income only. Income from U.S. sources includes interest on bonds, notes and other interest bearing obligations, all wages for services performed in the United States, dividends, rents, royalties and the gains from sale of property. The Canada — U.S. Tax Treaty sets forth the withholding rates, if any, on these sources of income.

The new treaty withholding rate is 10% on interest. The IRS has taken a position not to collect the treaty withholding tax on interest from all U.S. Banks, Savings and Loans and similar institutions providing the non-resident has filed an IRS Form W-8 with the payer of the interest. Form W-8 is the certification of foreign status and entitles you to this withholding exemption. As of January 1, 1997 all Canadians opening up any U.S. bank or brokerage account or filing any type of U.S. tax return must use IRS Form W-7 to apply for a Individual Tax Payer Identification Number

(ITIN). The ITIN is similar to a Social Insurance or Social Security number and is used to track payer and payee income tax reporting, as well as speed non-residents income tax filings. Most banks keep a good supply of W-7 and W-8 Forms or they can be obtained from any IRS office.

Non-residents earning dividends in the U.S. will face a 15% withholding rate, reduced from 30% by the Canada — U.S. Tax Treaty. Canadians may have to file IRS Form 1001, Reduced Rate Certificate, to ensure they get the treaty rate of withholding rather than the regular rate.

Gains on the sale of U.S. securities are exempt from United States capital gains tax, providing you have filed a W-8 form with your broker.

Canadians collecting rent have two options; either pay a flat 30% withholding tax on the gross rent, or file a non-resident tax return, Form 1040NR. They can net expenses against the rent and then pay regular tax rates on the net rental income at the applicable rate. Most Canadians with rental income will find that they will pay less tax, and perhaps no tax at all, if they file a U.S. return. Even if you clearly made no profit from your rental property and paid no withholding tax, you must still file a Form 1040NR, unless you enjoy playing Russian Roulette with the IRS. New IRS regulations have been enacted that will disallow any rental expenses 16 months after the normal filing deadline of June 15, each year. If the IRS catches up with you for failure to file, you would then be forced to pay tax and penalties on the gross rent collected.

Canadians selling real estate will be exempt from withholding tax if they are selling a personal use residence in the U.S., if it is valued under $300,000 and the buyer is going to occupy the home for their own personal use. Otherwise, the withholding rate is 10%, whether or not there will be any profit on the sale. Application can be made to the IRS to reduce or eliminate the withholding tax, if there is only a small gain or a loss on the sale of the property. The gross amount of the sale transaction is reported to the IRS on Form 1099-S and the details of any gains or losses must be reported to the IRS on Form 1040NR, for the year of the sale. If there is further tax to be paid on a gain it will be paid with this return and likewise, if there is a refund due of any withholding, this is the mechanism for applying for it. Canadians who owned their property prior to 1980, the date of the 1980 Canada — U.S. Tax Treaty revision, may use the treaty to exempt any gains prior to December 31, 1984, from taxation in the U.S.

Remember that exemptions from U.S. tax on any of the aforementioned income, does not mean it is exempt from Canadian taxation. A Canadian resident is taxable on their world income and must report all of these U.S. earnings annually to Revenue Canada whether exempt or not. You will receive a credit on your Canadian return for any taxes paid to the U.S.

Most Canadians investing to produce United States income will have no U.S. withholding tax to pay, or tax returns to file, if they use the exempt investments first mentioned in Chapter 2 and explained in detail in Chapter 6. The section headed *Who Must File U.S. Tax Returns* later in this chapter, will tell you exactly under what circumstances, and when you must file a non-resident tax return.

DUAL CITIZENS & GREEN CARD HOLDERS RESIDENT IN CANADA

Canada taxes its citizens on their world income, only when they are residents of Canada. The United States taxes its citizens and resident aliens or green card holders on their world income, with certain exclusions, regardless of where they reside in the world.

Many Canadians obtained United States green cards over the years, when they were handed out much more liberally than they are today. Some never used these green cards, while others may have used them but moved back to Canada to set up principal residence there. Chapter 7 deals with the immigration implications of a Canadian in this situation. From a tax standpoint, the IRS considers all green card holders as legal permanent residents of the United States, and subject to the same filing requirements as anyone else with resident status. That is, they must file annual tax returns in the United States on their world income. There can be numerous tax advantages of paying taxes in the United States rather than Canada, and these are covered later in this chapter, and in Chapter 8. However, Canadians in this situation need to determine as soon as possible, whether they should officially abandon their green card or use it to their best advantage. The best means to make the final decision about what to do in this situation, is to complete a full cross-border financial plan that addresses every issue, from the perspective of getting the best of both the Canadian and United States systems. If you do nothing, and continue to sit in the woods with your green card, you inevitably end up getting the worst of both systems, instead of the best.

Canadians who were born in the United States, or obtained U.S. citizenship from some other source (see Chapter 7, Derivative Citizenship and Dual-Citizenship) and who are also naturalized Canadian citizens, are dual-citizens of Canada and the United States. Dual-citizens living in Canada are in a similar situation tax wise to the green card holders described above. They need to file annual tax returns in both countries on their world income. Similarly, Canadians who are dual-citizens need to determine, as soon as possible, whether they should officially abandon their U.S. Citizenship, or use it to their best advantage. Our advice here is also the same. Complete a cross-border financial plan and use it to position your dual citizenship to obtain the best advantages between Canada and the United States. Chapters 8 and 9 will show you what your options are.

IRS GIVES U.S. CITIZENS IN CANADA AMNESTY

Canadian resident holding U.S. green cards, U.S. citizens, dual citizens and derivative U.S. citizens who have not been filing U.S. annual tax returns on their world income have been given a window of opportunity to come out of the closet and get back on the correct U.S. filing roles without penalty. This informal and unofficial amnesty program requires simply that the last six years tax returns be accurately filed with the international section of the IRS in Philadelphia. Future returns must be filed on a continuing basis by the required deadlines. If the past six years returns are filed, the IRS will waive basic penalties (but not interest) on tax due, if any, and reduce the normally unlimited statute of limitations for failure to file for the same six years by not asking any questions as to what happened to any income or taxes due prior to the six years. If you wait for the IRS to come after you, this limited amnesty program is not available to you and you will be nailed with the full tax, penalties and interest for perhaps further back than the six years. The new Canada — U.S. Tax Treaty rules will also allow the IRS to seize assets and bank accounts with Revenue Canada's obliging assistance. This makes it extremely important that Canadian residents who are citizens or green card holders take action immediately to get right with the IRS before the IRS finds them, and to know what their liabilities are to avoid a possible financial disaster. The IRS has hired thousands more auditors and have started coordinating records with the U. S. Immigration and Naturalization Service (INS) to bring more filers into compliance. Those who have ignored or were unaware of this IRS filing requirement will find one door slammed shut that may have once been open to them prior to February 6, 1995 with new expatriation legislation as explained in the next section of this chapter.

The requirement to file in the U.S. on world income does not necessarily mean that there would be taxes due to the U.S. on income earned in Canada. There are exemptions such as the earned income exemption of $70,000 US providing it was not U.S. sourced income. In addition to this employment income exemption, the Canada/U.S. Tax treaty allows for foreign tax credits for taxes paid in Canada on the U.S. return for the same income. Since Canadian tax rates have been significantly higher than U.S. rates in recent years, the foreign tax credits from taxes paid in Canada usually would cover any U.S. taxes due. However, there are certain circumstances where U.S. taxes can be due on income that would not be taxed currently, if the taxpayer/U.S. citizen was filing only in Canada. For example, if a U.S. citizen in Canada had a capital gain on stocks or mutual funds in Canada that qualified for the $100,000 lifetime capital gains exemption, prior to February 22, 1994, they may be exempt from tax in Canada. But since the U.S. has no equivalent exemption they would pay tax to the U.S. at the standard U.S. capital gains rate. A similar problem can arise when a Canadian resident/U.S. citizen takes advantage of the Canadian principal residence exemption in Canada since the U.S. principal exemption works quite differently.

U.S. citizens in Canada taking dividends from their closely held Canadian corporations in an attempt to zero out Canadian tax with the dividend tax credit, could also find themselves paying U.S. taxes on the dividends received. If a U.S. citizen resident in Canada has an RRSP, the IRS will consider interest, dividends, and capital gains earned in the RRSP income unless an election provided by the Canada/U.S. Tax Treaty is filed to defer the tax each year with the U.S. return (see Chapter 8 *Withdraw Your RRSP Tax Free* section). One can correctly surmise that the IRS regulations requiring U.S. citizens to file annual returns, in light of the differences in the applications of tax rules between Canada and the U.S., can provide for some very unpleasant surprises. The amnesty program will be of great advantage to any U.S. citizen who wants to get back into the good graces of the IRS and to avoid penalties. They may also want to prevent the IRS from scrutinizing financial transactions prior to the six years of required returns, that may require large tax amounts to be paid. Failure to take advantage of this amnesty program could be a costly mistake. The IRS is now tracking passport renewals and travel visa requests by U.S. citizens and is actively campaigning to ferret out and prosecute non-filers around the world. A U.S. citizen living in Canada, who has not been filing U.S. returns and who does not take advantage of the amnesty program, may find themselves facing severe penalties. Once the IRS catches up with them, they may also be forced to file U.S. tax returns for more than six years. The IRS may not even catch them until an estate tax return is filed after the death of the taxpayer. This is when they tend to audit more closely, and conceivably, the estate could attract large enough penalties, interest and taxes to reduce the inheritance to zero.

As a consequence, U.S. citizens in Canada require constant cross-border tax advice to avoid unnecessary tax and should construct a plan that takes best advantage of the of U.S. and Canadian tax systems while avoiding common pitfalls. Proper planning from a knowledgeable cross-border planner can turn these apparent tax problems into great tax saving opportunities. In general, the US citizen living in Canada is going to be hit with the worst of both the Canadian and U.S tax systems if they remain full time residents of Canada. If there is no intention to return to the United States, serious consideration should be given to renouncing their U.S. citizenship, but only after taking into consideration the new Expatriation Rules explained in the next section of this chapter. This step should only be taken after they have addressed all their options in a comprehensive cross-border financial plan. Green card holders living in Canada need to follow the same tax rules as U.S. citizens, but face the added burden of losing their green cards. Filing a U.S. tax return is one of the key indicators used to determine if residency rules required to maintain the green card are being followed.

This amnesty program remains open, but the IRS can revoke it at any time. Anyone who wishes to use it needs to check with their cross-border advisor to see if it is still available. If not, you might pursue other alternatives, like negotiating with the IRS to get current without penalty.

NEW U.S. TAX LEGISLATION CONCERNING EXPATRIATION FROM THE U.S.

New expatriation rules were passed into law in August 1996, retroactive back to the proposal date of February 6, 1995. This new U.S. expatriation law is meant to force U.S. citizens and long term residents who give up their citizenship or residency status to go through a capital disposition of assets at the time they give up their status. As a result, they would have to pay U.S.

capital gains tax on any unrealized capital gains at the time they give up their status in a similar manner to the Canadian deemed disposition or departure tax for Canadians leaving Canada to take up residence elsewhere as explained in Chapter 8. Under this U.S. Tax Legislation, U.S. long-term residents are those who were lawful permanent residents (green card holders) for at least 8 of 15 (current and prior 14) years. These rules apply and you are considered to be giving up your U.S. citizenship or green card status for tax avoidance purposes if your average tax liability for the 5 prior years exceeds $100,000 or your net worth on expatriation date is at least $500,000. In addition, expatriation for tax avoidance may mean you will never be allowed back into the U.S. again for any reason, even as a visitor. Persons expatriating the U.S. under these rules will pay the capital gains tax due to the IRS on the expatiation date and be subject to regular U.S. tax rates on any U.S. sourced income at regular US rates for 10 years after the expatriation date. There are certain circumstances in which expatriates can apply to defer or avoid the expatriation tax or receive tax credits to avoid double taxation. However, these circumstances are complex and

The Substantial Presence Test

Number of days present
this year .... $124 \times 1 = 124$

Number of days present
last year .... $124 \times 1/3 = 42$

Number of days present
previous to last year .... $124 \times 1/6 = 21$

Total days deemed present
in the current year 187

FIGURE 3.1

anyone in this situation must seek professional help to guide them through the mine fields.

NON-RESIDENT TO A RESIDENT IN THE U.S.

Canadians who regularly spend less than four months a year in the United States do not have to worry about becoming a resident of the United States for tax purposes. They will keep themselves void of any filing requirements other than the situations listed later in this chapter under the section heading *Who Must File in the U.S.*

From Chapter 1 under the section *How Long Can You Stay in the U.S. as a Visitor,* you may recall there are different sets of rules that apply to winter visitors, such as being considered a U.S. resident for tax purposes and yet having no right to remain in the U.S. as an immigrant. This section will examine the tax rules that make this apparent contradiction possible.

The Substantial Presence Test. A winter visitor is considered to be a resident of the United States for tax purposes, if they meet the substantial presence test. The winter visitor satisfies this test if they have been present in the U.S. for at least 183 days during a three year period that includes the "current year." The current year is the particular tax year for which the winter visitor is determining their resident status. For purposes of the substantial presence test, a winter visitor will be treated as "present" in the U.S. on any day that he or she is physically present in the U.S. at any time during the day. This would include any cross-border trips you make to the United States being counted as a full day, even if you were present in the United States for only a few hours. Note that the days present in the U.S. need not be consecutive.

Each day of presence in the first preceding year, is counted as one-third of a day and each day of presence in the second preceding year is counted as one-sixth of a day. For example, Figure 3.1 illustrates the results of these calculations for a winter visitor who spends four months in the U.S., plus a few shopping days in the adjoining border town. Even though this winter visitor never came close to spending six months in the U. S., they can be deemed to have spent 187 days in the current year, and are therefore a U.S. resident for tax purposes under the substantial presence test.

In computing the days of presence in the U.S. under the final rule, certain days are not considered as days of presence. These include any day that an individual is prevented from leaving the U.S. because of a medical condition that arose while the visitor was in the U.S.

If an individual is not physically present for more than 30 days during the current year, the substantial presence test will not apply even if the three-year total is 183 or more days.

Closer Connection Exception. A winter visitor who meets the substantial presence test, may nevertheless be considered a non-resident alien for the current year if they: (1) are present in the U.S. for fewer than 183 days during the current year; (2) maintain a "tax home" in a foreign country during the year; and (3) during the current year have a "closer connection" to the foreign country where they have a tax home other than in the U.S. This closer connection exemption is available only to those winter visitors who file IRS Form 8840, The Closer Connection Exception Statement, by June 15 of each year for the previous calendar year. (See Figure 3.2)

A tax home is considered to be located at the visitor's regular or principal place of business. If the individual has no regular place of business because of the nature of their business, or because the individual is not engaged in any business, the visitor's tax home is their regular place of abode "in a real and substantial sense." The tax home maintained must be in existence for the entire current year.

A visitor will be considered to have a closer connection to a foreign country, if the individual or the IRS establishes that the visitor has maintained more "significant contacts" with the other country than with the U.S. Factors to be considered in determining this include the location of the visitor's home, family, personal belongings, routine banking activities, and organizations to which the visitor belongs. Also, the closer connection exception is unavailable to a visitor who has taken steps to change their status to permanent residence during the current year.

TAX TREATY PROTECTION FOR NON-RESIDENTS

The Canada — U.S. Tax Treaty affords all Canadian visitors a great deal of latitude from filing in the United States and paying taxes on income not sourced in the United States. In addition, that income which is effectively sourced in the United States is prevented from being double taxed; once in the United States, and again in Canada. The treaty accomplishes this in three key ways:

Form **8840**

Closer Connection Exception Statement for Aliens

▶ Attach to Form 1040NR or Form 1040NR-EZ.

Department of the Treasury
Internal Revenue Service

For the year January 1Ð December 31, 1996, or other tax year
beginning _____ , 1996, and ending _____ , 19 ____ .

OMB No. 1545-1410

1996

Attachment
Sequence No. 101

Your first name and initial	Last name	Your U.S. taxpayer identification number, if any

Fill in your
addresses only if
you are filing this
form by itself and
not with your U.S.
tax return

Address in country of residence	Address in the United States

Part I General Information

1 Enter your U.S. visa number, if any ▶ ....

2 Of what country or countries were you a citizen during the tax year? ....

3 What country or countries issued you a passport? ....

4 Enter your passport number(s) ▶ ....

5 Enter the number of days you were present in the United States during:
1996 _____ 1995 _____ 1994 _____ .

6 During 1996, did you apply for, or take other affirmative steps to apply for, lawful permanent resident
status in the United States or have an application pending to change your status to that of a lawful
permanent resident of the United States (see instructions)? . . . . ☐ Yes ☐ No

Part II Closer Connection to One Foreign Country

7 Where was your tax home during 1996? ....

8 Enter the name of the foreign country to which you had a closer connection than to the United States during 1996
▶ ....

Next, complete Part IV on the back.

Part III Closer Connection to Two Foreign Countries

9 Where was your tax home on January 1, 1996? ....

10 After changing your tax home from its location on January 1, 1996, where was your tax home for the remainder of 1996?
....
....
....

11 Did you have a closer connection to each foreign country listed on lines 9 and 10 than to the United
States for the period during which you maintained a tax home in that foreign country? . . . . . . ☐ Yes ☐ No
If ªNo,º attach an explanation.

12 Were you subject to tax as a resident under the internal laws of (a) either of the countries listed on lines
9 and 10 during all of 1996, or (b) both of the countries listed on lines 9 and 10 for the period during
which you maintained a tax home in each country? . . . . ☐ Yes ☐ No

13 Have you filed or will you file tax returns for 1996 in the countries listed on lines 9 and 10?. . . . . ☐ Yes ☐ No
If ªYesº to either line 12 or line 13, attach verification.
If ªNoº to either line 12 or line 13, please explain ▶ ....
....

Next, complete Part IV on the back.

For Privacy Act and Paperwork Reduction Act Notice, see page 3.   Cat. No. 15829P   Form **8840** (1996)

FIGURE 3.2

Form 8840 (1996)   Page 2

Part IV   Significant Contacts With Foreign Country or Countries in 1996

14   Where was your regular or principal permanent home located during 1996 (see instructions)? ....

15   If you had more than one permanent home available to you at all times during 1996, list the location of each and explain ▶ ....

16   Where was your family located? ....

17   Where was your automobile(s) located? ....

18   Where was your automobile(s) registered? ....

19   Where were your personal belongings, furniture, etc., located? ....

20   List social, cultural, religious, and political organizations you currently participate in and the location of each:

   a _____ Location _____
   b _____ Location _____
   c _____ Location _____
   d _____ Location _____
   e _____ Location _____

21   Where was the bank(s) with which you conducted your routine personal banking activities located?

   a _____ c _____
   b _____ d _____

22   Did you conduct business activities in a location other than your tax home? . . . . ☐ Yes ☐ No
   If "Yes," where? ....

23a   Where was your driver's license issued? ....
   b   If you hold a second driver's license, where was it issued? ....

24   Where were you registered to vote? ....

25   When completing official documents, forms, etc., what country do you list as your residence? ....

26   Have you ever completed:
   a   Form W-8, Certificate of Foreign Status? . . . . ☐ Yes ☐ No
   b   Form W-9, Request for Taxpayer Identification Number and Certification? . . . . ☐ Yes ☐ No
   c   Form 1078, Certificate of Alien Claiming Residence in the United States? . . . . ☐ Yes ☐ No
   d   Any other U.S. official forms? If "Yes," indicate the form(s) ▶ .... ☐ Yes ☐ No

27   In what country/countries did you keep your personal, financial, and legal documents? ....

28   From what country/countries did you derive the majority of your 1996 income? ....

29   Did you have any income from U.S. sources? . . . . ☐ Yes ☐ No
   If "Yes," what type? ....

30   In what country/countries were your investments located (see instructions)? ....

31   List any charitable organizations to which you made contributions and their locations:

   a _____ Location _____
   b _____ Location _____
   c _____ Location _____
   d _____ Location _____

32   Did you qualify for any type of government-sponsored "national" health plan? . . . . ☐ Yes ☐ No
   If "Yes," in what country? ....
   If "No," please explain ▶ ....
   If you have any other information to substantiate your closer connection to a country other than the United States or you wish to explain in more detail your response to lines 14 through 32, attach a statement to this form.

Sign here only if you are filing this form by itself and not with your U.S. tax return	Under penalties of perjury, I declare that I have examined this form and the accompanying attachments, and to the best of my knowledge and belief, they are true, correct, and complete. Declaration of preparer (other than taxpayer) is based on all information of which preparer has any knowledge.
	▶ _____ ▶ _____
	Your signature Date

FIGURE 3.2

1. Foreign Tax Credits. The treaty allows for a system of credits such that tax paid to one country on specified income, will be allowed as a full credit against any tax due on that same income in the country of residence. For example, a non-resident who earns a taxable rental income in the United States, files and pays tax as required by the IRS. The tax paid to the IRS is converted to Canadian funds and is used on the Canadian return as a full credit, to reduce or eliminate any Canadian taxes due to Revenue Canada on that same rental income adjusted for Canadian depreciation rules.

2. Exemptions. The Canada — U.S. Tax Treaty provides for certain exemptions from filing or reporting income of a non-resident in the United States, that would otherwise be taxable by the IRS. The Substantial Presence Test, without any treaty protection, would apply to a large number of Canadian winter visitors who regularly spend four to six months each year in the American Sunbelt. Under the Canada — U.S. Tax Treaty, there is an exemption from the Substantial Presence Test for Canadians who without the treaty protection would be required to report their world income in the United States under the terms of this test. New IRS rules, implemented for the 1992 tax year, will require Canadians who are using the Canada — U.S. Tax Treaty as protection from the substantial presence test, to file a Closer Connection Exception Statement, IRS Form 8840 (see figure 3.2) and/or Form 1040NR declaring they are treaty exempt.

3. Withholding Rates. Provisions in the treaty establish the amount of maximum withholding either country can take on various forms of income. These withholding rates were detailed earlier in this chapter under the *Taxing Non-Resident Aliens* section. The provisions for maximum withholding rates prove very useful when doing cross-border financial planning, as you will see in Chapters 8 and 9.

The exchange of information capabilities between Canada and the United States, as provided for in the Canada — United States Tax Treaty, often traps those who do not report income earned in one country to the other, where applicable. Canadian and U.S. tax authorities can currently ask for and obtain a complete tax profile of anyone they choose who lives in the other respective country at any time. The new Canada — U.S. Tax Treaty contains provisions to enforce the tax judgment from one country in the jurisdiction of the other through the facilities of the local taxing authorities. Revenue Canada will be able to exercise its collection authority in the U.S. and the IRS in Canada with nearly the same powers they already have in their own respective countries. This was not possible under the 1980 Canada — U.S. Treaty. Under the prior rules, if a taxpayer owed tax to one country but lived in the other, it was difficult for the country owed the tax to collect it unless they could find assets within the tax owed country to seize.

WHO MUST FILE IN THE UNITED STATES?

The purpose of this section is to make you aware of the situations and the types of income on which you as a non-resident, are legally required to file a tax return of any form in the United States. You must file a return under the following circumstances:

- The sale of any United States real property requires that the seller file IRS Form 1040NR before June 15 following the year of the sale. Form 1040NR must be filed whether or not there was any gain or withholding tax collected on the sale. There are no exceptions to this rule.

- Any non-resident who spends four to six months per year in the United States, and is deemed to be a resident under the Substantial Presence Test, and who is claiming to be exempt under the Canada — U.S. Tax Treaty, must file Form 1040NR or the Closer Connection Exception statement (see Figure 3.2) by June 15 every year they are subject to the substantial presence test. Refer back to discussions about the Substantial Presence Test in previous sections of this chapter.

- A Canadian who spends more than 183 days in the U.S. is considered a resident for tax purposes, and must file a U.S. tax return, Form 1040, declaring their world income. The treaty will be of little help in preventing world income from being taxed in the U.S., but will help to eliminate most, if not all, of the taxes due to the IRS. Canadians in this situation, should review Chapter 7 on Immigration, with a view to obtaining permanent residency in the U.S., so they may take full advantage of the lower U.S. tax rates as outlined in the last section of this chapter.

- Any non-resident who collects rental income in the United States from any owned property, including their own personal use home, must file Form 1040NR by the required deadline, unless the lessee is withholding the 30% non-resident withholding tax on the gross rental income.

- Any non-resident who carries on a business of any form in the United States, must also file Form 1040NR regardless of whether or not that business is profitable. This filing requirement applies even though you may not have any legal immigration status to work in the United States.

- If a non-resident has had withholding tax withheld incorrectly or at an improper rate, they must file Form 1040NR for the year in which the error occurred if they wish to obtain a refund. Be sure to keep all the reporting slips that any withholding entity must provide you with. Generally, these would be 1042S, 1099 or 8288A slips which are similar to Canadian T-4 or T-5's. Lottery and gambling winnings are considered taxable income in the U.S. and are subject to non-resident withholding tax. If you hit a jackpot in Las Vegas, this filing method could make you an even bigger winner by giving you some or all of your withholding back. Planning Tip for Gamblers: Keep detailed daily records of both winnings and losses. The losses can be useful when filing for a refund of withholding tax from a jackpot. Without good records, the IRS will not allow an offset of losses against winnings as now allowed under the latest amendment to the Canada — United States Tax Treaty.

- The estate of a non-resident decedent that has a U.S. taxable estate of greater than $60,000 must file IRS Form 706NA within nine months of the death of the decedent. See Chapter 4 to determine the taxable estate of a non-resident.

- Any non-resident who gifts taxable U.S. property over $10,000 total in one year to any single person, or $100,000 to a spouse, is subject to U.S. gift tax and must file IRS Form 709 the gift tax return, to pay any taxes due by April 15 after the year end in which the gift was made. The gift tax rates are equal to the estate tax rates. See Chapter 4 for a more complete discussion of gift taxes.

HOW AND WHEN TO APPLY FOR A U.S. SOCIAL SECURITY NUMBER

Generally speaking, Canadians do not need a U.S. taxpayer identification number, commonly known as a Social Security Number (SSN) or Individual Taxpayer Identification Number (ITIN). But starting January 1, 1997 you will be required to have at least a ITIN if you are going to open a bank or brokerage account or conduct any other financial transaction in the U.S., including the filing of U.S. tax returns/forms. SSNs and ITINs look alike, but ITINs are now for those non-U.S. persons who have no visa, green card or other immigration status in the U.S. Those who have obtained SSNs in the past may continue to use them, but it is quite incorrect for Canadians under any circumstances to provide the Canadian Social Insurance Number (SIN) to any U.S. entity for any reason. Doing so is not only illegal from the stand point of providing a false SSN, but it throws the IRS computers for a loop. Your SIN number may be the same as some American's SSN, or there may no record of it at all! When you open a bank or brokerage account ask for IRS Form W-8, Certificate of Foreign Status, which will satisfy any legal tax reporting requirements. See the *Taxing Non-Resident Aliens* section, earlier in this chapter.

There is no real disadvantage to having an American SSN/ITIN unless having another number to keep track of bothers you. A SSN/ITIN is not only required as noted above, but it can be a convenience to you in certain financial transactions, such as filing tax returns or selling property. It may also be to a person's advantage to have a taxpayer identification number, to obtain increased assurance the IRS has properly recorded certain facts that could be helpful in the future, such as tax losses which are permitted to be offset against future profits. In fact, the IRS, with the new requirement to have a SSN/ITIN, will hold refunds or delay return processing for those who have failed to supply a SSN/ITIN.

To obtain your own permanent ITIN you will need to complete and file IRS Form W-7 and your number will be provided in 4-6 weeks.

If you have a U.S. Visa or other legal immigration status, you can take your Visa to the nearest Social Security Administration office and complete Form SS-5 and obtain a SSN. All residents of the U.S. are required to have a SSN.

CANADA - UNITED STATES INCOME TAX COMPARISON

There are two main issues to consider when it comes to the actual amount of tax you pay; the tax rates and the income on which those rates are applied, called your taxable income. No comparison between Canada and the United States would be complete without considering both these factors. Since there are fifty states and ten provinces, a detailed comparison of each state and each province is beyond the scope of this book. Appendix

B includes the tax rates from all provinces and the key Sunbelt states. However, we will provide you with a guide to the major opportunities of cross-border financial planning. We will also compare the tax rates of Ontario and Florida, the two locations that generate the most winter visitor traffic (Quebec also accounts for a similar amount of visitors to Florida). Other provinces and state tax rates will vary somewhat from the Ontario and Florida tax numbers, but the trends will be the same. The states in the U.S. which do have a personal income tax, collect their tax on a separate return in the same manner as Quebec.

Figure 3.3 charts the tax rates and income brackets of Ontario and Florida. The rates shown are for 1997, and include all provincial and federal surtaxes. For the purpose of our comparison, we assume that the Canadian is married to a spouse who has too much income to qualify for the married exemption in Ontario, and that the Florida person is also married, and filing jointly with their spouse.

CANADA - U.S. TAX RATES 1997

ONTARIO CANADA

Taxable Income	Tax Rate
$29,590 or less	30%
$29,591 - $59,180	44%
$59,181 and over	52%

FLORIDA UNITED STATES

Married Filing Jointly

Taxable Income	Tax Rate
$41,200 or less	15%
$41,201 - $99,600	28%
$99,601 - $151,750	31%
$151,751 - $271,050	36%
$271,051 and over	40%

FIGURE 3.3

As you can see from Figure 3.3, a Florida taxpayer in the highest income bracket has a strong advantage over the Ontario taxpayer because the Florida tax rate is 12% lower than Ontario's and it takes a much larger income to reach the highest bracket in the U.S. On the same income stream, a high income earner would cut their total taxes by nearly 40%, if they had the choice of paying their taxes in Florida. Chapter 8 will show you some direct comparisons using actual cross-border tax situations, to provide a more complete picture for those considering permanent residence in the United States. Florida has no personal state income tax (but has a small intangible property tax of approximately 1/10th of one percent on certain personal property), so the rates reflect the actual United States federal tax rates. Appendix B compares the provincial tax rates with those of popular Sunbelt states.

As we previously noted, you must look at taxable income as well as the tax rate, to get a complete picture of the total taxes paid. Now, we will look at the deductions that reduce your gross income to your taxable income. This list of deductions is by no means a complete summary of all the deductions available in both Canada and the U.S. but it does cover major tax deductions that apply to a married couple at, or near retirement age.

PERSONAL EXEMPTIONS

Canada has converted the basic personal exemption of $6,456 to a non-refundable federal tax credit of $1,098. The age exemption for those over 65 has been reduced to a tax credit of $592 and, after the 1994 Federal budget, has been eliminated for those with incomes exceeding approximately $26,000. For a spouse or a dependent with no income, there are credits available of $915 and $71, respectively. The benefits of credits are enhanced by the applicable provincial tax rates. For any Canadian above the lowest tax bracket in Figure 3.3, the old personal exemptions would have meant a greater net tax reduction than the current credits.

The United States has a standard deduction total of $6,900. If the taxpayer itemizes certain deductions rather than taking the standard deduction, a greater total deduction may be taken. Add $1,600 to the standard deduction, if you and your spouse are over age 65. Add another $2,650 for yourself and each dependent including your spouse, regardless of his or her income, for personal exemptions. The U.S. is more liberal with their dependent deductions. You may claim adult children, grandchildren, parents and other close relatives for whom you supply over 50% of their financial support. The basic personal exemptions are phased out for married persons with incomes between $181,800 to $304,300. Certain itemized deductions will also be reduced up to 80%, for incomes starting at $121,200.

PENSIONS

Canada has the $1,000 pension deduction converted to a non- refundable federal tax credit of $170. This deduction is scheduled to be eliminated in 2000 with the introduction of the new Income Security changes to OAS and GIS. Old Age Security is taxed up to 100% due to a claw back starting at incomes exceeding $53,214. This pension credit is scheduled to be eliminated in 2001 when a new Senior Benefit rate takes effect.

The United States has no standard pension deduction, and allows a tax-free return of contributions to contributory pension plans making these pensions partially tax-free. United States Social Security payments are totally tax-free, until a married couple's income exceeds $40,000, and then up to 85% of these benefits will be taxed at the regular tax rates. Those in the top tax brackets will pay a 34% maximum tax on Social Security payments.

MORTGAGE INTEREST AND PROPERTY TAXES

Canada: these are not deductible in any amount.

United States: mortgage interest on up to two homes is fully deductible as an itemized deduction. The definition of a residence could also include an RV or a yacht. Total mortgages on these residences cannot exceed $1,000,000. Property taxes are deductible regardless of the number of homes involved.

PROVINCIAL OR STATE INCOME TAXES

Canada: provincial taxes cannot be taken as a deduction from federal taxes paid.

United States: state and municipal taxes are deductible as an itemized deduction.

EARNED INTEREST DEDUCTIONS OR DEFERMENT

Canada — the $1,000 earned interest exclusion and the ability to defer interest in investment vehicles such as Canada Savings Bonds and annuities have both been eliminated for all Canadian taxpayers several years ago.

United States — any amount of interest earned on certain municipal bonds is tax-free on both the federal, and in most cases, the state level. Interest on United States Savings Bonds or other federal government securities is tax-free at the state level. Any amount of interest, dividends or capital gains can be deferred as long as desired through the use of various forms of annuities.

CAPITAL GAINS DEDUCTIONS

In the February 22, 1994 federal budget, Canada eliminated its life time $100,000 capital gains exemption on gains from securities other than real estate (this deduction was available for real estate prior to February 1992, and those who owned qualifying property before that date, have limited grandfathered rights to use the exemption for gains accumulated prior to this date but not after February 22, 1994). Persons who own a qualified small business, for the time being, may obtain $400,000 in additional capital gains exemptions on the sale of the shares of their company. Only 75% of actual gains are taxable, making the maximum capital gains tax approximately 40%, depending on the province. All capital gains on the sale of a principal residence in Canada are tax-free. On the date of a taxpayer's death, all their capital assets are deemed as sold at fair market value and any capital gains are fully taxed. If there is a surviving spouse, the capital gains can be deferred to the second spouse's death.

The United States taxes capital gains at a reduced rate, with a maximum federal rate of 28%. In August 1993, Congress reduced the maximum capital gains rate on certain qualified small businesses to 14% and is now attempting to reduce the overall maximum capital gains rate to around 20%. There is a lifetime capital gains exemption of $125,000 for those over 55, on the sale of their principal residence. In addition, any gains on the sale of a principal residence can be rolled tax-free into a new home of equal or greater value. There is no capital gains tax on deemed dispositions at death, and beneficiaries receive appreciated property without any income tax due. However, some assets of larger estates may be subject to the estate tax. See Chapters 4 and 8 for more details.

MEDICAL EXPENSES

In Canada, medical expenses that exceed 3% of income are allowed by converting the deductible expenses to a non-refundable federal credit at the 17% computation.

In the United States, medical expenses that exceed 7.5% of adjusted gross income are deductible as an itemized deduction. Premiums paid for health insurance are included as a deductible medical expense.

REGISTERED RETIREMENT PLANS

Canadians with earned income can contribute 18% of their last year's earnings to a maximum of $13,500 to a Registered Retirement Savings Plan (RRSP) each year.

Americans with earned income can contribute up to the lesser amount of 100% of their income or $2,000 to their own, and $2,000 to a spouse's Individual Retirement Account (IRA). There are numerous other related qualified plans that can allow contributions of up to 25% of income to a maximum of $30,000 per year, depending on your employment status.

CHARITABLE DONATIONS

In Canada, donations to qualified Canadian charities, not exceeding 75% of income, are allowed by the non-refundable federal credit at the 17% computation for the first $250, and 29% for the remainder.

In the United States, donations to qualified charities, not exceeding 50% of income, are allowed as an itemized deduction.

MISCELLANEOUS DEDUCTIONS

Canada - Union and professional dues, safety deposit box fees, interest on funds borrowed for investment purposes, and fees for investment advice are deductible expenses.

United States - tax preparation fees*, vehicle licenses, property and casualty losses exceeding 10% of income, unreimbursed employment expenses, trustee fees*, safety deposit box fees*, interest on funds borrowed for investment purposes to the extent of portfolio income, IRA administration fees* and fees for investment advice* are deductible expenses.

(*denotes expenses that are totalled and deductible only to the extent the total exceeds 2% of adjusted gross income).

The net effect of the differentials in tax rates and deductions between Canada and the U.S. can be best illustrated by example, or by an exact calculation based on your personal situation. Chapter 8 will provide some typical cross-border tax situations that will show you how the application of different tax rates to the same income source, can result in substantial net tax differences between the two tax systems.

CROSS-BORDER Q&A

Many of the issues covered in the preceding chapter of this book have been touched upon in the author's weekly column *Cross-border Q&A,* which appears in *The Sun Times of Canada,* published in Tampa, Florida and circulated throughout the U.S. Sunbelt for Canadians living or wintering there. The majority of these questions have been posed by readers of the Sun Times and/or readers of the previous editions of *The Border Guide.* Most were looking for advice relating to their own specific problems or situations. At the end of this chapter, we have included some typical reader questions, along with our response, to illustrate and broaden the concepts presented in the preceding chapter.

CHOOSE TAX FILING WISELY

If you have any information on the following question, I would appreciate receiving it from you. I believe that if all of my income is from Canada, and Canadian income tax rates are higher than the American, then there is no point in filing a U.S. return. That's because a reciprocal agreement between the two countries allows one to deduct the amount paid in Canada from the amount payable in the U.S. and the Canadian amount would always be more. I have read a variety of U.S. and Canadian publications on this subject and none of them covers this point.

—*Margaret L., Satellite Beach, FL*

You did not state what country you are a resident of and whether or not you were a U.S. citizen or green card holder. If you are a Canadian resident and non-U.S. citizen/green card holder, you are correct that there is little point in filing a U.S. tax return, unless you had U.S. sourced income. However, if you are a green card holder or U.S. citizen, there are several important points as to why you should look at filing U.S. tax returns.

1. You are required by law to file U.S. returns when your world income exceeds the total of your standard deduction ($4,100 for 1997) and personal exemption ($2,650 for 1997).

2. You may be able to receive an overall reduction in taxes paid by using the Canada — U.S. Tax Treaty to your best advantage thus getting the lowest tax rate available to you.

3. Proper foreign tax credit planning may help you recover some of the higher taxes paid to Canada on future U.S. returns, since unused foreign tax credits can be carried forward for up to 5 years.

There is not a lot of literature out there that can help you on this matter but you should try both Revenue Canada and the IRS publications included in the appendix of *The Border Guide* as well as *The Border Guide* itself.

REMARRIAGE LEGALITIES NEED ATTENTION

I am a Canadian citizen who winters in Florida. My income comes from my late husband's Canadian Pension Plan (CPP), company pension and some investment income. I am going to be married this spring to an American and we plan to reside in Florida year round.

I wish to maintain my Canadian citizenship. Do I need to apply for a green card in order to stay in the U.S. for more than 6 months each year or will my marriage qualify me for residency? Also, will I pay income tax in Canada or in the U.S. (my income is all from Canadian sources)? Are there other legal repercussions of which I should be informed? We plan to be married in Canada and will have a pre-nuptial contract drawn up by my Canadian attorney.

— *Shirley L. Lakeland, FL*

In order to reside legally in the U.S., your new husband will need to sponsor you for a green card. You do not have to give up your Canadian citizenship to do this, even if you apply later for U.S. citizenship.

If you no longer reside in Canada on a permanent basis you do not have to file Canadian tax returns after you file a final exit return. You will report all your world income on only your U.S. return. You will have to notify the payers of all your Canadian pensions that you are a non-resident. They will then apply 15% non-resident withholding on your company pension and

25% on CPP and OAS. You will get a credit for the withholding tax paid to Canada when you file your U.S. returns which will likely cover most if not all of any U.S. federal income tax you may have to pay.

There are some other issues, both good and bad, relating to Medicare and estate planning that you should discuss with a certified cross-border financial planner to make sure you maximize benefits and minimize pitfalls.

NON-RESIDENT WITHHOLDING A FACT OF LIFE

We are Canadian citizens by birth, and we received permanent U.S. residency in 1977. In 1992 we applied and received U.S. citizenship, giving us dual citizenship. When we left Canada in 1977 to become U.S. residents, we filed U.S. tax returns including all our world income. We have not filed any Canadian tax returns since we left Canada in 1977.

If we have to pay a new 25% non-resident withholding tax to Revenue Canada on the government pension benefits we receive under the 1995 Canada — U.S. tax treaty, will they deduct this from the pension payments we receive, or will we have to pay this tax ourselves to Revenue Canada? Will this withholding tax be available to us as a tax credit on our U.S. tax return to the IRS.?

— *Myron C., North Miami, FL*

Normally, if you provide Health and Welfare Canada with your correct non-resident address, they will deduct the 25% non-resident withholding tax at source before you receive your cheques. If they do not deduct it or you fail to give them proper notice of your Canadian non-resident status, you will have to send them the withholding on a regular basis. The withholding tax may be available to you as a tax credit to use against foreign source income of the same or similar type, otherwise you should be able to deduct it as an itemized deduction on Schedule A of your U.S. return, provided you are not using any foreign tax credits from the same year in the same return. Regular pensions other than OAS or CPP will still be subject only to a non-resident withholding rate of 15% by Revenue Canada.

TAX FILING STRATEGY COULD SAVE MONEY

My wife (deceased in August, 1993) and I bought a condo in Florida in 1976. We received our green cards as resident aliens in 1978, through my sister in L.A., who has been a U.S. citizen since 1946. Since then we have spent six months in Florida and six months in Canada. I elected to file Canadian income tax and also U.S. income tax relative to reciprocal tax laws. All taxes paid to Canada (federal and provincial) were used as a credit on U.S. tax forms, adjusting the income each year for the current exchange.

All of my income, investments, bank accounts and family are in Canada. We do not own property in Canada as my son has ample room in his residence, and we spend the six months with him. On the U.S. side, I own the condo, with about a $48,000 value.

A year ago a consultant advised me that I have dual resident status. Also, I have been given Power of Attorney by the State of California to look after my sister's affairs in Los Angeles. She is 98 years of age and ruled not competent to attend to same.

My questions are: 1) What is the situation regarding capital gains? 2) Should I sell my condo? 3) In effect it is my principal residence for six months and the only property I own. Isn't your principal residence exempt from capital gains? 4) Dual residency in Florida calls for my will to be probated in Florida. I only have a Canadian will, can that will be probated in both places?

— *Howard S., Ft. Lauderdale, FL*

Your U.S. condo can be both your Canadian residence and U.S. principal residence for tax purposes. Consequently, any gain on the sale of this residence would not be reportable to Revenue Canada. In the U.S. you could use your lifetime exemption of up to $125,000 allowed for all U.S. taxpayers. Consequently, you should not have any tax to pay either country on the sale of your Florida residence. If you hold the condo at your death, it will be income tax-free in both countries under current rules.

By filing returns both in Canada and the U.S. as you currently do, you may be paying more tax than necessary. You should look into this with a competent cross-border accountant or planner as there may be some substantial annual income tax savings if you arrange your affairs correctly.

Your will, if it is a valid Canadian will, is generally usable to settle your Florida affairs. If you have both Canada and U.S. property, it may be advantageous for you to put all your assets into a U.S. living trust so your estate is not required to go through probate in either country saving a great deal of cost and aggravation for your heirs.

BETTER LATE THAN NEVER

I read your informative article "Save on Currency Exchanges" in *The Sun Times of Canada*. If possible, I would appreciate an answer to the following questions. A person born and living in the U.S. for 25 years, moves to Canada 30 years ago, received Canadian citizenship, still retains his U.S. citizenship, lived and worked in Canada all of those 30 years but now lives in the U.S. about five months each year.

If this person decides to purchase property in Arizona and builds a house on that property are there rules and regulations that he should be aware of before he starts this project? Is this dual citizen required to file his Canadian income with the IRS even though he had no U.S. income? If so, what is the proper procedure for doing this? Thank you for your assistance.

— Ralph A., Apache Junction, AZ

As a citizen of both Canada and the U.S., you are subject to the tax rules of both countries at the same time. Canadian citizens pay tax on their world income only when they are residents of Canada, whereas U.S. citizens pay tax on their world income regardless of where they are resident. Consequently, you are subject to filing returns in both Canada and the U.S. unless you exit Canada to become a resident of the U.S. only.

The requirement to file in the U.S. is not negated based on the fact that all your income was Canadian sourced. This requirement to file has always been there even since you left the U.S. 30 years ago, so in effect you are quite overdue with your IRS filings. Please remember that just because you were required to file U.S. returns it does not mean that you necessarily have any tax owing to the IRS. There are certain exemptions and foreign tax credits from taxes paid to Canada for U.S. citizens living outside the U.S. that can greatly reduce or even eliminate U.S. taxes payable. However, the only way to find out if you have taxes due is to actually go back and file returns. There is an amnesty program currently available from the IRS that can allow you to get back in their good graces without filing 30 years returns that you should take advantage of before they pull the program.

Getting square with the IRS needs to be your top priority regardless of whether or not you build a place in Arizona. There may be some tax savings in store for you in the future if you file in the U.S. and exit Canada for tax purposes. There are no particular issues you need to be concerned about by building your new place in the Sun Belt except that you might consider using a living trust to hold title to your property so it does not have to go through probate in Arizona or Canada.

Some of the issues you need to deal with are quite complex and I would recommend you seek out some assistance from a qualified person knowledgeable in both the applicable Canadian and U.S. matters.

DOES A GREEN CARD HAVE AN EXPIRATION DATE?

My wife and I moved to Florida in 1991 on a permanent basis as retirees. My wife is a U.S. citizen and I have a green card issued in 1953. I do not intend to work. I returned to Canada in 1954, retaining my green card and filed Canadian income tax returns from 1954 to 1990. I will file a U.S. return for the year 1991, and subsequent years. I will not file a Canadian return. My questions are:

1. Is my green card still valid, or do I have to re-apply for another one ?

2. Do I apply in Tampa or do I have to go back to Toronto?

3. When I file my U.S. return, am I liable to be asked why I did not file a return since 1954 and if so, how do I answer? And depending on the answer, will the Internal Revenue Service (IRS) inform Immigration and Naturalization (INS) of my status?

4. Will I be able to apply for U.S. citizenship after three years?

— *Edward P., Venice, FL*

Since you did not surrender your green card, and it has no expiration date, it is technically still valid. However, you were supposed to surrender the green card in 1954 when you left the United States.

Your best bet is to tread softly with the Immigration and Naturalization Service for awhile, and just start using the green card again each time you cross the border. According to new INS rules you do need to file an INS Form I-90 to obtain a new green card with updated pictures and a ten year expiration date. Since you have a permanent Florida home, the Immigration and Naturalization Service will likely not bother you.

The Internal Revenue Service may question you though, as to where all your tax returns were since 1954. If you hurry you can also take advantage of an amnesty program with the IRS which requires you file the last six years U.S. returns. You will pay no penalties but will pay the taxes due, if any, with interest for the six years. The IRS will forgive any taxes that may have been due prior to the six years. You need five or more continuous years of U.S. residency before applying for U.S. citizenship.

AVOIDING U.S. ESTATE TAXES

I am a Canadian citizen, and a resident of Canada. I own a property in Florida that is valued in excess of $100,000 U.S. I would like to sell this property to my daughter so that no estate tax will be payable on my death.

The property has increased in value by about $50,000 since I purchased it. This transaction will take place in Canada between two Canadian citizens. I know I will have to pay a capital gains tax in Canada but what are my liabilities in the U.S. as far as capital gains?

— *Todd A O, Montreal, PQ*

You would be subject to Canadian capital gains tax of approximately $20,000 U.S. not including any currency gains or losses on this transaction. If you have crystallized your $100,000 capital gains exemption election on this property while it was still available, you could possibly avoid paying tax to Revenue Canada by selling it to your daughter.

Under the Canada — U.S. Tax Treaty, your first obligation for taxes on this sale, would be to the IRS. Since the property is in the U.S. you will be subject to U.S. tax on the gain in the year of the sale. A $50,000 gain would accrue a total tax bill in the U.S. of approximately $12,500. This U.S. tax paid will provide an offsetting foreign tax credit against the $20,000 due in Canada.

Consequently, if these numbers proved accurate, you would pay $12,500 tax to the IRS and an additional $7,500 ($20,000 minus $12,500) to Revenue Canada for a total of $20,000 U.S.

Your goal is avoidance of the U.S. non-resident estate tax, but your current U.S. non-resident estate tax liability on this specific property is only $10,800. Paying $20,000 at current tax rates to save $10,800 (or even zero under the new Canada-U.S. Tax Treaty estate tax rules) in estate tax at some point in the future seems economically self-defeating. Selling the property to your daughter does not eliminate the estate tax, it only transfers the tax obligation to her estate. If she were to predecease you, the tax would be paid at her death, and if you inherited the property back, it would be taxed a second time at your death.

You would likely be better off looking at alternatives other than selling your residence to your daughter. For example, if you are currently around the age 60, take the money you would have paid in taxes and buy a single deposit no-load life insurance policy with your daughter named as beneficiary. This would provide her with as much as $100,000 in tax-free death benefits, enough to pay any estate taxes several times over. If you decide to sell the property to a third party before your death, you can cash out the policy and get your money back with interest.

If you are uninsurable, investing the $20,000 capital gains tax that you would pay at 7% interest doubles the amount over 10 years; enough to pay estate tax. Just make sure the investment is exempt from U.S. estate tax.

The new 1994 Canada — U.S. Tax Treaty, will allow you to offset U.S. non-resident estate tax liability with a credit for Canadian capital gains taxes if you hold property until death in the United States, thus avoiding any double taxation.

EFFECTS OF DUAL CITIZENSHIP

What effects does dual citizenship have on Canadian citizens regarding income tax, etc.

— *Candy O., Tampa, FL*

Although your question is a short one, there are no short answers. There are a large number of tax issues which will need to be addressed if a Canadian becomes a dual citizen, including your country of residence, the size of your estate and the types of income you are receiving.

Probably, the first question you need to address is, why become a dual citizen? Unless you intend to reside in the United States more than six months a year and Canada less than six months, you will not likely benefit tax-wise by becoming a dual citizen. You may even expose yourself to some unnecessary tax complications.

Canada taxes its citizens only when they are actual residents of Canada. United States citizens are taxed wherever they live in the world, with tax credits allowed against foreign taxes paid by the United States citizens in another country of residence. Consequently, if you become a dual citizen, and still intend to reside in Canada, you will be required to file tax returns in both countries on world income. Filing in both countries affords you no tax advantages since you will pay the Canadian tax rate and take a credit for those taxes paid on the United States return. Your total tax paid between the two countries, under most circumstances, will not be any greater, but why complicate your life unnecessarily?

The real tax advantages of dual citizenship come when you become a non-resident of Canada and are no longer subject to Canadian tax rules. Depending on your sources and amounts of income, you can realistically cut your annual income tax bill in half or more, with good cross-border financial planning.

Under the Canada — United States Tax Treaty, you can be a dual citizen and maintain a lifestyle of winters in the Sunbelt and summers in Canada, without being subject to taxes in both countries. Consequently, dual citizens can arrange their financial affairs in such a way that they pay tax on their world income only in the United States. Once you have completed an exit tax return from Canada, your tax situation becomes much clearer. CPP and OAS are tax-free in the U.S. and are subject to a non-resident withholding tax of 25% by Revenue Canada. Taxes on RRSPs and RRIFs withdrawals drop to 15% or 25%, depending whether they are periodic or lump sum withdrawals. Canadian dividend and corporate pensions are subject to a non-resident withholding tax of 15%. Under the new treaty, interest withholding has been reduced to 10%. You can also take advantage of a large variety of tax-free, tax deferred or tax sheltered investment options in the United States, to substantially reduce or eliminate any tax on investment income.

The tax advantages of becoming a dual citizen and paying your taxes in the United States need to be greater than the net cost of United States Medicare, approximately $3,600 US each per year, or less if you qualify for U.S. Social Security. There are many complex estate planning issues that should be addressed before making the move to dual citizenship, particularly if you and your wife's total estate is over $1,600,000 CDN. Over this amount, United States estate taxes will have to be taken into account.

Because of the complexity of the issues involved with becoming a dual citizen, I don't recommend you attempt such a move without a written plan completed by a knowledgeable cross-border financial planner. Talking to an attorney or accountant in either or both countries may only give you a part of a much larger puzzle, and can be confusing, especially if they lack knowledge of the other country's systems.

CANADIAN CITIZENS VERSUS LEGAL RESIDENTS

Are there any differences in the legal situation (in Canada or the U.S.A. as well) between legal residents of Canada, and Canadian nationals travelling and/or investing in the United States? Do the Canadian federal or provincial governments differentiate between these two categories other than during elections?

— *Flora B., Largo, FL*

You didn't say what situation you are in now so I will attempt to answer your question by reviewing the most likely scenarios.

Please note there is more than one set of rules from at least two United States government agencies that may apply to you, depending on what you are attempting to do; so sorting out what rules apply to your situation may be difficult.

The first set of rules to consider are tax rules from the IRS in the United States. The IRS doesn't differentiate between legal residents of Canada and Canadian citizens, unless the legal Canadian resident happens to also be a United States citizen. Canada taxes its citizens only if they are residents of Canada. The United States taxes its citizens regardless of where they reside in the world. Non-residents of the United States investing in the United States have certain tax withholding and filing requirements they may be subject to, depending on what they are investing in, and what country they come from. There is a Canada — U.S. Tax Treaty that segregates Canadian residents and citizens from other non-resident investors in the United States, with respect to what withholding rates are on investment income, and what tax credits are allowed.

Legal Canadian residents or Canadian citizens travelling in the United States are subject to essentially the same Immigration and Naturalization regulations. Canadians are allowed to visit the United States without formal visa requirements. However, there are rules that apply such that Canadians travelling in the United States are technically on a B-2 visitors visa, which lasts up to six months and can be renewed by simply re-entering the United States again, to start the six months over. If you are immigrating to the United States, then your status in Canada as a landed immigrant or a citizen does have some bearing on what status you may apply for in the United States.

Canadian federal or provincial governments do not generally have any separate tax rules that apply to Canadian landed immigrants or citizens. Under Revenue Canada rules, citizens and non-citizens, as residents of Canada, are taxed identically.

WITHHOLDING TAX COMPLIANCE ON U.S. RENTAL INCOME

What options are available to Canadian owners/renters in Florida, who through ignorance, have failed to comply with the 30% withholding tax, and who wish to square themselves immediately with the Internal Revenue Service?

— Ed F., Williamsburg, ON

Your question is a very good one, and a situation we run into quite often. Anyone who rents out their United States property for longer than two (2) weeks per year, is subject to taxation on this income in both the United States (under the Internal Revenue Code) and Canada (under the Income Tax Act).

First, you must decide which of the two methods, explained below, is appropriate for you. The first method has the renter withhold 30% of the gross rental income received, and forward it to the IRS Service Center in Philadelphia, PA. The onus is on the renter to withhold the tax if you are a non-resident landlord, but the IRS will come after both the renter and the landlord, if the tax is not paid as required.

The second method is to make an election under Section 871 of the Internal Revenue Code to be taxed as effectively conducting business in the United States, and file annually a Form 1040NR tax return in the United States.

On this return, expenses incurred to earn the rent such as property taxes, utilities, mortgage interest, travel, etc. and allowable personal exemptions, are taken as deductions to arrive at a net taxable income for non-resident United States tax purposes.

By filing Form 1040NR for both the current and past years, the non-resident taxpayer will generally pay less tax. In fact, most people in this situation make little or no profit after all expenses have been deducted and therefore no tax is due. Even if you do have some net rental profit the tax rate after deducting personal exemptions of $2,650 starts at only 15%.

A husband and wife can split this income on separate United States returns, and both take personal exemptions if the rental property was purchased jointly.

The forms for filing a return, the Form 1040NR and the necessary rental income Schedule E, may be found at any IRS office or may be requested by calling the IRS toll-free number, 1-800-829-3676. If you do not already have a United States Social Security Number for tax purposes, or Taxpayer Identification Number (TIN) you need to apply for one by completing IRS Form W-7.

Form 1040NR is relatively easy to complete, however, if you do not file your own Canadian return, you will likely need someone experienced in the Canada — U.S. tax treaty to assist you.

THE LONG ARM OF THE LAW

Is there a statute of limitations for not reporting rental income for non-residents?

— Wanda M., Kitchener, ON

There is a statute of limitations of 3 years with the IRS if you have filed a completed Form 1040NR. If you have not filed or you filed without reporting all income, the statute of limitations does not apply, and the IRS can go back as far as they like to collect prior taxes. Prior to 1990, people in your situation had little to fear if the IRS ever caught up with them, because they typically made no net profit on their rental income.

So, all you would need to do, is file a return for the years in question, and prove there was no net income.

However in 1990, the IRS came out with new regulations that do not allow non-resident filers the ability to file a new return deducting rental expenses against rental income longer than 16 months past the due date of the return. Consequently, beyond the 16 months allowed, tax on the gross rents, plus interest and penalties would apply irrespective of whether you made any net profits. To reconcile with the IRS, you need to first ensure you file your 1997 tax return by June 15, 1998 (the deadline for the Form 1040NR). I would also recommend going back and filing for the previous years in which you had rental income.

Regardless of whether you pay the withholding tax of 30%, or choose to file the Form 1040NR, you must still report the income earned to Revenue Canada on your annual T-1 return. You can take a foreign tax credit against the Canadian taxes due, for taxes paid in the U.S. Remember, filing a United States return and paying United States taxes does not exempt you from Revenue Canada reporting requirements.

RESIDENCY FOR TAX PURPOSES

Do I need to have a "green card" or other visa before I am considered a U.S. resident for tax purposes? Are there other regulations that apply to becoming a resident for tax purposes without actually immigrating?

— *Oscar G., Sun City, AZ*

Residency for tax purposes does not relate to permanent resident status, but rather to your physical presence within the United States. The following is the general explanation offered by the IRS in its Publication 927, "Tax Obligations of Legalized Aliens." If you are in the United States as a lawful permanent resident (have a green card) at any time during the year, you are considered a resident alien for tax purposes and are taxed just like a U.S. citizen. That is, you are taxed on your income from any source throughout the world.

Even if you do not have a green card, you are still treated as a resident alien, if you are actually in the United States for enough days during the year. Generally, if you are in the United States for 183 days during that year, you are considered a resident for tax purposes for that year. But, you may also be considered a resident for a year, if you are in the U.S. for less than 183 days during that year, provided you were there for a certain minimum number of days, over a three year period. You do not count the days you were there under a diplomatic, student, or teacher visa. Since the United States and Canada have a newly ratified tax treaty, most Canadian visitors to the United States who stay less than the 183 days, would not be considered residents of the United States under the terms of the treaty. Consult a tax advisor if you are in doubt about your status.

ALIENS AND THE 1040NR

My wife and I are Canadian citizens. In 1978, we bought a condo in Hallandale, Florida, which we have enjoyed in the winter for a three to four month period each year. This year we sold our condo, realizing a small capital gain. We have no other investments in the U.S.

In "Publication 519, U.S. Tax Guide for Aliens" (1989), which was provided to us by the IRS in Hallandale, one paragraph mentions that if "aliens have been in the U.S. for less than 183 days during a taxation year, gains from sales of capital assets are exempt from tax."

— *Ingomar H., Hallandale, FL*

You have done a good job in researching what your U.S. tax consequences are for selling your Florida condo. The "capital assets" that IRS Publication 519 refers to that are exempt from tax for non-U.S. residents are stocks, bonds and other such assets. Real estate and other real property are not included in this exemption for capital assets.

Consequently, your small capital gain on your condo may be subject to tax. However, before you calculate whether you have a gain or not you can add improvement and selling costs plus other related expenses to the cost basis or total amount you paid for the property. Regardless of whether you had a net gain or loss, you need to reconcile your sale with both the IRS and Revenue Canada. In the U.S. you are required to file IRS Form 1040NR, the non-resident tax return for the year in which the property was sold, by June 15th the next year.

If the property was held in joint ownership with your spouse, you both will have to file, each reporting half of the gain (or loss). Since both you and your wife each are entitled to personal exemption of $2,650, your gain would have to exceed $5,300 before any tax would be due. If you did pay any tax to the IRS, you would receive a foreign tax credit on your Canadian return for the total tax paid. For Revenue Canada you will report the gain (or loss) on Schedule 3 of your T-1 tax form.

SHARING THE WEALTH OF TAX INFORMATION

My wife, a Canadian citizen, sold a condominium in the USA in 1995 at a small loss from the original 1990 purchase price. She did not report the sale to Revenue Canada due to the loss, although she did to the IRS. I obtained an exemption from withholding tax because a loss was incurred. She has just received a letter from Revenue Canada requesting copies of the Purchase & Sale documents and the reason why the disposition was not reported on her 1995 tax return.

Is it necessary to report the sale of property in the USA (not principal residence) to Revenue Canada when no profit results? Also, if an "equity membership" in a golf club is sold for more than the original cost is this deemed to be income or profit? Am I required to report it for Canadian tax purposes?

— *Don R. C. Naples, FL*

You didn't tell me which country your wife is a resident of for tax purposes. Canadian citizens only have potential tax obligations to Revenue Canada on foreign dispositions if they are residents of Canada. Your wife should not have to report the sale of a condominium or golf club membership to Revenue Canada if she has exited Canada for tax purposes.

By the tone of Revenue Canada's request, they still consider your wife to be a Canadian resident. If they are wrong and your wife is a non-resident, you need to provide them with information to prove she has left - such a US green card, sale of Canadian residence, etc. If she is still a resident of Canada, Revenue Canada is correct in their requests. Residents of Canada must report their world income to Revenue Canadian including both the sale of the condominium and the golf club membership. Tax could be due to Revenue Canada on the net gain on the sale of these two items, adjusted for Canadian dollars on the difference of the purchase and sale.

This is a good example of Revenue Canada and the IRS sharing your tax information as allowed under the Canada/US Tax Treaty.

TAXING CANADIAN RESIDENTS ON US SOCIAL SECURITY BENEFITS

You have covered the matter of Canadian citizens living in the U.S. and drawing Canadian pensions. I'm wondering if you could do "the other side of the coin" and review the tax agreement for Canadians living in Canada and drawing U.S. Social Security benefits such as my wife and I.

We lived and worked in the U.S. for many years and paid into Social Security. We also filed returns with the Internal Revenue Service and paid every year since 1958. Now with the new agreement they are withholding 25% of our monthly payments which amounts to $2,100 per year. This is in addition to the amount we pay on other income from the U.S. Under the old agreement I didn't have to pay anything on Social Security because my income was under about $40,000 per year. I wouldn't mind the monthly deduction if I received a tax credit for that amount but according to a letter from the U.S. Treasury Department, I can't do that. There is "currently no basis for appeal" although now I do not have to declare half of my U.S. benefits on my Canadian tax return. My accountant says even so, the new agreement will cost me about $650 CDN per year.

I know a Canadian couple who are elderly (80 yrs.) and their situation is much like mine except they have very little Canadian income. The new agreement is costing them about $2,000 per year because of the U.S. withholding on their Social Security. Not having to declare the 50% on their Canadian tax return doesn't do them much good, if any good at all.

In the light of this information, I ask you if you think this new agreement is fair to us Canadians living in Canada and drawing U.S. Social Security?

—Baron M.W. Abbotsford, B.C.

Your assessment of the new tax treatment of your Social Security under the Canada — U.S. Tax Treaty is quite accurate. You did not mention why you are still filing U.S. tax returns, but if you are filing because you are either an American citizen or Green Card holder, you can qualify to have the 25.5% withholding tax on Social Security eliminated. Just contact a Social Security office.

There is however, a real problem for those who are not U.S. citizens or Green Card holders and who do not file U.S. resident returns. Revenue Canada only provides Foreign Tax Credits for taxable income and Social Security is no longer taxable from a Canadian perspective. Therefore, no Foreign Tax Credits are available when you file Canadian returns. If your friends are not U.S. citizens, the 25.5% Social Security tax applies. Under the terms of the treaty, they along with many others, began paying higher taxes on their Social Security income as of January 1, 1996.

Fortunately, relief may be on the way thanks to the grass roots efforts of the estimated 50,000 Canadians who collect U.S. Social Security benefits. As a result their campaign, both governments have agreed to amend the U.S. — Canada Tax Treaty, providing tax relief for many Canadians collecting U.S. Social Security. The changes were approved in April 1997, and will probably be in place by January 1, 1998. Details are still sketchy, but changes will likely be targeted at those in the low and middle income range. There is also said to be a provision for these Canadians to receive a tax refund from the U.S. government.

You Still Can't Take it with You

NON-RESIDENT ESTATE PLANNING

C anadians have not had to deal with any true inheritance or estate taxes since the Capital Gains tax was introduced in 1972. The provinces which had an inheritance tax at the time opted out of their own tax programs in favour of collecting the provincial portion of the Capital Gains tax from the deemed disposition at the death of a taxpayer. However, Canadian citizens (or Americans) owning property in Canada, need to be aware of the increasingly heavy hand of the tax man encroaching into their estates, when transferred to heirs, regardless of which country they permanently reside.

The first step in understanding cross-border estate planning is comprehending all the forces of Canadian law that come into play, and the need for estate planning in the first place.

Many Canadians are complacent and believe estate or inheritance taxes concern only Americans. However, on estates of less than $1,600,000 CDN, the Canadian inheritance or estate tax can be much greater than in the U.S. See Figure 8.11 in Chapter 8 for more details.

What, you say? There is no inheritance tax in Canada. Look again. The deemed disposition at death of capital assets with capital gains, and retirement programs such as RRSPs and RRIFs, create a substantial tax liability at death. In some cases, these hidden taxes can exceed 53% of the value of the estate. Revenue Canada and the provinces do not call these taxes inheritance taxes but — if it looks like a duck, and walks like a duck... The Ontario Fair Tax Commission has recently made the following recommendation to the federal government on a Canadian estate tax:

"Ontario should seek the agreement of the federal government and other provinces to establish a national wealth transfer tax. This tax should be fully comprehensive and should apply to gifts as well as transfers at death. The tax should exempt spousal transfers. It should have a generous exemption but should contain no credit for capital gains taxes on deemed dispositions." The new Conservative government in Ontario has not yet stated its position on this matter, so hopefully they will drop the initiative altogether. If you think the federal government is not seriously considering this or similar proposals, think again. A wealth transfer tax is one of the last "politically correct" taxes it has not imposed on the Canadian taxpayer and they would love to get a piece of the action as baby boomers begin to inherit an estimated one trillion dollars from their aging parents.

The province of residence of the deceased collects approximately half of this deemed disposition tax at death. Several provinces however, don't seem to be happy with their share of the tax, and have implemented new taxes disguised as user fees.

British Columbia led the way by implementing a probate fee, with many other provinces getting quickly in line. The probate fee is a cleverly disguised inheritance tax, since the majority of one's assets go through probate either at their time of death, their spouse's death or both times; hitting the estate twice. Family heirlooms can be taxed every time they are passed on to the next generation. As recently as June 1992, Ontario increased its probate fee by 300%. Alberta, in October 1993 raised its maximum probate fee by 600%. Because this so-called probate fee is an administrative type issue, it doesn't need to come before provincial legislators for a proper debate. The general public is kept in the dark until the fee is already in place. Since there are few publications which include all the provincial probate fees I'll include a brief summary of them here:

- Newfoundland: $50 for the first $1,000 and $4 per $1,000 thereafter with no maximum fee.

- Nova Scotia: $75 for the first $10,000 progressing to $800 for estates of $200,000 and $5 per $1,000 thereafter with no maximum fee.

- Prince Edward Island: $50 for the first $10,000 progressing to $400 for estates of $100,000 and $4 per $1,000 thereafter with no maximum fee.

- New Brunswick: $5 per $1,000 with no maximum.

- Quebec: has a different legal system with no probate or probate fees.

- Ontario: $5 per $1,000 for the first $50,000 and $15 per $1,000 thereafter with no maximum.

- Saskatchewan: $12 for the first $1,000 and $6 per $1,000 thereafter with no maximum fee.

- Alberta: $25 for the first $10,000 progressing to a maximum of $6,000 for estates of $1,000,000 or more.

- British Columbia: no fee for the first $10,000. For estates between $10,000 and $25,000 there is a fee of $100. And there is a fee of $6 per $1,000 thereafter with no maximum fee.

Canadians or Americans who live in one country and own property in the other, face additional tax rules, which can leave them exposed to double tax. The double tax arises from Canada's deemed disposition tax stacked on top of the United States resident/non-resident estate tax, if applicable. This multiple death tax can total up to 80% of the property value in the other country. The new amendment to the Canada — United States Tax Treaty goes a long way to eliminate most of this potential double tax whammy for Canadians and Americans in this situation. See the section titled *The Double Estate Tax* later in this chapter.

Canadians, particularly those who own property in both the U.S. and Canada, are setting their estates up for trouble in the form of high taxes,

Estate Shrinkage

Name	Gross Estate	Net Estate	% Sh.
John Rockefeller	$26,905,182	$9,780,194	64%
Elvis Presley	$10,165,434	$2,790,799	73%
Walt Disney	$23,004,851	$16,192,908	30%
Henry J. Kaiser, Jr.	$55,910,973	$54,879,958	2%

FIGURE 4.1

liquidity problems and high legal fees, if they ignore current or future inheritance taxes. Use the examples in Figure 4.1 to see what happened to the estates of some well-known people, as measured by estate shrinkage. Estate shrinkage, as the name implies, is simply the amount of the estate that was consumed by probate fees, legal fees, accounting fees, and estate taxes, before the beneficiaries actually inherit the estate.

From Figure 4.1, you can also see that there is a great deal of difference in estate shrinkage between these wealthy deceased persons. Why did Elvis Presley have a 73% shrinkage while Henry Kaiser, with a much larger estate, only 2%? The answer is simple; proper estate planning techniques.

There are a number of planning techniques you can use to reduce or eliminate inheritance taxes — regardless of your residency and whether you have property in both Canada and the U.S. This Chapter will provide you with some basic guidelines, and direct you to some of the most appropriate estate planning techniques for your situation. Remember that attempting to implement an estate plan without the assistance of a financial planning professional familiar with both U.S. and Canadian estate planning techniques, is analogous to reading up on removing your gall bladder, and then doing the procedure by yourself.

THE U.S. NON-RESIDENT ESTATE TAX

On November 11, 1988 President Reagan, in his last major formal announcement, signed the Technical and Miscellaneous Revenue Act (TAMRA) of 1988, making adjustments to the Tax Reform Act of 1986. There are two major provisions in TAMRA which affect Canadians who own U.S. property such as real estate, stocks, bonds or businesses. The first provision is a dramatic increase in estate or death taxes for non-residents on their U.S. property.

The second provision is the loss of the unlimited marital deduction by Canadians or non-U.S. citizens who are residents of the U.S. They can no longer transfer assets, estates or gifts tax-free to a Canadian citizen spouse during their lifetime, or upon death. For gifts made after July 14, 1988, only the first $100,000 of gifts per year to a non-citizen spouse will not be taxed under this new provision. Prior to this revision in TAMRA, there were no tax disadvantages for Canadians who resided in the U.S. and who chose not to become U.S. citizens.

This dramatic increase in U.S. estate taxes — which applies after November 11, 1988, affects Canadian and other foreign owners of U.S. real estate, company shares, debt securities and other property. Under this reform, estate tax rates on these investments jumped from between 6% - 30%, up to 18% - 55% (depending on the taxable estate value).

Estate tax can be analogous to income tax; there are two main factors which determine the amount of tax that is actually paid. These are, the tax rate in any given bracket and the amount of the estate that it applies to. We will deal with each of these issues separately, and then combine them with some examples.

THE TAXABLE ESTATE

Estate tax in the United States is technically a transfer tax on property owned at death. If the property is transferred during one's lifetime, it is subject to a gift tax at the same rates as the estate tax, with some minor exceptions noted in the section titled *What is a Gift Tax?* United States citizens and residents of the U.S. are subject to estate taxes on their worldwide assets, while non-resident Canadians are subject only to tax on their property deemed to be situated in the United States. The Income Tax Rules and Estate Tax Rules covered in Chapter 1 details what situations Canadians may be considered residents of the United States for estate tax purposes. Estate tax is based on the fair market value (not just the appreciation) of all assets either on, or exactly nine months after the date of death. The property subject to estate tax includes: real property located in the United States, personal property normally located in the United States such as autos, jewellery, boats, RVs, furniture and artwork, shares of U.S. corporations, regardless of where they were purchased, or where they are physically held, and certain bonds and notes issued by United States residents and corporations.

Assets normally excluded from the estate of a non-resident include: U.S. Bank deposits; government and corporate bonds issued after July 18, 1984; and shares or notes of non U.S. corporations. Chapter 6 provides more specific details, under Exempt Investments, about which investments are exempt from both income tax and estate tax for non-residents.

The total of all taxable assets noted above, less any of the exempt assets and minus certain deductions for estate settlement costs and non-recourse mortgages, equals the taxable estate.

U.S. FEDERAL ESTATE TAX

Once the taxable estate has been totalled, the estate tax applies at the graduated rates, with the lowest rate being 18% and the highest 55% on taxable estates over $3,000,000. Refer to figure 4.2 which illustrates the tax for some sample estates.

UNIFIED CREDIT

Non-residents and non U.S. citizens are allowed an estate tax credit of $13,000 to offset any estate tax payable. This credit effectively exempts the first $60,000 of the estate from attracting taxation, as illustrated in Fig. 4.2 and Fig. 4.3.

Residents or citizens of the United States are subject to the same tax rates, but there is one significant difference. They are allowed a unified estate tax credit of $192,800, which effectively equates to a tax exemption of $600,000!

U.S. Estate Tax
(All figures in U.S. dollars.)

Taxable Estate	Tax (Before Credit)
$10,000	$1,800
$20,000	$3,800
$40,000	$8,200
$60,000	$13,000
$80,000	$18,200
$100,000	$23,800
$150,000	$38,800
$250,000	$70,800
$500,000	$155,800
$1,000,000	$345,800

FIGURE 4.2

THE NEW CANADA & U.S. TAX TREATY ESTATE TAX PROVISIONS

The new Canada — U.S. Tax Treaty hammered out in 1994 after six years of negotiations brings some good news for Canadians owning property in the U.S. The new treaty agreement corrects an oversight made in 1988, when the U.S. increased non-resident estate taxes to the level paid by U.S. residents, but did not increase corresponding exemptions. Thus, many Canadian non-residents saw taxes double or even triple after the 1988 tax package took effect.

The new treaty amendment increases the non-resident exemption, according to a specified formula, from $60,000 U.S. to $600,000 U.S. per person, retroactive to 1988. This means that most Canadians, those with total world wide estates valued at $600,000 U.S. or less won't be hit with the non-resident estate tax.

Example: Non-Resident Estate Tax Current U.S. Domestic Rates

Dorothy, a Canadian non-resident of the U.S., owns a villa in Hawaii her deceased husband had purchased for her over 15 years ago. The villa is valued at $300,000 fully furnished with a small mortgage of $50,000 remaining at a local bank. This property is all she owns in the U.S.

Dorothy's taxable estate is $250,000 (the $300,000 value of the villa less the $50,000 non-recourse mortgage).

Her estate tax from Figure 4.2 would be $70,800 less her unified credit of $13,000 for a net tax of $57,800 U.S.

FIGURE 4.3

DETERMINING EXEMPTIONS

When calculating the portion of U.S. non-resident exemption under the new treaty rules, compare your total world estate to your U.S. estate. You will get the same percentage of the $600,000 maximum exemption as the ratio of value of U.S. assets relative to the value of your world assets. As you may have already surmised, to get this higher exemption under this new formula, you must reveal your worldwide assets to the U.S. and be subject to an IRS audit. Since nearly 100% of all large estate tax returns in the U.S. are audited, executors will have this added burden which could prove to be time consuming and expensive.

Here's how it would work for a non-resident Canadian who owns U.S. property with a fair market value of $100,000 U.S. and a total net worth including the U.S. property of $500,000 U.S. Under the amended treaty, they would receive 20 percent or $120,000 of the $600,000 exemption (calculated by taking $100,000/$500,000 X $600,000 =$120,000). They

---

Non-Resident Estate Tax
According to the New Treaty Rules

Dorothy's taxable estate would remain the same as Fig. 4.3 at $250,000 and tax before equivalent exemption $70,800. Her new exemption would be:

($250,000 ÷ 1,000,000) x $600,000 = $150,000

Unified credit from Fig. 4.2 for $150,000 exemption $38,800.

Net tax due $70,800 - $38,800 = $32,000.

FIGURE 4.3A

would not be subject to any U.S. non-resident estate tax since their U.S. property is valued at less than the allowed exemption. They may still be subject to the Canadian deemed disposition tax at death, if the property had appreciated in value during the term of ownership prior to death.

While most Canadians will benefit from the larger estate tax exemption, those with larger estates could actually face a higher tax burden because the ratio of U.S. to world assets results in an exemption less than $60,000. For example a person with a world wide estate of $2,000,000 U.S. with the same $100,000 U.S. property would receive an exemption of only $30,000 (calculated by taking $100,000/$2,000,000 X $600,000 = $30,000). In this circumstance the higher net worth individual could bypass the treaty and revert to the domestic rules for the non-resident estate tax mentioned in the preceding sections of this chapter and receive the $60,000 exemption since it is higher. It's important that you consult with a financial planner who is up-to-speed on cross-border issues to determine your best options.

When determining the value of your world estate, you must follow U.S. reporting rules (i.e., including such things as the value of life insurance policies that you own on which you are the insured and the present value of all the future payments you might leave a spouse under the spousal benefit of your pensions). Since most Canadians do own the life insurance on their own life and do have some form of government and private pensions the value to their world estates for the purposes of figuring the size of their U.S. exemption under the new Treaty can be greatly reduced. Note that the treaty does not give Canadian residents with appreciated U.S. property any break from the Canadian deemed disposition tax (Canada's estate tax) at death. The sole exception is a credit that will now be allowed to offset this tax if any U.S. non-resident estate tax is paid. See the *Double Taxation Issue* in the next section of this chapter.

The treaty has some other positive changes. For example, it adds U.S. stocks to the list of investments that Canadians can make that will be exempt from the non-resident estate tax. This only applies to Canadians whose world estate is less than $1.2 million U.S. See Chapter 6 for a complete list of exempt investments.

Previously, exempt investments only included bonds and treasury bills issued by the U.S. government, bank deposits, life insurance and corporate bonds issued after July 18, 1984. The inclusion of U.S. stocks will enable most Canadians who are non-residents of the U.S. to freely hold a very diversified portfolio of U.S. stocks, bonds and mutual funds without being exposed to any non-resident estate tax. Figure 4.3A shows the effects of the new Canada — U.S. Tax Treaty. Compare it with Figure 4.3 which was calculated under the current U.S. domestic rules. We assume Dorothy has a world wide estate of $1,000,000 U.S. including her Hawaiian villa.

In summary, the new articles regarding non-resident estate tax in the Canada — U.S. Tax Treaty, provide some relief for Canadians owning U.S. property, but at the expense of complexity. The estate may incur legal and accounting fees that can be, in some instances, higher than the tax itself. The treaty will be of little relief to the double taxation status of U.S. citizens in Canada with Canadian appreciated property or for Canadians living in the U.S. as dual residents with U.S. property.

THE DOUBLE TAXATION ISSUE

Earlier in this chapter, we discussed the Canadian equivalent to estate tax, the deemed disposition tax on appreciated assets, including foreign assets at death. This tax is, in effect, an income tax on capital gains. By its own definition, the United States estate tax is not an income tax. Consequently, under current rules, Revenue Canada does not allow a foreign tax credit on estate taxes paid to the United States to offset the deemed disposition capital gains tax on foreign assets. In other words, there is no foreign income tax credit available from Revenue Canada since an estate tax cannot offset an income tax. Conversely, the American IRS will not allow the capital gains tax paid to Revenue Canada as a credit or deduction against U.S. estate taxes payable, for exactly the same reason. The new Canada — U.S. Tax Treaty will allow for a credit of these two dissimilar taxes and all but eliminate this double tax.

Canadians who own appreciated U.S real estate and other taxable U.S. assets, should no longer face two separate taxes on the same assets at the same time, without any means of obtaining offsetting credit.

Figure 4.4 illustrates this double tax more clearly. Let's use the examples of Figures 4.3 & 4.3A, and assume that the owner of the Hawaiian villa dies this year, both under the existing treaty and under the new treaty. As you can see from figure 4.4, Dorothy, according to the new Canada—U.S. Tax Treaty rules, would pay the equivalent total of the higher of either the Canadian deemed disposition tax or the U.S. non-resident estate tax. She would not pay a total of both taxes since she would take a credit for U.S.

taxes paid against her Canadian deemed disposition tax. Note that if the U.S non-resident estate tax is equal to or larger than the Canadian deemed disposition tax , no tax is due to Revenue Canada.

There are a number of estate planning techniques designed to assist Canadians to avoid or reduce the effect of this non-resident estate tax. These techniques will be discussed in the next section of the chapter.

HOW TO AVOID THE U.S. NON-RESIDENT ESTATE TAX

Each of the following techniques have their individual merits and drawbacks in dealing with the non-resident estate tax. There is no silver bullet solution for all people in all situations. We will briefly cover the circumstances under which each technique works best, and what to watch out for with each option. These options are given as a guide only and any attempt to apply these methods to your own situation, should be accomplished with the assistance of a qualified cross-border estate planning professional. The new Canada — U.S. Tax Treaty with its articles on estate tax may make the following strategies less necessary than in the past, since those Canadians with smaller estates should qualify for larger exemptions than under existing U.S. domestic rules.

BECOME A U.S. RESIDENT

In a previous section in this chapter, The U.S. Non-Resident Estate Tax, we mentioned the fact that residents of the United States receive an estate tax equivalent exemption of $600,000 compared to the non-resident exemption of $60,000 (unless the new 1994 Canada — U.S. Tax Treaty allows for a greater exemption, see the earlier sections of this chapter). A husband and wife who become United States residents would be eligible for a total exemption of $1,200,000 US or about $1,600,000 CDN, which is enough for many Canadians to be fully exempt from any estate taxes. Without further estate planning, persons with larger estates could still be subject to tax.

There are many other implications of becoming a United States resident besides estate tax reduction. These ramifications will be covered in greater detail in Chapters 7 through 9.

Example: Double Estate Tax - Old Treaty

Dorothy's deceased husband paid $100,000 for the
Hawaiin villa when he bought it 15 years ago,
now valued at $300,000:

Canadian Tax		U.S. Non-resident Estate Tax	
$300,000	Deemed Sale	$300,000	Value
-$100,000	Cost	-$50,000	Mortgage
		-$60,000	Exemption
$200,000	Capital Gain	$190,000	Taxable Estate
$80,000	Tax Payable	$57,800	Tax Payable

Total Tax Payable ($80,000 + $57,800) = $137,800

Example: Double Estate Tax - New Treaty

Canadian Tax		U.S. Non-resident Estate Tax	
$300,000	Deemed Sale	$300,000	Value
-$100,000	Cost	-$50,000	Mortgage
		-150,000	Exemption
$200,000	Capital Gain		
$80,000	Tax Payable	$100,000	Taxable Estate
	Credit for		
-32,000	U.S. Tax Paid	$32,000	US Tax Payable
	Net Canadian		
$48,000	Tax Due		

Total Tax Payable ($48,000 + $32,000) = $80,000

FIGURE 4.4

MORTGAGE YOUR U.S. PROPERTY

Examples given in Figures 4.3, 4.3A and 4.4, illustrate that non-recourse mortgages can be deducted from the taxable estate, and only the net equity will be taxable. A non-recourse mortgage is from a lender whose only security is the property itself. In case of a default, the lender cannot go after the borrower's other assets, if there is insufficient collateral in the property.

One side benefit of taking out a mortgage is that you may be able to deduct the mortgage interest on your Canadian tax return. If you invested the mortgage proceeds in growth investments outlined in Chapter 6, *Exempt Investments,* you would be able to deduct the interest as interest paid to produce investment income. This could go a long way toward producing United States investment income which can protect you from a falling Canadian dollar. For this to work most effectively the return on your investments must provide a return greater than the cost of your mortgage which may not always be possible.

You should also be aware of potential currency risks if you mortgage your property, and then take the proceeds back to Canada, since your loan obligation is in U.S. funds. In this situation, a falling Canadian dollar would require larger Canadian dollar conversions with each payment.

Mortgages advanced through Canadian banks, or non arms-length lenders such as a controlled Canadian corporation, will not work for this strategy, since the debt would not be non-recourse.

JOINT PROPERTY OWNERSHIP WITH CHILDREN

Since each individual non-resident has a $60,000 estate tax exemption, possibly more under the new Canada — U.S. Treaty, it sometimes makes sense to place all family members on the title of an existing United States property, or when purchasing a new one. A family of five for example, could combine their exemptions and own a vacation home worth $300,000, and none of them would be subject to a non-resident estate tax. On the surface, although this strategy appears to be very simple and basic, it can be wrought with pitfalls.

Much as we may not care to admit it, our children are only human, and they will experience some of the not so pleasant things in life such as divorce and bankruptcy. Many an unsuspecting parent has had to pay off an ex-spouse, or a child's creditors, so they could keep their own winter vacation home. Family discord of any substantial proportion can sometimes result in a battle over control of a family owned property.

Once you have carefully considered the drawbacks and still feel this is a suitable technique for you, there are several things to consider concerning the actual placement of adult children's names on the property title. If you already own this property, and want to place one or more children on title, there are both Canadian and United States tax implications to consider. First, Revenue Canada will consider this transfer subject to capital gains tax on the portion of the property being transferred. From a U.S. standpoint, the IRS will consider the transfer of the American property a gift and subject to gift tax. A more detailed description of the gift tax appears later in this Chapter under the heading *What is Gift Tax*. If both you and your spouse are not already on title, you can run into some of the same tax problems adding the spouse to the title.

Sometimes the best method to complete this type of a transfer is to sell a portion of the property to your children, even if you have to loan them the money in Canada at no interest. You can avoid the United States gift tax, but not the Canadian capital gains tax if the property has appreciated. The capital gains tax, if any, could be paid by the recipient children, who are likely getting a pretty good deal anyway.

If you are about to purchase U.S. property, this arrangement is much easier at the time of purchase, than after the sale is completed. One additional benefit of this technique, is that the estate will likely avoid probate at the time of both parent's death.

HAVE AN INSURANCE COMPANY PAY THE TAX

Life insurance benefits from a non-resident insured person are not included in their taxable estate. The recent development of no-load life insurance has made this planning option more practical than ever. Most people who buy life insurance are unaware that an average of 150% of their first year's premiums, and 20% of the next nine year's premiums go toward agent's commissions, manager overrides, marketing costs, sales trips to Hawaii and other related costs. No-load life insurance strips out all these unnecessary costs so you enjoy both lower premiums, and cash values equal to your paid premiums, plus interest at fair market rates. No-load life insurance works a lot like a term deposit, yielding slightly higher rates, but has the added benefit of a life insurance death benefit. It can only be purchased through some fee-only financial planners in the U.S. You pay a fee for their service, much as you would for hiring any professional, such as an accountant or an attorney.

No commissioned agent should be involved. If you sell your property later, you can generally cash in your policy, and walk away with all the premiums, plus a good rate of return.

This method is simple, and can be very cost effective for most couples. Used in combination with the next method, Establishing Appropriate Trusts, it provides a worry-free, easy to maintain U.S. estate plan.

There are no negative tax or legal complications with this method, other than the interest earned on your policy, under certain situations, must be reported to Revenue Canada, just the same as if you had earned the interest at a U.S. bank.

ESTABLISHING APPROPRIATE TRUSTS

The Canadian Spousal Trust allows the deemed disposition capital gains tax, ordinarily due at the death of the first spouse, to be deferred until the second spouse's death. In a similar manner, there is the opportunity to defer United States estate tax until the death of the surviving spouse.

The U.S. estate tax deferment is accomplished through the use of a Qualified Domestic Trust (QDT). This is a very simple trust created either during one's lifetime through a Living Trust with the QDT language, through a will, or by the executor of the estate. At the death of the first spouse, the QDT holds the decedent's share of the United States property in trust, under certain IRS guidelines, for the benefit of the surviving spouse for their lifetime. A further discussion of Living Trusts is included later in this chapter under the heading *Living Trusts — The Simple Solution to the Problems of Wills*.

If the QDT is created under a Living Trust arrangement, you will achieve the added benefit of avoiding U.S. probate of your estate at either spouse's death, if you have the trust hold all your United States property. If you are transferring property into the Living Trust, you may face a deemed disposition tax by Revenue Canada if it is not done correctly, please check with your cross-border advisor.

A Living Trust/QDT, along with a joint and last survivorship no-load life insurance policy, is easily the best solution for coping with the non-resident estate tax. It is simple, flexible, economical, easy to maintain, and does not operate in any untested or controversial areas of tax law.

USE EXEMPT U.S. INVESTMENTS

Chapter 6 provides the details of U.S. investments you can use to generate income that is free from both U.S. income and estate tax. Use of these investments will go a long way toward simplifying your estate plan.

Unfortunately, real estate does not fall under the category of exempt investments, so it must be dealt with, under some of the other estate planning techniques. Remember, exempt investments, unless held in a Living Trust could be subject to probate in the United States.

THE USE OF CANADIAN HOLDING COMPANIES

Many Canadians hold U.S. winter homes or similar property by purchasing or transferring the property through a Single Purpose Canadian Holding Company. This is by far, the most complex strategy, and coincidentally, the one most often recommended by lawyers and accountants on both sides of the border. Don't let this lure you into a false sense of security. You should also not think that because it is the most complicated strategy , it must be the best. Of all the techniques described in this chapter, this method has by far, the most pitfalls and potential problems.

The logic behind the use of holding companies is that the holding company will never die, and if the company is Canadian, it will not be subject to U.S. transfer or estate taxes, upon the death of its shareholders.

This line of reasoning does have some merit. A holding company can work if you're buying land or a business for investment purposes, but those are unusual circumstances for most Canadian winter visitors, who normally purchase personal use property such as retirement or vacation homes.

One of the great pitfalls of having a foreign holding company owning personal use property is, it may not free shareholders from non-resident estate tax, which is generally the entire reason for forming the company. The reason is simple. The IRS bases what is subject to estate tax on incidence of ownership. Thus, it will pierce the veils of a corporation, or a trust, under these kinds of circumstances to determine who actually owns the property. This is particularly true if corporate formalities have not been followed to a tee. Non-recognition rules, which are similar in both the U.S. and Canada, allow the IRS to technically reverse the transaction of placing the property in a foreign holding company, if it was created solely to avoid taxes, and there was no legitimate business purpose being served.

The second major pitfall concerns using foreign holding companies for personal use assets.

In a recent tax court case, the IRS ruled that individual shareholders living in corporation controlled property should have paid rent and had a formal rental contract with the company based on current market value rates. This ruling is in total conflict with the rules Revenue Canada makes compulsory for the owners of a Single Purpose Canadian Holding Company. Revenue Canada states very clearly, that the property cannot be rented out, or any income earned by the company.

Generally speaking, if you set up and operate your holding company in the United States to meet IRS rules such as formally registering the company to do business in the state, filing state and federal tax returns, keeping corporate books and rental contracts with the owner shareholders, you will breach the Revenue Canada regulations and vice versa. This is an impossible legal situation to resolve.

The message is clear, the IRS never intended to allow the use of foreign holding companies to avoid non-resident estate tax by their shareholders, and will continue to attack them.

Considering the pitfalls and the expense of setting up and maintaining a Single Purpose Canadian Holding Company, why do so many advisors continue recommending them? They may be unfamiliar with other solutions to the estate tax, or they justify their recommendations by saying that the holding company may not avoid estate tax, but not using one means the property is certain to be taxed. With all the other more economical and viable alternatives, why gamble your time and money on the one technique that is only a maybe method of avoiding estate tax?

We continue to recommend that Single Purpose Canadian Holding Companies be used under very limited circumstances. We believe they do little more than generate unnecessary paperwork, raises your costs, and are at best, a long shot. If you already have a holding company set up and running for this purpose you should seriously look at unwinding it unless the home in the company has highly appreciated and will produce an immediate tax liability if the corporation is unwound.

SELL YOUR PROPERTY AND RENT

Selling your property and renting it each year, may seem a bit drastic but it can be a very good alternative for some people. It is a simple solution and the only tax consideration is possible capital gains tax on the sale of your property, to the IRS and Revenue Canada. With the steep decline in real estate values in many areas during the past few years, there may not be any problem with capital gains either.

Proceeds from the sale of the home should be invested in United States tax exempt investments, to generate U.S. dollar income to finance future winter stays.

If the death of the property owner is anticipated in a short period of time, a quick sale to a family member in Canada could be a very smart estate tax saving move.

IS YOUR CANADIAN WILL VALID IN THE UNITED STATES?

There are plenty of legitimate concerns among Canadians owning property in the United States about whether their Canadian wills will be valid in the United States at the time of their death.

Generally speaking, if your Canadian will has been drafted correctly and is valid in Canada, it will also be valid in the United States. There is no real need to have separately drafted wills for American and Canadian property. There is some merit to having a separate United States will drafted in the state you normally reside in, to simplify the probate process, but having two wills can also create problems, like trying to convince the courts which one is the valid one. You will also have to pay for and keep track of two separate wills when it is usually unnecessary.

If you do not have a valid will in either country, your estate will be subject to the intestate laws in your place of residence. This creates double work for your appointed executor when there are assets in two separate jurisdictions such as a Canadian province and a U.S. state. Many people ignore the need for a will, or do not look at alternate estate planning vehicles, because they are under one or more misconceptions about wills, joint ownership and the probate process.

Probate comes from the Latin word meaning to "prove." After a person dies, probate is the process of proving how the deceased person wanted his or her property distributed. This "proof" is accomplished by presenting the will to court for probate.

Unfortunately, it isn't always that easy. You may know someone who has been through the frustration and the expense of probate. To help you better understand wills and the alternatives now available, here are twelve costly misconceptions:

- Misconception #1. Probate costs are small.

  Wrong! Most personal representatives hire an attorney to help with the paperwork of probate. Here's why: The laws relating to probate and estate administration are extremely complex for a lay person. So while provincial and state law does allow a personal representative to go through the probate without a lawyer's help, most personal representatives do not want to face this challenge alone. So they hire a lawyer. Legal fees for even a simple probate, taking less than one year, can reach $5,000 to $10,000. Provincial probate fees, depending on the province involved, can add 1.5% of the value of the probate estate to the total costs.

  Total legal fees and other estate administration costs can average from 3% to 10% of the total estate value, depending on the complexity of the probate. Owning property in both the United States and Canada definitely increases the complexity of the probate.

- Misconception #2. Your will and your assets remain private.

  Sorry! Probate is a matter of public record, so all of your assets and liabilities will be spelled out to the penny in court records. Names of beneficiaries and the amounts of their inheritance are all open to the public. Anyone can go to the court and ask to see your probate file. If you valued your privacy in life, you'd probably find probate uncomfortable.

- Misconception #3. A will can be probated in just a few weeks.

  No way! Even with a simple estate, probate can take from ten months to two years. During that time, the deceased person's property must be inventoried and appraised. Relatives and beneficiaries must be notified. Creditors must be notified and paid. Income taxes must be paid. Any contested claims and contested inheritances must be settled. Only then is the property distributed to the beneficiaries.

- Misconception #4. A will helps you avoid taxes.

  Dead wrong! A standard will does nothing to lower your taxes. A properly drafted will may take advantage of certain estate planning options such as setting up trusts that can save or defer estates taxes. A standard will simply indicates how you want your property distributed, and who you want to care for your children.

- Misconception #5. A will or a testamentary trust (a trust set up by your will) avoids probate.

  Not true! All property governed by a will must go through the probate process by law, before it passes to beneficiaries. The law does not allow minor children to inherit bank accounts, stocks and bonds, or real estate. That is why parents often set up a testamentary trust for their children, which holds the property until the children reach the age of majority. But since the testamentary trust is part of the person's will, it still must be probated by the court.

- Misconception #6. Joint tenancy is the safest way to own property.

  Not so! Joint tenancy with right of survivorship exposes each party to the debts of the other. For example, assume you own a home in joint tenancy with your child. Your child starts a business that goes broke. His creditors are chasing him trying to collect their money. The home you own with your child could now be taken away from you to satisfy your child's debts.

  Also, joint tenancy property must go through probate when the second person dies, or in the event both people die in a common accident.

- Misconception #7. Your permanent home and your vacation home can be handled through the same probate.

  Yes, but only if they are located in the same province or state. If you own a home or property in another province, or in the United States, you'll need to open a second probate, which means you'll hire another lawyer. This usually doubles the probate expense. And, if you own real estate in a third location, you'll need to open a third probate and hire a third lawyer.

- Misconception #8. A will prevents quarrels over assets.

  Not on your life! Wills are the subject of more lawsuits than any other document. Today, it is common for unhappy friends or relatives to contest a will, resulting in higher legal fees and added delays. This is one more reason why the average probate takes from ten months to two years.

- Misconception #9. Family members can sell property in the estate to raise money.

A fatal mistake! The court freezes the estate's assets until the probate has ended. The court may allow the personal representative to give family members small living allowances, but only up to the amounts allowed by provincial or state law. Permission to pay beneficiaries out of the estate must be granted by the court. Regardless of the outcome, asking the court's permission to sell property, increases the legal fees.

- Misconception #10. A will from one province is not legal in another or in the United States.

Untrue! If the will is legal in one province, it is also legal in another, and in the United States. However, if your will contains certain legal language, it can go through probate more quickly and smoothly. If you want to avoid delays in probate, you might want to have your will reviewed by a lawyer in each province or state, in which you own property that must go through probate.

- Misconception #11. The cost of planning your estate is only the cost of drawing up your will.

Not quite accurate! The cost of any estate plan is both the cost of drawing up the documents, and the cost of carrying out the plan. If your will costs $150.00 in legal fees, and the probate costs $5,000.00, the cost of your estate plan is $5,150.00. This is a lot more than merely the cost of the will. This will is not only the most common document in our legal system, it is also one of the most expensive.

- Misconception #12. You must name your lawyer as your personal representative.

Nope! When you name your lawyer as your personal representative, you are in effect, giving him your permission to get paid twice. Once, for acting as your personal representative, and again when he acts as your lawyer. You can select anyone you wish to be your personal representative. For convenience sake, you may want to choose someone who lives in your province or state.

LIVING TRUSTS -
A SIMPLE SOLUTION TO PROBLEMS WITH WILLS

A Living Trust is a legal entity that is formed to hold your property for your benefit while you are living. After an estate planning lawyer drafts your Living Trust, he helps transfer your assets into the trust. Property held by a Living Trust does not go through probate after death.

Here's why: The law says that any property owned when you die must go through probate, with a few exceptions such as joint tenancy property. When you set up a Living Trust, property is transferred into the trust and retitled in the name of the trust. So, after your death, the property doesn't have to go through probate, because the property is no longer in your name, it's owned by the trust.

If you want to manage the trust, name yourself as trust manager, or "trustee." A trust company's involvement is not needed at all. As trustee, you can (a) put property into or take it out of the trust, (b) change the trust, and even (c) revoke the trust — any time you wish. If you want someone to manage the trust for you, you can select a relative, friend, lawyer, bank, or trust company. Normally, both husband and wife are trustees while either are still living. In the case of death or disability, a successor trustee is named in the trust document, usually the same person who would be your personal representative in your will. While you are living, the operation of the trust provides you with all the same rights to your property, and your personal affairs operate pretty much the same as before.

When you form a Living Trust you accomplish the following:

- Save your family thousands of dollars in legal fees.
- Save your family months of lengthy court proceedings.
- Keep your family's legal affairs out of court records.
- Protect your family from the dangers of joint tenancy.
- Reduce the likelihood that your wishes will be challenged by unhappy friends and relatives.
- Give your family complete control over the property, because the trust assets are not frozen by the court.
- Avoid added probates for property you own in other provinces or states.

- Provide more efficient management of your estate in the event of death or disability.

As you can see, a Living Trust can be a very useful tool in cross-border financial planning, particularly when it has the Qualified Domestic Trust provisions, mentioned earlier in this chapter, for deferring non-resident estate taxes. Living Trusts are a very common estate planning vehicle in the United States, and are routinely recommended by estate planners at all levels. In fact, Canadians wintering in the United States see a continual barrage of advertisements for Living Trust seminars put on by banks, attorneys, brokerage firms and financial planners. Some use the Living Trust as a loss leader to sell other products or services.

A small number of Canadian lawyers and financial planners have started to realize the benefits of Living Trusts. They should not only be reserved for Americans. Canadian trusts, like wills, are generally valid in the United States and vice versa. However, if you are going to use your trust to hold property in both Canada and the United States simultaneously, we highly recommend that you use a cross-border financial planner, to help coordinate legal services such as drafting the documents and the transfer of the assets, in both your home Canadian province and U.S. state.

POWER OF ATTORNEY - SHOULD YOU HAVE ONE?

One of the simplest and most useful documents you can add to your estate plan is Power of Attorney (POA). These will be of great assistance to you in almost all U.S. states and Canadian provinces.

These very basic documents give some other person(s), whom you trust, the right to transact business or make medical decisions on your behalf, if you are physically or mentally unable to do so for yourself. Anyone who has had a spouse or a loved one in this situation may have discovered the long, costly and frustrating process of going to court to get authorization for a conservatorship or guardianship, so you can pay for this person's care. Correctly drafted, a Power of Attorney should eliminate the need for the conservatorship or guardianship.

To be effective, the POA must be a Durable or Enduring Power of Attorney. A Durable or Enduring POA means that it will be valid even after you become incapacitated, the point at which a non-durable POA would lapse.

Many lawyers in Canada and the U.S. recommend two separate Durable POAs, one for general financial needs, and one for medical needs. Good estate lawyers will routinely include the proper POAs with the wills and trusts they draft at no extra cost. Have the POAs reviewed by a lawyer in each of the jurisdictions that it is most likely to be used in, to insure they will be valid there.

Durable POAs are the kind of documents you hope you never have to use but when you need them, they are invaluable.

WHAT HAPPENS IF YOU DIE IN THE U.S.?

We've covered a lot of ground in this chapter on cross-border estate planning, but what actually happens when a death occurs? How does the IRS find out whether the deceased owned property in the United States?

Whether physical death occurs in Canada or the United States, there is technically no difference with respect to taxes or any other obligations. At the time of death, either your personal representative or, if there is a Living Trust your successor trustee, has certain responsibilities. These are:

- Make a separate list of assets in both Canada and the United States and arrange for appraisals of the property.

- If the decedent did not have a Living Trust holding their assets, probates in the province(s) or state(s) where they owned property would have to be initiated.

- Determine what, if any, estate tax is due to the IRS, and to the state(s) or to the province(s) where the property is located.

- Arrange for the filing of the final tax returns in Canada and if necessary, in the U.S. by the appropriate deadlines.

- Arrange for the filing of the federal and state estate tax returns in the United States if the taxable estate, as defined earlier in this chapter, exceeds $60,000.

- If property in the United States is to be sold, obtain estate tax clearances for both the IRS and the appropriate state department of revenues.

- Hire and coordinate the professionals needed to execute all of these responsibilities.

- Notify beneficiaries as to their rights under the will or trust.

The IRS will normally learn about a death during one or more of the above procedures. The Canadian executor, personal representative or successor trustee becomes personally liable for any estate tax due, if it is not paid correctly from the estate. If there is no specified executor, the tax code states any person in receipt of a deceased person's property is considered to be that person's executor, known as a "Statutory Executor".

There is an automatic estate tax lien attached on all U.S. property of the deceased. These liens must be satisfied before they are released. If a personal representative wants to sell the property before the estate is finalized, he or she will be required to obtain federal estate tax clearance, and may face withholding taxes of up to 60%. The withholding tax may be refunded after the estate is settled by filing the appropriate returns.

Revenue Canada gives the personal representative six months from the date of death or to April 30, the year following the date of death which ever is sooner, to file the final Canadian return of the deceased, and pay any tax due. The IRS requires the non-resident estate tax return Form 706NA be filed within nine months from the date of death. Most of the United States including Arizona, California, Florida and Hawaii have their own estate tax, which is called a pick-up tax because they tax only to the extent that the IRS will allow a credit for state taxes paid. This does not increase the total amount of tax paid, but does mean that the IRS and the state involved share the equivalent of the federal estate tax.

Incidentally, estate tax returns are audited at least ten times more often than regular tax returns. The IRS routinely audits nearly 100% of all larger estate tax returns because collecting the extra taxes can be very lucrative.

WHAT IS A GIFT TAX?

Throughout this chapter we have referred to gift taxes. This terminology is not familiar to most Canadians, but they hear it mentioned frequently in the United States. Gift taxes are paid by the giver not the recipient.

The U.S. gift tax is an off shoot of the U.S. estate tax. Gift tax is a transfer of property during one's lifetime, while estate tax is on transfer of property at one's death. The rates for gift taxes are identical to the estate tax rates provided in Figure 4.3 earlier in this chapter. Gift taxes have the same lifetime exemption as estate taxes, $60,000 (unless the new 1994 Canada — U.S. Tax Treaty allows for a greater exemption, see the earlier sections of this chapter) for non-residents and $600,000 for U.S. residents and citizens. The lifetime exemption or any portion thereof, if used up through gifting, is not available for use as an estate tax exemption after death.

There is, in addition to the lifetime exemption, an annual gift tax exemption of $10,000 of U.S. property per donor whether resident or non-resident of the United States, to any recipient they choose. For example, a married couple with one child could give $10,000 each to the child gift tax-free each year, and not reduce their lifetime estate/gift tax exemption. Non U.S. residents or non citizens, are allowed an annual tax-free gift of $100,000 U.S. in property to a non U.S. citizen spouse. U.S. citizens can gift unlimited amounts of cash or property to a citizen spouse, any time.

Canadians are subject to gift tax rules, whenever they give or transfer any U.S. located property. You should be careful and plan transfers of U.S. property accordingly. There are severe penalties for failure to pay this tax, and ignorance of the law will be of no help to you should you get caught.

CROSS-BORDER Q&A

Many of the issues covered in the preceding chapter of this book have been touched upon in the author's weekly column *Cross-border Q&A*, which appears in *The Sun Times of Canada,* published in Tampa, Florida and circulated throughout the U.S. Sunbelt for Canadians living or wintering there. The majority of these questions have been posed by readers of the Sun Times and/or readers of the previous editions of *The Border Guide.* Most were looking for advice relating to their own specific problems or situations. At the end of this chapter, we have included some typical reader questions, along with our response, to illustrate and broaden the concepts presented in the preceding chapter.

DOES A LIVING TRUST SATISFY REVENUE CANADA?

I have read your informative articles in the Sun Times of Canada, and the matter that most concerns me, is what will happen to my property, in terms of taxation when I die? According to information I have gathered from attending estate planning workshops, I could have a living trust. However, I need to know if this would satisfy Revenue Canada or the Ontario Government. These questions could not be answered by the American financial planners whom I have asked.

My house and property are located in Arizona, where I would like to live for eight months of the year instead of the usual six months less a day. How would I apply for resident alien status? My efforts to reach U.S. Immigration by telephone have been thwarted by their computer answering system.

— *Morris C., Lake Havasu, AZ*

You are correct in thinking that you should have a living trust as part of your estate plan. You can use this trust to hold both Canadian and U.S. assets. However, you need to be aware of some tax implications that Revenue Canada may catch you on. Revenue Canada considers most transfers into a living trust a deemed disposition. Consequently, if you have any potential capital gains in the property you are transferring into the trust, you will be subject to Canadian tax when you complete the transfer. If you are transferring your personal residence, you will have no Canadian tax to pay. Items like term deposits, GIC's and bank accounts can be transferred in without tax consequences and the tax on income earned after the transfer into the trust can be either paid by the trust or passed through to you individually.

If your trust is set up correctly, it will allow your estate to avoid probate in both Canada and the U.S., which is a desirable goal for most people.

Since you are likely to be Trustee of your own trust, the trust will be a resident of the same country you are. This means that if you are earning income from assets in the trust, you will be subject to different sets of reporting requirements depending on the residency of you and the trust. For example, if you have Canadian bank term deposits in the trust and you are a resident of Canada, your trust will file Canadian tax returns to report the interest earned. If you passed this interest through to you personally, the trust would issue you a T-3 slip and you would ultimately pay the tax on your personal return. The trust would pay no tax by offsetting the interest earned on the term deposit with a deduction for the interest paid through to you, but it would still have to file its own return.

It is much simpler if you are a U.S. resident with a U.S. bank deposit. The Internal Revenue Service does not require the trust to report interest earned if you report it on your own personal tax return, cutting out any unnecessary duplicate reporting. Also, transfers of property into a living trust are not considered deemed dispositions and are allowed without tax consequences.

As far as your chances of immigrating to the U.S., you will likely need either a business or family sponsor to provide you with a realistic chance at a green card. There are no green card lotteries in the near future that I am aware of that Canadians will be able to participate in.

WHERE THERE'S A WILL THERE'S A WAY

I am a Canadian citizen, and I own property in Florida. May I legally bequeath this property or money to a relative who lives in Europe? If so, is a will appropriate or is there another way to accomplish this?

— *Arne I., St. Petersburg, FL*

You certainly may bequeath your Florida property to a relative in Europe. You can pass the property via your will, or by forming a simple trust. From the information you've provided, the only real advantage of the trust would be to avoid the expenses of probating your will in Florida. Keep in mind your executor or personal representative will have to file a U.S. Estate Tax IRS Form 706NA, and pay any U.S. non-resident estate tax if your U.S. property exceeds the $60,000 exemption (unless the new 1994 Canada-U.S. Tax Treaty allows for a greater exemption). The tax, if any, would have to be paid before the property passes to your European beneficiary.

CHANGING TITLE & U.S. TAX OBLIGATIONS ON FLORIDA PROPERTY

I am a Canadian, who lives seven months per year in Ontario and five months in Sarasota. Our house in Florida was jointly owned with my husband who passed away recently. How do I remove his name from any ownership documents? Also, I think my house would sell for $125,000 - $150,000. Please tell me the Florida laws that apply to Canadians.

— *Doreen A., Sarasota, FL*

Since you owned your Florida property jointly with right of survivorship, and are now the sole owner, you can simply have the title changed at your local county recorder's office. They will require a copy of your deceased husband's death certificate, and have you complete a basic form which varies from county to county.

You didn't say whether you had filed IRS Form 706NA and paid the U.S. non-resident estate taxes. This form needs to be filed within nine months of a death unless you received an extension, or your husband's U.S. assets were less than $60,000.

Form 706NA will detail how to calculate the non-resident estate tax due. You would be wise to get an appraisal of the Florida property, including the contents, as of the date of your husband's death. If the value of your deceased husband's share of the U.S. assets exceeds the non-resident estate tax exemption of $60,000, you will have to pay tax starting at 26% of the amount over $60,000. Although your filing will be quite simple, I recommend seeking professional help to complete Form 706NA, as it can be rather intimidating. Remember, if you have taxes due, interest and penalties for late filing will keep accruing, so you should get started as soon as possible. The new 1994 Canada — U.S. Tax Treaty may allow your husband a greater exemption than the current $60,000. It will be retroactive back to 1988 so you could actually file for a refund if any tax has to be paid to the U.S. prior to the Treaty taking effect. Don't forget about the Canadian deemed disposition tax if you property had accrued any capital gains prior to your husband's death.

CANADIAN TAX OBLIGATIONS WHEN SELLING FLORIDA PROPERTY

As a recent widow, I plan on selling my Florida home in the near future, if the real estate market improves. I could use up-to-date information regarding the sale of real estate concerning Florida sales taxes and Canadian capital gains (or loss) taxes. What is the advisability of changing the deed to joint ownership to a family member to avoid paying estate taxes. Is this change made through a Florida lawyer or my lawyer in Ontario?

— Veruca S., Chatham, ON

This question is similar to the previous one with respect to U.S. tax obligations, and filing requirements for a widow with Florida property. In addition to U.S. obligations, you may have to pay Canadian tax on the deemed disposition at your husband's death. This would be the capital gains tax on the appreciation of your Florida property on your deceased husband's share, since the time it was purchased. If your husband died in 1997, this tax would be due to Revenue Canada no later than six months from the date of death or April 30, 1998, whichever comes first. The tax can be reduced or eliminated if your husband used his capital gains exemption while it was still available, to crystallize the gains prior to his death.

Changing the joint ownership with right of survivorship from your deceased spouse to another family member could cost you a hefty U.S. gift tax, if you do it all at once. If you are transferring U.S. property either while you are alive or via your will, you are subject to transfer tax in the form of a gift tax or estate tax, respectively. These taxes are levied at the same rates, with the gift tax having a $10,000 annual exclusion, and the estate tax a $60,000 once in a lifetime exemption for a non-resident (unless the new 1994 Canada — U.S. Tax Treaty allows for a greater exemption). Consequently, a gift of $50,000 would attract tax on $40,000. The tax starts at 18% and must be paid by filing IRS Form 709NA.

You would most likely be much better off selling a share of the residence to the family member and avoid this potential problem. If the family member has no money you can loan them the funds in Canada and take back a note.

As always, we recommend you seek professional advice before you make any changes. A good U.S. estate planning attorney in Florida should be able to advise you as to your best course of action.

COMPUTING NON-RESIDENT ESTATE TAXES

My wife and I are joint owners of beach property, which we purchased in 1979. A special valuation was done and submitted to the IRS via Form 6661, prior to December 31, 1984, which covered the period from 1980 onwards. Can you elaborate on the non-resident estate tax, and whether it works on a sliding scale; assuming that the gross market value of the property was $100,000, $120,000, or $150,000, what would the applicable rate be for these three figures?

Finally, I have heard the terms "Community Property Agreement" & "Qualified Domestic Trust", applied to processes intended to reduce or avoid estate taxes in the United States. What do these processes mean and could they apply in our case?

—James C., Redington Shores, FL

The U.S. non-resident estate tax is applied to the Fair Market Value of a decedent's U.S. situs property on the date of death. U.S. situs property includes the decedent's share of jointly owned real estate, personal property normally present in the U.S., and U.S. stocks or similar investments.

A brief summary of the tax tables is as follows:

Taxable Estate	Tax Rate
$60,000 - $80,000	26%
$80,000 - $100,000	28%
$100,000 - $150,000	30%
$150,000 - $250,000	32%
$250,000 - $500,000	34%
$500,000 - $750,000	37%

You do not reach the 55% rate until the taxable estate exceeds $3,000,000. The first $60,000 of the estate is not taxed (unless the new 1994 Canada — U.S. Tax Treaty allows for a greater exemption).

Since your property is located in Florida, and Florida is not a community property state, community property rules give you no advantages. In Florida, it is important that each spouse contribute equally from separately owned funds, if you are going to put property in joint ownership with right of survivorship between spouses. If both spouses do not contribute equally to the purchase of U.S. property, you can create other problems such as U.S. gift tax at the same rates as the above table, for the spouse who contributed the greater amount towards the purchase. Alternately, the IRS may consider the home to be owned by only the contributing spouse, for the purpose of calculating the non-resident estate tax.

A Qualified Domestic Trust can act as a mechanism to defer any non-resident estate taxes at the time of the first spouse's death. This can be set up either before or immediately after the death of the first spouse. You are required to have a U.S. individual or corporate trustee, and will need to hire an estate attorney to draft the documents you require.

A Qualified Domestic Trust will not reduce the estate taxes but you can delay them to the second spouses death in a manner similar to a Spousal Trust in Canada, with respect to capital gains tax at the first death of a spouse. There may be other, more viable alternatives to assist you to deal with non-resident estate taxes. However, this would require more information than contained in your letter. Take a close look at the new Canada — U.S. Tax Treaty. This treaty could possibly provide you relief from this non-resident estate tax.

KNOW FLORIDA RULES FOR FOREIGN COMPANIES

I am a Canadian subscriber to *The Sun Times of Canada* living in Florida for approximately half the year.

Recently I received a letter from a C.P.A. living in Boca Raton advising me that Canadians who own their U.S. property through a Canadian corporation to avoid U.S. Estate tax are required to have a Florida Registered Agent .

Can you tell me if there is any validity to these claims? I predict a number of Sun Times readers would be interested in this information.

— *Edgar J. G., Longboat Key, FL*

Using a Canadian holding company to own your personal use Florida real estate does not necessarily mean you will avoid non-resident estate tax. In fact unless you jump through such regulatory hoops as following state requirement for registering corporations, as you noted above, paying rent to the corporation under a lease agreement at fair market value rent, filing U.S. corporate tax returns, paying all expenses through the corporation amongst many other rules, the IRS will consider your corporation a sham and look right through it so you will be subject to the non-resident estate tax any way - as if the corporation doesn't exist. If your company is a Single Purpose Holding Company under Revenue Canada rules you will lose the special tax treatment afforded these corporations in Canada the minute you try to follow the U.S. requirements such as having the corporation collect rent. This conflict of laws makes it nearly impossible, if not very complex and expensive to use a Canadian holding company to avoid the U.S non-resident estate tax. There are numerous more simple, less tax problematic ways to get around the non-resident estate tax. I generally discourage the use of Canadian holding companies to avoid the non-resident tax because they have so many pitfalls and give those using them a false sense of security that they will work as planned when in fact the odds are very slim that they will work. Those persons such as yourself who already have their property in a Canadian holding company need to reassess your situation closely and either attempt to get the corporation to abide by all the regulations or wind it up and use one of the simpler and cheaper methods to reduce or avoid the U.S. non-resident estate tax. Most Canadian advisors recommending the use of these holding companies are not U.S. qualified estate planners and should not, nor be expected to, give such advice. They are unaware of the U.S. federal and state requirements with respect to these corporations to give them some possible legitimacy in avoiding the estate tax they were designed for in the first place.

If you wish to examine some of the alternative methods to the use of holding companies to avoid the non-resident estate tax, please write and we can discuss it in a future Q & A column.

SINGLE PURPOSE CANADIAN HOLDING COMPANIES

This concerns a recent Sun Times column about Single Purpose Canadian Holding Companies. Two Ontario readers asked what to do with their existing Canadian holding companies that were formed to avoid U.S. non-resident estate taxes on their Florida properties. They discovered, to their dismay, that the holding companies would not likely do what they were established to do, which is avoid the non-resident estate taxes. Could you tell me why? Please provide more details.

— *Billy A., Toronto, ON*

Because of this and numerous other inquiries, it is obvious there is a need to revisit this issue and discuss it in greater detail.

The two Ontario readers both had Single Purpose Canadian Holding Companies, which owned their Florida properties. For this type of holding company, Revenue Canada states that the company must be used only for holding the real estate, not for rental or income properties. Since this type of holding company does not have a source of income, upkeep, taxes and other related expenses are paid personally by the shareholder. For a holding company to have some hope of escaping the U.S. non-resident estate tax; the company must charge Fair Market Value rent to the shareholder, and all taxes and expenses must be paid by the company itself.

Appropriate United States federal and state tax returns must also be filed. From the contents of their letters, it appears that these two Ontario readers, were not fulfilling the United States requirements, and if they were, they would be in violation of the Revenue Canada's requirements for a Single Purpose Canadian Holding Company. Confronted with this conflict in laws, the best advice to these and other readers, is to unload their holding companies as soon as possible.

It is my experience that most Canadians who have holding companies for their United States vacation properties are in the same position and hence, this advice would be appropriate for all of them.

As one of the accountants who called me pointed out on the telephone, holding companies can have some useful purposes in estate planning for non-residents of the United States, but in isolated circumstances, and for non-personal use property. However, for the vast majority of Canadians who use their U.S. property for winter vacations, there are far better methods than holding companies to deal with the non-resident estate tax. In addition, holding companies are complex and costly to set up and maintain. Why get involved with something so expensive and complex that may not do the job, after all is said and done? Your heirs may be forced to litigate with the Internal Revenue Service to settle the issue. There are several less costly and/or simpler methods to avoid this tax.

One popular method is to create a living trust in the United States to hold the home. If the trust is drafted correctly, up to $60,000 (or more if the new 1994 Canada — U.S. Tax Treaty allows for a greater exemption) may be exempted for each family member. The trust also helps avoid the costs and hassles of U.S. and Canadian probate.

Another option is to have an insurance company pay the tax, rather than paying it directly. This can be done through a low cost, no-load, joint and last survivor life insurance policy designed specifically for this purpose. Because it is a non-commission paying policy, the cash values are approximately equal to, or greater than the amount paid in. As a result, if the property was sold or the estate tax eliminated, the policy would have a greater cash value than was paid in premiums.

There are several other methods Canadians can use to avoid the United States non-resident estate tax. Options range from becoming United States residents, to placing a mortgage on the United States property, or giving the property to children.

Regardless of which method is chosen, Canadian residents holding United States assets of any kind, should seek professional advice on how to handle these tax issues.

If, after examining every alternative, you still decide to set up a holding company for your United States vacation home, I recommend you attempt to get an advance ruling from the Internal Revenue Service, and if a favourable ruling is granted, follow it to the letter.

Doctor in the House

One of the most perplexing questions confronting Canadians wintering, or taking up permanent residence in the United States, is medical insurance. With new initiatives from the U.S. administration and private insurers jockeying for improved market share, U.S. health care plans are a complex and constantly changing topic. We must also keep making adjustments for Canada's rapidly changing out of province medicare coverage.

The last thing people need to worry about when they travel is becoming ill, or suffering an accident. Unfortunately, sickness and accidents respect neither your travel itinerary, nor your socio-economic status. A medical emergency can happen anywhere, at any time and to anyone!

Any unforeseen expense is important to today's traveller and you will want to be protected, no matter how great or small the potential loss. Minor problems, such as the loss of luggage, can be a traumatic experience for many travellers, ruining their holiday or business trip. A catastrophic illness or an accident outside Canada can turn a relaxing trip into a financial nightmare.

To make matters worse, provincial medicare programs are constantly being squeezed by rising costs and decreasing income. Even Saskatchewan, the pioneer of the Canadian medicare system, has introduced user fees to help defray costs. In 1991 and again in 1993, Ontario's OHIP sent the travel insurance industry reeling with a drastic cut in daily hospital and other benefits outside the province. Ontario's move threw several insurance carriers out of the travel insurance business, because they didn't like the increased underwriting risks. Others jumped on the bandwagon, hoping to make big profits by cashing in on travel insurance premiums that virtually doubled overnight. We can expect more of the same from all provinces. Quebec's Regie, which was the last remaining province with adequate out of province coverage, has also cut back its coverage following

Provincial Health Insurance Plans
Outside Canada Hospital Benefits

- **British Columbia** (604)387-3166: $75/day as well as a small payment by the B.C. Medical Services Plan for services rendered in the emergency room prior to admission.

- **Alberta** (403)427-1432: $100/day.

- **Saskatchewan** (306)787-3261: $100/day, outpatient - $50/day.

- **Manitoba** (204)786-7101: 1-100 beds - $280/day; 101-500 beds - $356 day; 501 or more beds - $570 day; pays the greater of 75% or per diem only in the case of referrals.

- **Ontario** (416)440-4410: $400/day for "high level" care; $200/day for out-patient care.

- **Quebec** (514)873-4006: $498/day (including surgery in a day hospital).

- **Prince Edward Island** (902)368-5858: $570/day regardless of bed capacity.

- **New Brunswick** (506)453-2161: $600/day; higher rate possible but requires prior approval.

- **Nova Scotia** (902)424-5670: $525/day for hospital bill 50% for ancillary charges such as x-ray and lab bills.

- **Newfoundland** (709)729-5971: $350/day maximum.

All Provinces Cover Medical
100% of Provincial Level.

FIGURE 5.1

OHIP's lead. Fortunately for Ontarians, the new provincial government has made good on a campaign promise and restored coverage back to 1993 levels. A table of current provincial out of Canada medical benefit coverage is listed in Figure 5.1 along with phone numbers to call for more recent updates and changes.

There are still many travellers who are unaware of the need for adequate travel insurance. While provincial health and hospital programs may provide adequate benefits at home, a Canadian who finds himself in trouble outside the country, may discover his provincial plan covers only a small portion of his medical expenses. As illustrated in Figure 5.1, provincial plans vary considerably with respect to the amounts paid outside Canada. British Columbia at $75.00 per day for a hospital bed, currently pays the least. This is but a small fraction of what hospitalization actually costs, especially in the United States, where medical expenses may easily exceed $2,000 per day. In most U.S. hospitals, $75.00 a day would barely get you a parking spot. Canadians should be aware that in many parts of the world, physicians and hospitals do not follow the Canadian system of billing, where the daily room charge is all inclusive and covers most services and treatments. Many hospitals outside Canada charge a fee for room and board, and then charge for every procedure and band-aid they use. Figure 5.2 displays a sample of some of the heath costs in the United States, and estimates what portion of these costs would be covered by OHIP. In the past OHIP not only reduced their portion of these costs but has made it more difficult to collect them. More people had to rely on their travel insurance for the entire medical bill. It remains to be seen whether this trend will reverse itself in the near future.

Travellers who purchase token medical insurance plans may discover that the plan they purchased is inadequate or does not cover them when they need hospital and medical treatment. Your bargain medical insurance may be instead, a simple trip cancellation or flight accident insurance policy. Many of you have heard stories of Canadians who were forced to mortgage their property in order to pay for U.S. medical expenses. Figure 5.2 certainly offers some dramatic examples, with respect to patient costs, for someone treated in a U.S. hospital without adequate medicare supplements. The purchase of proper travel insurance not only reduces financial risk, but provides peace of mind as well!

Many people purchase travel protection as a supplement to their provincial medical plans, prior to heading south for the winter. The typical insurance plan has an expiration date of less than six months. If an individual covered by these plans wishes to stay longer than six months, they either go without coverage or have to return to Canada to trick their insurance carrier into giving them extended coverage. Premiums have become quite costly, and a typical married couple aged 65 can expect to pay between $2,500 to $5,000 for a six month policy depending upon the company and the deductible chosen. Numerous travel insurance plans are available through travel agencies, insurance companies, the CAA, the Canadian Snowbird Association and premium credit cards. The types of coverage and premiums can also vary widely. Most plans have benefit limits of $1,000,000 for covered medical expenses, although some plans have no dollar limitations on benefits. Terms may range from twenty-four hours to a maximum of one year. Premiums are based on the age of travellers, usually with categories for those over age 65, and those under age 65, and may also be dependent on the number of people in a party. Nearly all carriers require you to purchase your coverage before you leave Canada. A very positive development in the travel insurance industry with all this new competition

Coverage of U.S. Health Costs by Ontario's Medicare

Ailment	Hospital Stay	Total Cost	Medicare Share	Patient Share
Heart Attack	28 days	$87,600	$13,700	$73,900
Fractures	9 days	$38,525	$5,000	$33,525
Gall Bladder	7 days	$17,825	$3,300	$14,525
Mild Stroke	2 days	$5,534	$934	$4,400

FIGURE 5.2

has been a much better choice of plans with deductibles ranging from $50 to $10,000. Choosing a high deductible policy can reduce annual travel insurance costs by 50% or more without a significant increase in risk. See Appendix F for a listing of the names, addresses, and phone numbers of the major Canadian travel insurance providers.

The Canadian Life and Health Insurance Association publishes a very helpful brochure on health insurance for travellers, and what they should know before leaving Canada. This brochure can be received free of charge along with a complete list of insurers by calling 1-800-268-8099 toll free in Canada. The best sources of information for insurance company selection, policy choices and premium comparisons comes from the special travel insurance editions published in August or September each year by both The Sun Times of Canada, 1-800-253-4323, and the Canada News, 1-800-535-6788. In addition the Sun Times publishes the Canadian Travel Health Directory and the Sunbelt Health Guide for $2.95 U.S. The Canada News also publishes The Insurance Book, an excellent travel insurance guide for $7.50 U.S.

All policies are not alike, and you often need to work through a maze of costly options to ensure coverage for all major travel hazards. Here are some pointers to help you through that maze:

- In general, you get what you pay for. Buying the lowest premium, may get you inadequate coverage. However, just because a plan is expensive, doesn't mean it won't have gaps in its coverage. Premium alone, should not be the sole criteria for purchasing travel insurance.

- Check with your credit card company since some gold or premium cards will provide limited medical travel coverage for travel stays between two weeks and sixty days. These are sometimes included in the annual credit card fee. We must caution you to check out this type of coverage carefully, since many plans are inadequate.

- Look for a policy that covers all expenses your provincial plan does not, with no limitations on standard doctor's fees or daily hospital expenses.

- Check the upper limit of the policy. Many policies have total benefit limitations as low as $25,000, so you'll have to pay any costs over that amount that your provincial plan doesn't cover. Even a brief emergency stay in a U.S. hospital can exceed this limit. The largest single claim paid recently by a travel insurance company has been about $300,000, for a heart bypass operation. So as long as your upper coverage limit is around this amount, you should be okay.

• Choose the highest deductible available from an insurance carrier. Canadians are conditioned to think they must have no out of pocket expenses regardless of how small the claim. Since small claims are relatively expensive to process, you'll pay through the nose for a low or no deductible policy. You'll pocket big savings from sharing a small amount of risk, while limiting you exposure to smaller bills. If an insurer offered you a six month, maximum $4,750 medical policy for $392 you'd think it was outrageous, yet one major insurance carrier will offer you a $392 reduction from an $873 premium if you take a $5,000 deductible rather than a $250 deductible. A difference of only $4,750 more in total coverage costs you $392! Other insurance plans provide similar savings if they offer a choice of deductibles.

• Review the "exclusions" clause of your policy very carefully. Many policies will exclude coverage for any prior medical condition, or pre-existing condition as insurance companies like to call them, that has been treated by a doctor within the past year, or some other specified time period. If you had a bypass several years ago, and receive an annual check up from your doctor, any hospital stays that are even remotely related to your heart may not be covered.

• If you have a pre-existing medical condition, look for a policy that will at least provide you with emergency coverage for that illness. If you are uncertain how your pre-existing condition will be covered, pick up the telephone and call the home office underwriting department of the company in question. Their telephone number is normally listed on their brochure or policy. Or, check Appendix F in the back of this book. A five minute telephone call may save you thousands of dollars. Be very leery of insurance companies that don't complete some form of medical underwriting by detailed questioning in their applications. These companies are the most likely to decline claims due to pre-existing conditions even though it may appear on the surface they were easier to apply for and obtain.

• Talk to friends and other travellers who have made a claim through the insurance carrier you are considering, to see whether they were treated fairly, and their claims paid on time.

- Don't expect miracles from insurance companies when submitting claims. Most companies will pay only according to the letter of the policy and have highly structured claims systems in order to prevent fraud. Some companies pay only after the provincial plans have paid their portion of the claim. Only British Columbia, Ontario and Quebec allow insurers to bill them directly on your behalf. With payments from Ontario and some other provinces running many months behind, payment from private carriers will as a consequence, also be slow. The better travel insurance carriers will pay your claims quickly, without waiting for provincial plans to pay up.

- Look for a few of the better travel insurance carriers who have set up claims paying offices, and negotiated payment schedules with hospitals in the more heavily populated winter visitor areas in the United States. This will often mean much quicker claims processing. Instead of you paying the hospital and waiting months for reimbursement, you pay nothing and the hospital gets paid directly from the carrier. This valuable service is worth asking for, when shopping for travel insurance.

- Some provinces have reduced the repatriation allowance for returning Canadians back to Canada for further medical treatment. It currently costs about $10,000 to fly a patient back to their home province from the Sunbelt. Check your policy to see whether you are covered for the portion of the costs that your provincial plan won't pick up.

- Look for a plan that has a toll free or collect emergency assistance telephone number manned by the insurance carrier themselves, and not by a third party. It can be very reassuring to have a 24 hour hotline that you can call, if you need assistance or wish to verify coverages. Often hospitals will call this line for you, and establish any necessary liaison between you and your insurance provider.

REMAINING IN THE U.S. OVER SIX MONTHS

There are presently no Canadian provinces that allow you to remain covered by provincial medicare plans after absences of longer than six months. This is a real dilemma for those who want to remain in the U.S. for an extra month or two. Most travel insurance policies will cover you up to a maximum of six months, and will only pay if the provincial plan pays. There are really only three options for someone in this situation:

- Do nothing and hope the province will not find out that you were out of the province longer than you should have been. In the past this option would have been much less of a gamble, but with hungry provincial medical administrators looking to cut costs, we do not recommend this strategy.

- Find an insurance carrier that will cover you when medicare may not cover you, and for longer than six months at a time. At the time of this writing, we know of only one company in Canada that offers such a policy. We did not want to mention company names in any portion of this book except in Appendix F, but this unique service offered by Ingle Health's Nomad Travel Insurance in Toronto warrants special mention. The company was founded by John Ingle in 1960, after his entire family experienced a major medical emergency driving back from a Florida holiday. They have grown to be the most innovative Travel insurance company in Canada. They provide an insurance policy called Nomad Plan 103, that will cover Canadians outside of Canada, who are not covered by any provincial medicare. You can even purchase this coverage without having to return to Canada. There are some exclusions and limitations, as there would be with any policy. Pre-existing conditions are covered on an 80/20 co-payment basis to $25,000 maximum per policy period. However, if you have pre-existing conditions you may be required to register with a local doctor and hospital who are members of the John Ingle preferred provider program or have those conditions excluded from coverage. The Nomad Plan 103 will pay a maximum benefit of $150,000 per year with a $100 deductible and can be purchased to age 80.

- Become a resident of the United States if you are eligible (see Chapter 7), and enrol in an American health care plan. This will be discussed in the next section of this chapter under Insurance For Canadians Moving to the United States.

INSURANCE FOR CANADIANS MOVING TO THE UNITED STATES

There are a great many myths concerning Canadians finding effective and affordable medical insurance, when they take up permanent residence in the United States. We have prepared plans for Canadians, both winter visitors and permanent residents, for a good number of years and have successfully discredited most of these myths. We have been able to develop a variety of alternatives that insure Canadians receive the best of both the Canadian and United States medicare systems. By combining the two country's benefits, you can obtain the best protection, with increased flexibility.

Canadians over 65 who have resided in the United States for at least five years, or are United States citizens, are eligible for complete United States Medicare regardless of any pre-existing conditions. The cost is approximately $300 U.S. per month each, or $40 per month if you or your spouse have contributed the minimum amount to U.S. Social Security programs. See Chapter 9 for more information about qualifying for U.S. Social Security. There are also numerous private insurance carriers that provide Medicare supplements, to fill any gaps in U.S. Medicare coverage. If you do not qualify or are waiting to qualify for U.S. Medicare and are over 65 there is very little choice of coverage available for you with most of the policies coming from outside the U.S. including the Nomad Plan 103, from Ingle Health Insurance noted in the previous section. Be sure to secure this coverage prior to becoming a U.S. resident so that it is effective when you leave Canada and there are no gaps in coverage.

For those under the age of 65, there are a wide variety of health insurance options. Health insurance works much like car insurance in the United States. If you want zero deductible, with your auto insurance company paying for the slightest scratch, you will pay a substantially higher premium than someone with a $1,000 deductible. With health insurance in the United States, you can choose your coverage and your deductible. For example, a person age sixty can get a health policy with a $2,500 deductible and a $2,000,000 coverage limit from an A.M. Best rated "A" company for less than $150 per month.

If you are under 65, and have a pre-existing condition, expect to pay higher premiums and/or have some conditions excluded from coverage or be denied coverage all together. When choosing a health insurance carrier in the United States, stick to an *A.M. Best* rated company with an A or A+ rating, that has been providing health insurance for at least 10 years. Read over any policy and its sales literature very carefully.

There is much debate in the United States as to whether the current medical system should be changed to make it more accessible to more people. The major concern is how will the new system work, what will it cost and who will pay for it? Revamping the American medicare system would have a likely outcome of giving Canadians who become residents of the U.S. better access to the U.S. medical system. Some recent U.S. legislation now in effect improves the chances of someone under 65 with pre-existing conditions of obtaining new health insurance or maintain existing coverage until they can get on Medicare at 65. In addition, there are several U.S. states that will provide special provision for persons with pre-existing conditions. For example, we just had a client, age 55, with a serious pre-existing condition who normally would have been refused health coverage from any health insurance company in the U.S. The client took up residence in Washington state and because of the state laws she was able to obtain adequate medical coverage at a reasonable cost in spite of her medical condition.

WHAT HAPPENS IF YOU GET SICK IN THE U.S.

Contrary to what you may have been lead to believe by some Canadian media, you will not be left to die in the streets because you do not have large buckets of cash with you when you arrive in the emergency room of a U.S. hospital. It is the law in every state that you cannot be turned away from an emergency medical facility because of your ability, or lack thereof, to pay for your emergency treatment.

If you are using a travel insurance company with an emergency assistance line, your first call should be to them, as soon as possible after entering the hospital.

If you are unable to make the call, instruct someone else to do it for you. The travel insurance company can be invaluable in providing you with reassurance, finding medical specialists, or just getting you home in the shortest possible time.

If you do not have travel insurance, contact your provincial medicare office during business hours at the first possible moment. It won't be quite as easy as contacting a private insurance provider with a 24 hour hotline, but you should receive some valuable assistance nonetheless.

Be careful not to over do it with medical treatment that can be deferred until you return to Canada. Out of province medical insurance will likely not cover elective type procedures, so you could be doing it at your own expense. Once again, if you are not sure what is or isn't covered, call the emergency assistance line and confirm the treatments that will be covered.

If your condition has been stabilized and your doctors agree that you are well enough to travel, your insurance company and /or the provincial medicare services will make the necessary arrangements to have you flown back to Canada for follow up treatment. The insurance company will normally make return to Canada arrangements for loved ones, and your automobile, if necessary.

Generally, you are exempt from any adverse consequences from the IRS or U.S. Immigration, if your stay in the U.S. has to be extended beyond normal limits as a result of medical reasons.

CROSS-BORDER Q&A

Many of the issues covered in the preceding chapter of this book have been touched upon in the author's weekly column *Cross-border Q&A,* which appears in *The Sun Times of Canada,* published in Tampa, Florida and circulated throughout the U.S. Sunbelt for Canadians living or wintering there. The majority of these questions have been posed by readers of the Sun Times and/or readers of the previous editions of *The Border Guide.* Most were looking for advice relating to their own specific problems or situations. At the end of this chapter, we have included some typical reader questions, along with our response, to illustrate and broaden the concepts presented in the preceding chapter.

SOME CAN MAKE USE OF BOTH OHIP, U.S. MEDICARE

Your "Cross-Border Q & A" column in a recent issue of "The Sun Times of Canada" responds to a query concerning U.S. Medicare. The nature of your reply prompts me to submit the following information and question(s) to you:

My wife and I are U.S. citizens by birth, and have resided in Ontario for 18 years, with landed immigrant status. By virtue of our residency and my working prior to retirement, we enjoy full benefits of several senior programs, including of course, OHIP, and the Ontario Drug Benefit Plan.

Since retirement, we have been spending our winters in Florida. Each year we purchased "out-of-country" supplemental health insurance. Two years ago, as these premiums began escalating, we reinstated our U.S. Medicare insurance, both Parts A & B. My reasoning at that time was that while in the States, Medicare would be our primary insurance provider, with OHIP as the supplemental coverage. I then confirmed that this was a valid approach; first by asking Medicare (Social Security office), followed by the questions to OHIP.

Medicare advised that primary coverage would be forthcoming at the time of need, the same as any U.S. citizen with the same coverage; however they could not respond to the supplemental coverage from OHIP. OK, I understand, and it firms up 1/2 of the equation.

Now to OHIP — The office I spoke to advised that yes indeed, it is a valid plan. The routine would be to obtain duplicate originals of all bills, so that after submitting them to Medicare and receiving reimbursement, the second set of originals, along with documentation showing Medicare reimbursement, be submitted to OHIP. OHIP would then determine their allowable share of the costs and reimburse accordingly.

My questions is: Have you had any information from correspondents that would indicate problems with this arrangement? If not, it might be helpful for others in like circumstances to look into. We do pay a small penalty for not having taken Part B at age 65, but it's negligible compared to buying supplemental insurance on the Ontario market! Thanks very much - we appreciate your column, and have profited from it.

— *Lee F., Port Huron, MI*

Your Medicare strategy is a sound one that gives you full access to both the U.S. and Canadian medical systems any time you have a need. Since U.S. Medicare has no rules requiring that you must be present in the U.S. a certain time period each year, you only have to ensure you follow OHIP rules and be residents of Ontario without being out of province more than six months each year. The economics of using U.S. Medicare instead of travel insurance supplements to OHIP also makes sense since 12 months at

$40 per month for U.S. Medicare is a lot less than 6 months of travel insurance regardless of which company you're comparing.

HEALTH COSTS OFTEN RAISE U.S. COST OF LIVING

In a recent edition of *The Sun Times of Canada,* you invited readers to forward their queries about cross-border living. My concern is whether it is affordable for dual citizens to live here year round. As you know, medical costs are covered in Ontario by OHIP. I have never paid towards medical coverage in the U.S.

My understanding of your recent article in the paper on this matter is that our cost would be $3,600 per year, plus an HMO or such supplement, which could easily double that figure — all in U.S. funds.

I would much appreciate obtaining additional information and clarification if what you indicate is possible.

— *L.M.A., Lauderhill, FL*

U.S. Medicare, available to all U.S. citizens and legal residents of at least 5 years after the age of 65 does cost nearly $300 per month, if you have never paid into the U.S. Social Security system. However, HMO's (Health Maintenance Organizations) usually do not charge extra and are contracted to provide you complete medical coverage for only the Medicare premium you are paying to Medicare plus small fees for doctor visits and drugs. U.S. Medicare does not provide for long-term care beyond 100 days, so private insurance should be obtained for this, which can add $100-200 per month more in premiums. Insurance premiums can be a deductible expense for those U.S. filers who itemize their deductions.

Even though OHIP appears to be free, it is not. It is paid for by income tax, employer health tax and other tax revenues. Those looking to live in the U.S. need to understand exactly what they are paying for in Canada and just how much it is costing them. You should calculate whether the U.S. taxes you'd pay at your income level, would drop sufficiently to produce a net savings, after accounting for increased U.S. medical expenses. Generally speaking, if you have not paid enough U.S. Social Security to receive Medicare at no additional cost., lower U.S. income taxes will not be sufficient to cover the medical costs, unless your annual income is over $60,000.

RESIDENT ALIENS MAY FIND MEDICARE PROBLEMS

I have read your articles in *The Sun Times of Canada.* Perhaps you can advise me. I am a Canadian citizen, 72 years of age, with resident alien status and social security number in the U.S. I have tried and failed to get Medicare. I pay my taxes in Canada, and return to Ontario for the mandatory period to retain OHIP. My son is a U.S. citizen, and for what it is worth, a commander in the U.S. Navy. I have no family or relatives in Canada, he was the one who sponsored me.

I am in good health, but the problem could arise that I would become incapacitated. There is no one to care for me in Canada, and my family worries about this. Is there any point in discussing this with OHIP? I am prepared to continue paying my taxes in Canada, and fulfil any criteria that may be necessary. Your help in this matter would be appreciated.

—P.M.S., St. Augustine, FL

You didn't say how long you have held your resident alien status or more commonly called a green card. If you've had your green card for at least five years and if you are over age 65, you are entitled to apply for and receive U.S. Medicare. Assuming you qualify for U.S. Medicare, you would have to pay the full premium of approximately $300 per month. You didn't say whether you were ever employed in the U.S., or have a spouse who was employed there. Those who contributed to Social Security through wage deductions, or whose spouse contributed, pay only $40 per month for both parts of U.S. Medicare. A Medicare supplement is generally also recommended, which can cost you another $100 to $150 per month depending on the company and extent of coverage taken. A Health Maintenance Organization (HMO) which contracts with Medicare, can provide the supplemental coverage at no additional monthly cost.

U.S. Medicare does not cover long term nursing care so if you are going to give up OHIP, you should purchase insurance from a wide choice of private insurance companies to cover this potential risk. You can buy this now whether or not you have U.S. Medicare.

If the cost of U.S. Medicare with supplement and long term care insurance is less than the savings in income tax and annual travel insurance premiums, you will come out ahead financially by moving to the U.S. Aside from not having to file returns in Ontario, you will also achieve your goal of being close to your family in the United States.

There is no provision in OHIP to allow for persons in your situation and in fact they continue to restrict out of Canada coverage more and more.

If you don't have your green card for five years, there are least two or three insurers who will cover you for an annual premium comparable to that of U.S. Medicare and supplement until you do have the qualifying time. Please write us again if you need more information.

RESIDENT ALIENS MAY FIND MEDICARE PROBLEMS

I have attended a couple of your seminars. I am under the impression that in order to use your advice, the planning has to start sometime before the actual date of leaving Canada. Is this correct?

My wife and I are quite happy with our present situation of living 6 months each in the USA and Canada. If for financial or medical reasons however, we had to choose one place, it would be Florida. But we want to be prepared.

I can get fairly good medical only coverage through my former place of employment. Is it possible to obtain hospital only coverage down here? Our ages are 73 and 72.

— *John W. Fort Pierce, FL*

Yes, there are several good companies with hospital indemnity type policies for anywhere from $100 per day to several thousand dollars per day for hospital stays. Also, check with the AARP. Most policies of this kind cannot be applied for after age 75, so don't wait much longer to start your planning with a knowledgeable cross-border financial planner before you leave Canada. If you need some help locating an insurance company for this coverage please give us a call and we can put you in touch with a broker.

Take The Money & Run

AN INVESTORS GUIDE TO THE U.S.

6

T he Canadian dollar has been fraught with uncertainty for most of the past two decades. In recent years, it has declined to near record levels against its U.S. counterpart. This came at a time when the American dollar was experiencing steep declines against most major world currencies. Few experts are willing to predict any significant increase in the value of the Canadian dollar in the near future. The major reason is that Canada's $600 billion national debt represents nearly 74% of the gross domestic product as compared to 32.9% for the United States. If you were to add provincial debt (a large number of the U.S. States, by law, cannot run deficit budgets), Canada's total debt comes to over 100% of GDP — a higher proportion than any major industrial country in the world, except Italy. Despite all the political rhetoric about deficit cutting, recent federal budgets still call for deficits well into double digit billions of dollars. Fortunately, some Canadian provinces are getting close to or have balanced budgets and are actively trying to pay down their debts.

Canada has to pay a premium to finance this debt and has had its credit ratings reduced by major rating services. It must therefore keep interest rates relatively high to reduce inflation, and attract foreign investment to bolster the Canadian dollar. The results have been economically punitive as currency exchange rates tend to closely follow interest rates.

Like the U.S., Canada has reduced interest rates in hopes of stimulating the domestic economy, thereby driving down the Canadian dollar. It could decline even further, as political uncertainties grow and Canadian policy makers try to make goods and services more competitive. The real truth of the matter is that no one really knows which way the Canadian dollar will head. At best, experts can predict general trends in its direction.

If the Canadian dollar continues to suffer wide swings in relative value against the U.S. dollar, you may want to take a good hard look at investment opportunities across the border.

THE INVESTMENT OPTIONS

Canadians often lack the confidence to invest across the border. They may opt for putting available U.S. funds into U.S. currency savings accounts at their local Canadian bank, where they'll earn a meagre 1/4% - 2% interest. By doing this they also give up the security of Canadian Deposit Insurance Corporation (CDIC) insurance. Contrary to what some bank employee may tell you, no Canadian Bank or Trust Company offers CDIC insurance on any U.S. dollar account.

This chapter is intended to help Canadians take advantage of U.S. investment opportunities, while minimizing or eliminating any adverse income tax and non-resident estate tax consequences of such investments. Chapter 2 discussed the need to protect yourself against a fluctuating Canadian dollar, and how to obtain the fairest rate of exchange. Now, we will focus directly on the major investment options in the United States, in consideration with income and estate tax implications for Canadians who reside there part-time. These tax consequences were previously discussed at great length in Chapters 3 and 4.

CERTIFICATES OF DEPOSIT

Term deposits, or GICs as they are known in Canada, are called Certificates of Deposit (CDs) in the United States. CDs are issued by most U.S. banks, or by Savings and Loans (S&Ls) which are very similar to Canadian Trust Companies.

Interest on CDs is guaranteed, and rates currently range from 3% to 6%, depending on the term selected. CDs are insured in the U.S. by an agency of the U.S. government, the Federal Deposit Insurance Corporation (FDIC), for up to $100,000 U.S. per bank, and per account-holder. The FDIC is similar to the Canada Deposit Insurance Corporation (CDIC). However, the CDIC's insurance limit is $60,000 CDN.

By filing an Internal Revenue Service (IRS) Form W-8 (provided by the bank), Canadian non-residents who invest in CDs or other similar accounts, are totally exempt from U.S. income and non-resident estate taxes. Before you open your first account at any bank, you will now need to obtain an Individual Tax Identification Number (ITIN) by filing form W-7 with the IRS if you do not already have a U.S. Social Security Number (SSN). Again, please don't give any U.S. financial institution your Canadian SIN.

Once you have a ITIN or SSN, it is good for life.

Unlike most Canadian term deposits and GICs, funds invested in CDs are not locked in and are fairly liquid. However, if you withdraw principal before a CD matures, you may be penalized and could lose one to six months interest earnings.

MUTUAL FUNDS

Mutual funds are diversified portfolios of professionally managed investments of any variety or mix of stocks and bonds. Also known as Investment Funds, these funds are very similar in both Canada and the United States. However, the mutual fund investor in the U.S. has a much broader choice, with more than 8,000 funds currently available. That should be more than adequate to suit any investment objectives with any level of risk.

Some U.S. dollar mutual funds are available through your Canadian broker/advisor, provided you do not mind paying higher commissions.

Many mutual funds in the U.S., have reduced commission levels from around 8% to 4% over the past five years, and many are available to the investor at no sales cost either on purchase or on liquidation. These are known as no load funds. When investing in mutual funds, read the prospectus before you invest and be aware of all the fees payable at the time of purchase, upon withdrawal and on an annual on going basis. There is a great diversity in how individual funds charge their fees, so careful shopping can save you a great deal of money. Canadian mutual funds on average charge management and administration fees typically in the 2-3% range per year while U.S. funds are typically half that with some good index funds available for less than 0.25% per year. These lower costs can be a great incentive to look at adding some U.S. domiciled funds to your investment portfolio. In a flat or down market, paying the higher Canadian Management fees can absorb a majority or even all of your total return available from that particular market.

If you are considering investing in mutual funds in the U.S., you'll find that most mutual fund companies and fund representatives are unfamiliar with non-resident accounts, including the use of IRS Form W-8. The use of a qualified investment advisor or Certified Financial Planner who is familiar with Canadian investment in the U.S., and who works on a fee basis rather than commission, is recommended.

Returns from mutual funds are not guaranteed, and will fluctuate accordingly. Many growth funds have averaged 12% to 18% on an annual basis over the last 10 years. Returns on growth funds will generally have one negative year for every two positive years so they should be considered long term investments not to be dropped at the slightest down turn. These returns are a result of the type of fund managed, and economic conditions.

Interest from U.S. mutual funds, and dividend distributions earned by non-resident investors, is subject to a 15% U.S. withholding tax which can be taken as a full tax credit on your Canadian tax return. Mutual fund investments in the U.S. — whether purchased in Canada or the U.S. — are also subject to non-resident estate tax on amounts over $60,000 US including all other U.S. property. The 1994 Canada — U.S. Treaty has added U.S. stocks including mutual funds to the list of investments that Canadians can make that are exempt from non-resident estate tax. This applies only to Canadians whose world estate is less than $1.2 million U.S. The next section of this chapter takes a closer look at exempt investments.

MONEY MARKET FUNDS

Money Market funds are offered by both banks and mutual fund companies. When purchased through a U.S. bank or a Savings and Loan, these accounts are merely daily interest savings/chequing accounts. They are currently paying 4% to 5% interest, and are insured by the FDIC if purchased through a bank.

Money market mutual funds generally yield 1/2% to 1% higher than bank money market accounts, but hold various types of short-term government and corporate securities directly. There is no FDIC insurance on money market mutual funds, but if you select a portfolio of strictly U.S. government securities, you have the same government guarantee without the FDIC's $100,000 limit.

Money market mutual funds are fully liquid, and impose no sales charges to get in or out of a fund. Many also provide free cheque writing services.

LIMITED PARTNERSHIPS

U.S. Limited Partnerships (LPs) are similar to Canadian LPs. They offer an opportunity to participate directly, with limited liability, in various businesses and investments, while providing professional management.

A non-resident investing in American LPs, will be required to file a U.S. non-resident tax return, whether or not any taxes are due. Taxes paid in the U.S. will provide Canadian taxpayers a corresponding credit on their Canadian tax return.

Rates of return and safety factors for the LP investor will vary as greatly as the myriad of types of LPs available. Great caution is advised when choosing an LP, and professional advice from a qualified investment advisor or Certified Financial Planner is highly recommended.

LPs are considered long-term investments and generally require you to commit your investment until the LP matures, normally 5 to 7 years or beyond. They are more suited to resident investors, but a large number of them will accept non-residents. The fair-market value of an LP is subject to non-resident estate tax on estates in excess of $60,000 unless the underlying securities in the LP are exempt investments (or if the new Canada U.S. Treaty allows for a larger exemption).

REAL ESTATE

Real estate investments in Canada and the U.S. are dependent on the same three principals: location, location, location! Investors must do their homework in order to be successful.

Canadians choosing to invest in the U.S. will find much more paperwork than they may be accustomed to, and some unfamiliar terminology.

For instance, rather than using an attorney to complete the paperwork, most U.S. investors are required to use the services of a title insurance company. These companies complete the necessary paperwork and provide trust services for the equitable exchange of funds between buyer and seller. They also provide the mandatory title insurance required to ensure there is clear title to the property. The buyer typically pays for this insurance, which can range from $500 to $1,000 or more on an average residence.

Marriage has much less paperwork than divorce, and real estate is much easier to purchase than to sell. When a non-resident sells, or is deemed to have sold property in the U.S., they are required to file a non-resident U.S. income tax return, reconciling any capital gains or losses in the year of sale. Without proper clearance certificates from the IRS, the non-resident may be subject to federal and state withholding taxes.

If you are placing a mortgage on your property, you should find an institution familiar with the unique requirements of U.S. non-residents. You will likely be confronted with additional mortgage costs known as "points or closing fees." Points and closing fees are the institution's way of covering the up-front costs of handling the mortgage, and may reduce or discount your mortgage interest rate.

The equity value of your real estate, together with your other U.S. assets, is subject to estate taxes over the $60,000 exemption on property held by non-residents. The new Canada — U.S. Tax Treaty exemption formula may provide some Canadians with an exemption greater than $60,000.

SPECIALTY FUNDS

A handful of mutual fund families have recently created a variety of investments aimed specifically at the non-resident U.S. investor. With these funds, which are registered outside the U.S., Canadian investors can enjoy the advantages of U.S. dollar investments and investment advice while avoiding any adverse tax consequences. They are fully exempt from any United States income or estate tax, plus there is no need for IRS Form W-8 and no income tax reporting requirement to the IRS.

Because these funds are managed in the same way as standard mutual funds, they give you access to professionally managed portfolios corresponding to various asset classes. For example, there are funds specializing U.S. government bonds, or Japanese stocks, Canadian stocks, German government bonds, and so on. The mix of funds you choose will depend on your investment objectives. Once you have opened an account, deposits and withdrawals can be made easily, and periodic dividend cheques can be mailed to you anywhere, or deposited in your local bank account.

Specialty funds are only available to non-residents and/or non-citizens of the U.S., and cannot be purchased while you are in the United States. If you want to maintain their exempt status, you must open your account while outside the United States. Purchases must be directed through U.S. stockbrokers. Commissions can be substantial, with front-end sales loads as high as 5%, and redemption fees of up to 4%. Many of these funds sport high annual expense ratios of up to 3%! Selling brokers are compensated from one or more of these expense categories. There are some good no-load funds now available in the specialty fund area but you need to find a fee only planner to get them for you or go directly to the company.

SPECIALTY PORTFOLIOS

Specialty portfolios are professionally managed portfolios solely comprised of the exempt investments listed below, and tailored to each investor's personal objectives and preferences. Investors with $250,000 U.S. to invest, who want international diversification, quick access to funds, and managers who work on a fee basis rather than commissions, should consider this alternative. These portfolios are managed only for non-residents. Only a limited number of investment firms manage specialty portfolios. Finding the right firm may be time consuming, but the increased flexibility, safety, and cost savings can be well worth the effort.

EXEMPT INVESTMENTS

Throughout this book, we have periodically referred to exempt investments, meaning U.S. investments that are exempt from both income and estate tax for non-resident. You should already be familiar with the fact that exposure to U.S. taxes can be a direct function of the type of investment you make in the United States.

The list of the exempt investments detailed below can be your guide to eliminate those investments that can create unnecessary tax burdens for the non-residents, while at the same time allowing them a number of choices to develop a safe, income producing portfolio of U.S. investments. Exempt investments include:

- Banking and Savings & Loan deposits, including CDs, savings accounts, and money market funds. A completed Form W-8 must be filed with the savings institution.

- U.S. Treasury bonds, notes, bills, and agency issues if issued after July 18th, 1984.

- U.S. Corporate bonds, if issued after July 18th, 1984. A completed Form W-8 must be filed with the company issuing the bond or the brokerage account where you purchased and hold the bond.

- Specially structured mutual funds. These are the specialty funds explained in detail in the previous section of this chapter titled Specialty Funds.

- Some investment companies or brokerage houses offer money market funds where the securities in the portfolio consists of only government and corporate bonds that have been noted above as exempt securities. A completed Form W-8 must be filed with the brokerage firm.

- Life insurance death benefits regardless of the amount.

- Canadians whose world estate is less than $1,200,000 U.S. ($2,400,000 for husband and wife with joint property) under the new 1994 Canada — U.S. Treaty, will be allowed to add U.S. stocks, including mutual funds shares, to this list of exempt investments for estate tax purposes only. The U.S. stocks or U.S. mutual funds will still be subject to the Treaty withholding on dividends of 15% unless they are purchased through your Canadian broker where all dividends are reported directly to Revenue Canada on T-5 slips.

UNDERSTANDING INVESTMENT RISK

Investors think of risk in two erroneous ways. The first is that investment risk reflects only potential downward movement in the value of an investment. In reality, risk is a measure of market volatility. Therefore risk reflects both the probability of upward and downward price fluctuations.

The second assumption is that "market" risk is the only kind of risk that exists in today's investment marketplace. Market risk is the degree an investment's price behaviour correlates with the general market for that investment. A good example of this is stock, whose value will generally reflect upward or downward movements in the stock market as a whole.

This section will outline at least seven types of investment risk and place special emphasis on those types of risk, which can most effect retirees or persons planning for their retirement.

- Specific Risk reflects risks inherent to one investment in particular. A purchaser of GM stock would be concerned about problems peculiar to GM, such as the amount of debt, potential labour problems, effective management, and so on. This type of risk may be eliminated by properly diversifying a portfolio.

- Market Risk is best exemplified by the stock or real estate markets. Market values of individual stocks or parcels of real estate tend to follow movement in the stock market or regional real estate markets in general. Market risk can pose a substantial short-term risk to investment principal. If your investment horizon is greater than three years, market risk in the stock market decreases rapidly, and continues to decrease the longer the time period of your investment.

- Inflation Risk is the most insidious and harmful risk to retirees, largely because its effects are not immediately obvious. Inflation reflects a loss of purchasing power, and it primarily affects fixed investments such as bonds, term deposits, GICs, CDs, and annuities. If an investor had $10,000 in Canada Savings Bonds which yielded 10% per year in income, and inflation averaged 5% that year, what happens to the value of the bonds? The bonds will still be worth $10,000 on the investor's annual statements, but will the investor still be able to purchase $10,000 worth of goods and services? No, because of the 5% annual inflation, the investors $10,000 is worth 5% less, or $9,500! Income from the bonds is also worth 5% less, compounded for each year of inflation! If the investor held these bonds for ten years, and inflation averaged 5% per year, the investor would get a check from the Canadian government for $10,000, but the bonds would purchase only $6,139 worth of goods and services. This type of risk may be reduced by adding inflation hedges to a portfolio.

- Interest Rate Risk reflects how movements in interest rates affect the value of investments. Anyone whose income depends primarily on interest rates has seen their income effectively cut in half from 1991 to 1992 and again from 1994 to 1996. as their term deposits came due for renewal. Interest rate volatility over the last 15 years have made bonds and term deposits much more risky to hold, particularly in a portfolio that has little or no diversification.

- Currency Risk is similar to inflation risk in the way that it affects investments. This type of risk is especially important to Canadian retirees and was exemplified in Chapter 2. Changes in the value of currencies can affect purchasing power the same way inflation does. For instance, if the Canadian dollar were to depreciate 5% in a year relative to the American dollar, Canadians could purchase 5% less in American goods. Over $1 trillion of currency is traded each day all over the world, up from almost nothing in the 1970s. This type of risk may be eliminated by diversifying a portfolio in the global sense.

- Economic Risk affects investments much like market risk. Stocks and real estate tend to do well when the economy is brisk. Gold and utilities are examples of "counter cyclical" investments, which perform well when the economy is down.

- Government Risk affects both Canadian and American residents. This type of risk results from both government's frequent changes to the tax laws — often with negative effects for the investor. The most recent example was the Tax Reform Act of 1986, in the United States, where many tax shelter investors lost their tax preferences, and were not grandfathered from the effects of the new law. Real estate is still struggling to recover from this change after eleven years. This type of risk may also be reduced by properly diversifying your portfolio.

By knowing all of the risks inherent to investing, and prudently diversifying investments, the informed investor can enjoy a high, tax-favoured income at low levels of risk. The effects of inflation and wide currency swings can be minimized.

THE REWARDS OF GLOBAL INVESTING

In 1990, Merton Miller, William Sharpe and Harry Markowitz won the Nobel prize in economics for their pioneering work in quantifying returns and risk from a portfolio perspective. Their research turned up some rather surprising results. It turns out your grandmother was right after all; don't put all of your eggs in one basket. The market may not compensate you for the additional risk with higher returns. There is also no such thing as a free lunch. Decrease your overall risk, you will also decrease returns over the long run.

Most surprising, were the results attained by combining two assets that behave differently. Take a stock that performs well during economic downturns, and take a cyclical stock. Both are expected to return 11% over the long run. If you buy equal portions of both stocks, the long-run return will be 11%. But year to year volatility will decrease, because one stock does well when the other does poorly. In fact, adding an asset that may be considered risky by itself, may actually reduce the total risk of the overall portfolio!

What does this have to do with international investing? International stock and bond markets do not move in lockstep with the U.S. and Canadian stock markets. Many European markets, as well as the Japanese market did poorly in 1991, while North and Central American markets skyrocketed. By combining foreign stocks and bonds with U.S. and Canadian investments, we lower risk and enhance returns over the long run.

Invest in foreign securities and you attain diversification through exposure to different economies. Over the last 20 years, many markets have grown faster than the U.S. or Canadian stock markets. This means added profits for investors. Opportunities may also emerge with the opening of eastern European countries and former republics of the Soviet Union.

Currency risks are also hedged. Canadian investors in foreign securities would have benefited greatly from currency gains when the Canadian dollar dropped from $0.89 U.S. to $0.83 U.S. in less than six months from late 1991 to early 1992 and then from $0.83 in 1992 to below $0.71 in 1994. In a global economy, diversifying currency risk is very important.

More aggressive investors may find excellent opportunities in "emerging markets". Some of these markets have boomed during the last few years. Many Latin American countries freed up their economies with skyrocketing stock markets as a result. Mexico, Chile, Argentina, and Brazil are recent examples. Indian and Israeli markets have also exploded. While we don't recommend that a portfolio contain only emerging market stocks, an exposure of 10% or so may aid returns and lower portfolio risk.

How do you select and purchase shares of stock or bonds in these markets? By using a mutual fund, stock selection is left to experts who focus on the country in question. This expertise can be crucial since financial disclosure and accounting standards are rarely as investor-oriented as they are in the U.S. and Canada. Information on foreign companies is also difficult to come by. Funds buy large blocks of stocks or bonds and transaction costs are reduced. Shares can be bought and sold quickly and inexpensively, and offer instant diversification.

With U.S. and Canadian stocks markets looking more overvalued every day and lower interest rates, now would seem an ideal time to consider the higher potential returns of foreign stocks and bonds. As always, we recommend you seek professional advice before implementing any of these ideas.

CHOOSING AN INTERNATIONAL INVESTMENT MANAGER

The key to successful investing is formulating a long-term, internationally diversified portfolio policy based on your own objectives and preferences. The first words out of a potential investment manager's mouth should be questions related to your personal investment objectives. These objectives should contain concise information regarding the returns you expect, and the level of risk or volatility you are willing to undertake in exchange for these returns.

It is also important to consider present and future income needs from the portfolio, investment time horizon, liquidity requirements, income and estate tax information, and your current estate plan. You should be active in these early stages when portfolio policy is being formulated, and again when your individual situation changes. Charles D. Ellis' book Investment Policy, 2nd edition, published in 1993, by Business One Irwin, is considered a classic in this area.

Unfortunately, in the real world, most advisors may be little more than sales people enjoying up-front commissions based solely on sales volume. Clearly, there is little or no incentive for an advisor to monitor a client account after a commission is received.

Moreover, advisors working on a commission basis earn more by selling or shifting existing investments. This latter procedure, if done excessively, is called "churning" and is illegal.

The key to successful investment performance is active, professional portfolio management; with the most important considerations being the manager's investment philosophy, and the client's comfort with that philosophy.

Why is formulation of a long-term portfolio policy emphasized here? Because some recent studies from the Financial Analysts Journal (Gary Brinson, L. Randolph Hood and Gilbert L. Beebower, "Determinants of Portfolio Performance", July-August 1986, and Gary P. Brinson, Brian D. Singer and Gilbert L. Beebower, "Revisiting Determinants of Portfolio Performance: An Update", May-June 1991) show that more than 90% of investment returns generated by large pension plans are due to following a long-term investment policy. Less than 10% of portfolio returns were attributed to "stock picking," or market timing (switching funds between investments or asset classes in response to perceived changes in the economy). The successful investment advisor will pay close attention to those decisions that will generate 90% of their portfolios' return.

There seems to be an inherently unfair bias in the way the investment marketplace treats "retail", or individual investors versus "wholesale" or institutional investors. What are these differences, and how can investors overcome them? How can you ensure equal treatment?

First, let's examine some of the differences. The retail marketplace is largely transaction-based. Stockbrokers, commissioned financial planners, and insurance salespeople are compensated by the number of financial transactions they effect. Put another way, the more they sell you, the more they make. The focus is not always on managing an investor's funds for the long-term, but on switching from investment to investment.

Even banks collect commissions indirectly. Term deposits or bank CDs return an interest rate plus a guarantee of principal for a specified period of time. The banks invest the funds in government and corporate debt securities, mortgages, and leases, and other investments. The return is often significantly higher than what is paid out to bank depositors.

The institutional marketplace, which includes pension funds, insurance companies, and mutual funds, is performance based. Portfolios are often managed by one or more managers, whose compensation is based on how big the portfolio gets. They are paid for performance rather than buying or selling investments. Here, the incentive is to reduce commission costs, since commissions reduce the size of the portfolio they manage.

Individual investors are constantly bombarded by the media and salespeople with information about the latest investment guru, the hottest stocks, or the best market pundit. They often buy under the premise that the broker, salesperson, or financial planner can pick "hot stocks" or other investments (why is life insurance so often the hot investment?) and can time favourable moments to switch between stocks, bond or cash, depending on market conditions. If market timing and security selection contribute less than 10% of a typical portfolio's return, why does the media and retail investment marketplace focus so much time and energy promoting these advisors who claim to have exceptional abilities in these areas? Because strategies that lean heavily on security selection and market timing generate many, many more transactions (read: commissions) than establishing and sticking to a long-term investment policy.

Although many institutional investors use stock-picking and some form of market timing, more have become asset allocators. This involves the diversifying investments between cash equivalents, stocks, bonds, real estate, and other asset classes. Asset allocators do not try to predict the markets, the economy, or interest rates, since they believe these markets and indicators are unpredictable over the long run. They also diversify their holdings, and use a buy-and-hold strategy to minimize transaction costs.

How can you level the playing field? Find an investment advisor who focuses on formulating a long-term investment policy based on your needs and preferences, which is 90% of the ballgame. In choosing an investment manager, you should consider the following:

- Choose a manager compensated on the basis of performance, not commissions.

- All other things being equal, choose the manager with lower management fees.

- Make sure the manager cannot make "big bets" with your portfolio. Choose a fund or firm whose management philosophy requires the manager to be diversified to some degree.

- Choose a manager who uses no-load mutual funds and/or a discount brokerage arrangement to transact securities trades, thus minimizing your investment costs.

CROSS-BORDER Q&A

Many of the issues covered in the preceding chapter of this book have been touched upon in the author's weekly column *Cross-border Q&A*, which appears in *The Sun Times of Canada*, published in Tampa, Florida and circulated throughout the U.S. Sunbelt for Canadians living or wintering there. The majority of these questions have been posed by readers of the Sun Times and/or readers of the previous editions of *The Border Guide*. Most were looking for advice relating to their own specific problems or situations. At the end of this chapter, we have included some typical reader questions, along with our response, to illustrate and broaden the concepts presented in the preceding chapter.

DOES U.S. LAW FORBID NON-RESIDENT BROKERAGE ACCOUNTS?

I have searched in vain for a way out of my dilemma; the Florida broker I had dealt with for about a year was forced to close my account. Apparently regulations prohibit a non U.S. resident brokerage account, with or without a W-8, no matter which address I use. As a Snowbird and a former stock broker, I am familiar with all of the information in your recent article "Relax While Your Money Works." Please explain how I can resolve this.

— *Edward S., North York, ON*

Your dilemma can be solved by calling Charles Schwab — the United States' largest discount brokerage firm. Charles Schwab has what is called a NRA account (NRA stands for Non-Resident Alien) that you may use without restrictions. There is a little more paperwork involved to set up this account than an ordinary brokerage account, but it gives you full access to trade in your account, as you require. If you want more information about Charles Schwab, they have offices in major cities throughout Florida, and the U.S., and are listed in your local phone book. You may have luck with other brokerage firms for these NRA accounts as well.

I believe your stock broker was confusing his company's policy and procedures with that of the regulatory bodies, as there are no laws, that I am aware of, prohibiting non-resident accounts if they are done properly.

HOLDING SECURITIES IN STREET FORM & U.S. TREASURY NOTES

If I hold U.S. securities in street form, in my Canadian account, are they still subject to the $60,000 limit for estate tax? Technically, the answer is probably yes, but are there reporting procedures between the two countries? Finally, I have read about U.S. Treasury notes. Are these available to Canadians? If so, where and how?

— *Ronald Z., Corunna, ON*

Holding securities in street form, as you already guessed, does not exempt them from non-resident estate tax. Any United States securities, unless they are specifically exempt, add to the taxable estate of non-residents. Tax exempt securities that would likely be purchased through a brokerage firm include Certificates of Deposit from United States banks, U.S. Government Treasury Bills, Treasury Notes and Treasury Bonds issued after July 1984. U.S. Securities are taxable for non-resident estate tax purposes, whether the securities are held in Canada, the U.S. or anywhere in the world. Canadians whose world estate is less than $1,200,000 U.S, under the new 1994 Canada — U.S. Treaty, can hold U.S. stocks as exempt from the non-resident estate tax.

There are no automatic formal reporting procedures between Canada and the United States with respect to brokerage accounts. However, the Canada — United States Tax Treaty allows for the exchange of tax information in either country at any time. The Internal Revenue Service has been using this treaty clause quite frequently to catch United States taxpayers for not reporting taxes due. The answer to your final question about purchasing U.S. Treasury notes is that you can hold as many as you desire, and if you open the NRA account with Charles Schwab, or another broker, you can purchase them there at a very reasonable cost.

SPECIALTY FUNDS FOR NON-RESIDENTS

I am semi-retired, and like to devote time to my business and leisure. I spend 5 months of each year in the U.S., so I need U.S. dollar income. I am afraid that the Canadian dollar will continue to decline in value against the U.S. dollar. Are there investment advisors in the U.S. who manage accounts specially for non-residents?

— *Tom C., Phoenix, AZ*

A number of U.S. based mutual fund companies have started specialty mutual funds for non-residents. These funds are registered offshore in places like the Cayman Islands or Guernsey. They may only be purchased by non-residents of the U.S. while outside the U.S. and only through a U.S. broker. All of the funds we have examined are load funds, and exact their pound of flesh through one or more of the following ways:

* up front commissions,

* commissions incurred when fund shares are sold, and

* high annual costs, some of which are passed through to brokers.

To date, we have not encountered any no-load specialty funds that are available to the general pubic. Although somewhat expensive, specialty funds can be useful to investors with $100,000 or less, who understand that diversification is important to the realization of their financial objectives.

Another alternative is to choose an investment advisor who can manage a diversified, international portfolio specifically tailored to each investor's needs and preferences. This type of professionally managed portfolio generally requires $250,000 or more to be invested. These accounts can be specifically tailored for each individual, but should invest only in exempt investments, such as U.S. Treasury securities and corporate bonds issued after July 18, 1984, bank certificates of deposit, exempt money market funds, and specialty mutual funds. Accordingly, specialty portfolios should be exempt from U.S. income tax reporting and withholding, and not included in the non-resident's U.S. estate. Funds should only be invested in marketable assets that can be turned into cash within a week or two.

Specialty portfolios are appropriate for investors who desire:

• A custom tailored, long-term investment policy.

• Personal, one-on-one attention.

• Prudent, professional management of their investments.

• Privacy.

• Increased safety and returns of international diversification.

• Quick access to funds.

• Minimal commissions.

• Exemption from U.S. income tax reporting.

• Exemption from U.S. income tax withholding.

• Exemption from the U.S. non-resident estate tax.

Investors typically pay management fees of 0.5% to 1.5% per year, depending on the manager and the size of the account.

CAN CANADIAN BROKERS ACT FOR US RESIDENTS

I am a retired Canadian and a recent Green Card resident of Florida. My income (except for U.S. Social Security) is all Canadian and I have an investment portfolio with a Toronto brokerage firm. This account consists of bonds and mortgage backed securities. Trading in this account is infrequent and usually only to replace investments which have matured.

My broker has recently advised me that SEC regulations prohibit him from making Canadian trades for a US resident! Is this a unique situation? There must be a great many Canadians in the U.S. who own Canadian securities. This creates a very serious situation for me and I would appreciate your comments and your advice as to what steps I might take. Are there Toronto firms which could do trades for me if necessary?

— *Darwin M. Sarasota, Florida*

Your broker is correct, in order for him to legally deal with a U.S. resident both he and his company must be licensed in your state of residence. Many Canadians in the U.S. have gotten similar notices from their brokers.

This can easily be solved by setting up a U.S. brokerage account and transferring the cash and securities into it through a broker to broker transfer. U.S. brokerage firms can and do hold just about any listed Canadian bonds and stocks. Those they can't accept should be converted to cash before the transfer.

CAN CANADIAN BROKERS ACT FOR US RESIDENTS

I am retired with no employment income. I do however, trade commodity futures through a U.S. based broker, using a computerized system. The net results are reported to Revenue Canada.

I intend to carry on this activity during the winter months from my temporary U.S. address and would like to know if the results (hopefully good) might be construed as being income earned in the U.S. and therefore liable to be reported to the IRS!

A complicating factor is that the income might never be actually received in the U.S. since a trade could be initiated in one country but come to fruition in another! Would appreciate your insight into this.

— *Gordon C., St. Catherines, ON*

You pose an interesting and unusual set of questions. If you are able to insure that your trading is simply a capital transaction and is subject to tax as capital gains (or losses), then you have no worries with respect to being taxed in the U.S., providing you don't spend more than 183 days a year in the U.S. and file the Closer Connection Form 8840 with the IRS annually by June 15th. If you follow these two requirements, the Canada/U.S. Tax Treaty clearly states that your capital gains are only taxable in Canada, regardless of the fact that you may be in the U.S. for part of the year.

If this trading is regular enough that it might be considered your only job, there is a possibility any income could be classified as business income. You would be considered to be doing business in the U.S. meaning that the business income would be taxable in the U.S. and included as part of your world income in Canada. I suggest you check to see if your U.S. broker is licensed to do business in Ontario by the Ontario Security Commission. If not, you could have little or no consumer protection for inappropriate advice or someone running off with your funds.

TRANSFERRING ACCOUNTS AND FINDING A U.S. BASED BROKER

I and my family became U.S. residents in 1995 on a L1 Visa. For stocks and securities trading we dealt with Green Line Investor Services while in Canada, but they insist that they can no longer trade on our behalf. They blame U.S. SEC rules, but I have seen conflicting information about this.

Green Line does offer a U.S. division which will carry my accounts in Canadian dollars, but I am not certain that I should go through the necessary exercise, or that all the downside has been made clear.

Are there any alternatives for someone in my position? Is there any significant risk or loss of flexibility in transferring my accounts? Can you recommend anyone in the Detroit area to provide financial advice?

Thank you for your excellent book and whatever comments you can provide on the above.

— *Murray K. Farmington Hills, MI*

Your brokerage firm is correct. They cannot legally trade accounts for U.S. residents unless both the broker and the firm are licensed in your particular state in the U.S. Also, there are generally some state securities requirements that could make it illegal for them to deal with you.

Your alternatives depend on your personal goals regarding the kind of investor you are, whether the accounts are RRSPs, and if you plan to be a permanent U.S. resident. Generally, it will simplify your financial life immensely if your account is in the U.S. It will be much easier for you to manage and administer, particularly for income tax reporting. You should also be able to reduce your brokerage costs as competition in the U.S. tends to keep transaction costs very low. We like to recommend Charles Schwab as the best all-around discount broker in the U.S. You can provide Charles Schwab with a list of your securities and they should be able to tell you which ones can be held in the U.S. They can also initiate the transfer of your account. Generally, most listed Canadian stocks and bonds can be held in your U.S. account. Mutual Funds will have to be liquidated and turned into cash to transfer to the U.S. If you need specific money management assistance in the U.S., call or write us for help and give more particulars as to what your goals are and the type and size of the accounts you need to have managed.

Coming to America

MOVING TO THE UNITED STATES

7

M any Canadians would never dream of moving to the United States, while others spend thousands of dollars attempting to obtain legal status as U.S. residents. There are other Canadians who live in the U.S. illegally year-round, or who stay longer than Immigration and Naturalization Service (INS) rules allow for a winter visitor. With the relative ease of crossing the border, and the ability to remain in the U.S. for extended periods of time, why should anyone consider becoming a legal resident of the United States?

For some people, United States residency means a new business opportunity. Others have had enough of paying more than half of their earnings to high Canadian taxes; while others just prefer the warmer climate. Whatever your motives, this chapter is designed to assist those people who have thought that at some stage in their life, they might like to emigrate from Canada to the United States. Chapters 8 and 9 will help you to determine whether United States residency would be a good move financially, after taking into consideration the key cross-border issues of income tax, estate tax and medicare. For those who are seriously contemplating a move, all of the issues in this and the next two chapters need to be addressed simultaneously, for maximum benefit.

This chapter will serve as a general discussion of American immigration rules and policies. Individual factors can greatly influence the course of any immigration undertaking. Immigration can be a complex and lengthy procedure under current law, and should not be attempted without the services of a good United States immigration attorney.

HOW TO BECOME A LEGAL RESIDENT OF THE U.S.

There are normally two ways to immigrate to the United States. The first is through a business or a professional relationship. The second is through the sponsorship of a close family member. This is about as simple an explanation as it gets, about who is entitled to immigrate to the United States. After that, the whole process starts becoming complex and contradictory. Figure 7.1 provides a chart of the basic business categories, under which you may acquire either a permanent or something less than permanent resident status.

You can see from Figure 7.1, that there are numerous opportunities for U.S. immigration for persons with business contacts. Business and professional immigration categories will be explained in greater detail in the next section. Where does this leave the retired person who wants to immigrate and retire in the United States Sunbelt? That's where some advance planning can pay big dividends. For those who have recently retired, or are about to retire, you should consider keeping open any business or professional relationships long enough to assist you in getting permanent immigration status. Those of you who are retired but feel they wouldn't mind operating a business, investing in a small U.S. business and hiring a full time manager, can be a very suitable means of obtaining a visa that allows you to legally live in the United States, year round.

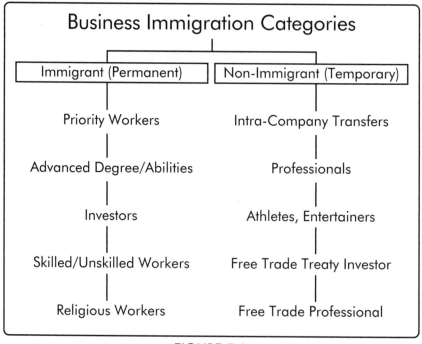

FIGURE 7.1

Those with no applicable business or professional means, may wish to look for any possible family connections that can provide legal status in the United States. Figure 7.2 addresses the key family relationships that can prove useful for immigration purposes.

IMMIGRATION CATEGORIES

This section lists some of the basic qualifications for each of the business and family immigration categories that are outlined in Figures 7.1 and 7.2.

Immigrant or Lawful Permanent Resident (LPR) status is also known as a "green card." This is similar to Landed Immigrant status in Canada. The green card is no longer even green, this year's model is pink, or more accurately, deep salmon. Every so often, the green card is given a new look to impede fraudulent reproduction. Current versions of the green card now include an expiration date. This means the card is now like a drivers license, and must be renewed before the expiration date.

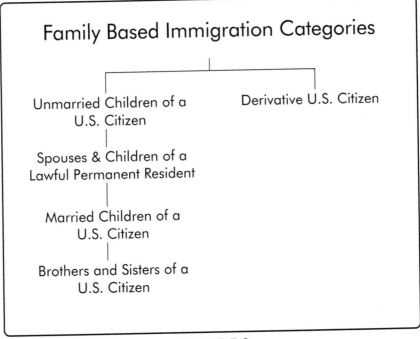

FIGURE 7.2

Congress, under President Bush, substantially revised the immigration laws, effective October, 1991. This revision greatly expanded the number of categories, and eligibility requirements for entering the United States and obtaining a green card. So many new green card categories were created, that the INS had difficulty providing proper regulations under which people apply for the various employment based categories. Now after six years, most of these regulations have been provided by INS.

GREEN CARD - EMPLOYMENT BASED IMMIGRANT CATEGORIES

FIRST PREFERENCE

1. Priority Workers. There are three priority worker classes known to the INS as EB - 1-A, 1-B, and 1-C categories:

    1-A. Extraordinary ability immigrants in the sciences, arts, education, business and athletics. The regulations define extraordinary ability as a level of expertise indicating that the individual is one of that small percentage who have risen to the very top of their field of endeavour. No employer sponsorship or labour certification is required for a person in this category.

    1-B. Outstanding professors and researchers. Applicants in this category must be coming to the U.S. to conduct research for a private firm in full time research activities or for a university. They must display documented achievements in their field. The university or the private research company applies to INS for this visa.

    1-C. Executives and managers. An executive or manager employed at least one of the three years preceding the application by the U.S. employer's Canadian affiliate, parent, subsidiary or branch office qualifies for this category. This is a good opportunity for obtaining a green card for those business people who have a business in both Canada and the United States. This category is very similar to the L-1 intra-company visa in the non-immigrant petitions.

SECOND PREFERENCE

2. Professionals Holding Advanced Degrees, 2-A. or Exceptional Ability Immigrants, 2-B.

2-A. Advanced Degree. This category includes people with Ph.Ds and Masters degrees. Five years or more experience of progressive work may be accepted in lieu of the advanced degree providing a Bachelors degree has been acquired. Unless they qualify for the national interest waiver discussed below applicants for this category must have an employer (i) petition on their behalf for a position that requires this advance education and (ii) obtain a labour certification from the U.S. Department of Labor. To obtain labour certification the employer must demonstrate that there are no U.S. workers who are qualified and available to fill the position.

2-B. Exceptional Ability Immigrants. INS provides for admission of a person with exceptional ability in the arts, sciences or business. If you can convince INS it is in the United States national interest (because of your significant positive contribution to the U.S. economy) to waive the employment and labor certification requirement, this petition can be submitted directly without an employer sponsor. Like many aspects of immigration rules, the term "exceptional ability" has not been clearly defined. It is a lower standard than "extraordinary ability" but still requires a degree of expertise significantly above the ordinary. Like the 2-A category 2-B applicants must have an employer petition for them and they must obtain a labor certification unless they are granted the national interest waiver of those requirements.

THIRD PREFERENCE

3. Skilled and Unskilled Workers. This catch-all category is for immigrants with offers of employment. This category is further subdivided into:

3-A. Professionals with Bachelor's degrees and labor certifications.

3-B. Skilled workers performing a job requiring at least two years of higher education, training or experience.

3-C. "Other workers." This sub-category is for positions that require less than two years of higher education, training or experience.

FOURTH PREFERENCE

4. Religious Workers. Must have been a member of and worked for a denomination for at least two years and seek entry as (a) minister (needs

a baccalaureate degree); (b) professionals working in a religious capacity or (c) other religious organization workers.

FIFTH PREFERENCE

5. Immigrant Investors. This is sometimes referred to as the "gold card." It is similar to the program Canada has used for years for attracting foreign business entrepreneurs. This category is a Conditional Lawful Permanent Residence for two years until all the requirements listed below are met, then full green card LPR status is granted:

- Establish a new or expand an existing commercial enterprise; with:

- An investment of $500,000 (in rural or special high unemployment areas) or one million dollars in other areas that will;

- Benefit the U.S. economy; and

- Create at least 10 full time jobs for U.S. authorized workers.

EMPLOYMENT BASED NON-IMMIGRANT CATEGORIES

1. Intra-Company Transfers. This category is classified as the L-1 Non-immigrant Status and can last, with renewals up to seven years. This visa requires an ongoing relationship between a Canadian company and a United States parent subsidiary, branch office or affiliate. The visa applicant must be an executive, manager or a person with specialized knowledge or training needed for the U.S. company, and the applicant must have worked for the Canadian affiliate for at least one year out of the three years prior to the transfer to the United States.

2. Professionals and Other Temporary Workers. This category is divided into five categories and can last, with renewals up to six years. The five categories of this visa are as follows:

   a. H-1A - Professional registered nurses; (slated to expire Sept. 30, 1997)

   b. H-1B - Professionals in special occupations requiring a college degree or equivalent in work experience;

   c. H-2A - Temporary agricultural workers in short supply;

   d. H-2B - Temporary non-agricultural workers that are in short supply;

   e. H-3 - Trainees

The H1-A and H-1B categories can be granted for an initial three year period, extendable to six years maximum. The H-2A, H-2B and H-3 categories can be granted for up to one year initially, extendible to three years for H-2A and H-1B or two years for the H-3. There is a numerical cap on the numbers of these visas granted.

3. Artists, Entertainers and Athletes. There are two non-immigrant statuses available for these emigrants from Canada. These are known as the P and O Status and both are limited to the time period of a particular event(s). The O Visa is for extraordinary artists, entertainers and athletes and can last for three years initially then yearly renewable thereafter or the time period of the event(s), whichever is less. The P non-immigrant status can last for up to five years extendible to ten years maximum. There is a numerical cap on these visas.

4. NAFTA Free Trade Agreement Treaty Traders and Investors. The Canadian Free Trade Agreement with the United States became effective January 1, 1989 and was superseded by the North American Free Trade Agreement (NAFTA) which came into effect January 1, 1994. The Immigration Section of NAFTA provides for the temporary entry of business visitors, eliminates barriers to trade, facilitates across-the-border investment, provides for joint administration and dispute resolution, and emphasizes trade and the movement of people.

This means that Canadian citizens can now obtain the equivalent of E-2 visas, which are usually indefinitely renewable as long as the qualifying investment remains ongoing, and is considered the next best thing to permanent residency. Requirements for an E-2 Visa are:

- Canadian citizen.

- A substantial investment in a bona fide U.S. enterprise must be made. A substantial investment is not clearly defined but the State Department has issued a sliding scale guideline. If the value of the enterprise is less than $500,000 the applicant must provide 75% of the investment. The amount of the investment must be an amount normally considered appropriate to establish a viable enterprise of the nature contemplated.

- The investor must be in a position to "develop and direct" the entity into which he or she has invested. Generally, that means the investor must have 50% ownership or control interest.

- Certain "essential employees" of the investor may also be eligible for E-2 status. Essential employees must be employed in a supervisory or executive capacity or have special skills needed by the employer.

- There is no requirement for a minimum number of employees to be hired, but the number of employees required to operate the business in addition to the E-2 investor must be sufficient to make the enterprise successful. The investment must do more than support the investor and his or her family.

- The company or employer of the visa applicant must be at least 51% Canadian owned and controlled.

NAFTA FREE TRADE AGREEMENT PROFESSIONALS

This category is a unique one and is called the TN status. It permits people to come in as non-immigrants on the basis of their being a "professional" as listed on a schedule to NAFTA. The TN visa is valid for one year and may be renewed annually for an unlimited duration as long as the visa holder maintains his or her non-immigrant intent. The list of professionals includes accountants, engineers, scientists, research assistants, medical/ allied professionals, psychologists, scientific technicians, disaster relief insurance claims adjusters, architects, lawyers, teachers, economists, computer systems analysts, management consultants and others. The list includes professors but omits high school level teachers. The professionals require at least a bachelors degree. Work experience will be allowed to replace educational requirements only for the management consultants.

FAMILY BASED IMMIGRANT CATEGORIES

Family based immigration is predicated on the fact that a family member who is already a U.S. citizen or green card holder can sponsor other family members for permanent residence in the United States. There is also the possibility that a person looking to immigrate to the United States may already be a derivative citizen due to their family history. Derivative citizenship will be covered in detail in the next section of this chapter. There are five main categories for family sponsored immigration.

The immediate relative category is separate from other family-based immigration because it is not numerically restricted. This category belongs to spouses, unmarried minor children and parents of U.S. citizens. New spouses obtaining a green card by marrying a U.S. citizen will receive a two year temporary green card and must go through an interview process after the two years before a permanent card is issued. The purpose of this process is to thwart marriages of convenience whose purpose is to fraudulently obtain legal immigration status. Those who saw the movie Green Card will have a better understanding of what this process entails with its detailed questioning of the spouses to ensure they are truly married.

In all but one of the other four categories, the family member sponsoring the green card LPR of another family member must be a U.S. citizen (see the section Becoming a U.S. Citizen later in this chapter). These categories are subject to quotas and waiting lists of a few months to several years. They work on a priority or preference system and are in order of preference:

- 1st Preference. Unmarried sons and daughters of U.S. citizens. At the present time there is a waiting list of nearly a year in this category.

- 2nd Preference. This category is broken down into two sub-categories.

  A. Spouses and minor children of Lawful Permanent Residents or green card holders. There is currently a wait of about four years in this category.

  B. Adult unmarried sons and daughters of Lawful Permanent Residents or green card holders. There is a waiting period of over six years in this category.

- 3rd Preference. Married children of U.S. citizens. There a waiting period in this category of over three years.

- 4th Preference. Siblings of U.S. citizens. There is a waiting period in this category of over ten years. Even though the waiting list may be quite long it is worthwhile getting on this list as a change in legislation could either reduce the waiting period, and/or increase quotas, and people already on the list could move much more quickly. There are currently proposals before Congress to eliminate the 4th Preference altogether.

DERIVATIVE CITIZENSHIP - ARE YOU A U.S. CITIZEN?

With Canada and the United States being so closely related in geography and past history, there has been a substantial migration of residents back and forth across the 49th parallel. As a result, many Canadians, although they may never have lived in the United States, may be a U.S. citizens solely on the basis of their ancestry. This is known as Derivative Citizenship, obtaining U.S. citizenship by inheritance or derivation.

Derivative citizenship was first established into law by the United States Congress in the late seventeen hundreds. Since then, Congress has amended the rules as to who is eligible for derivative citizenship status, at least a dozen times. Consequently, the rules to determine derivative citizenship can be quite complex.

Figure 7.3 illustrates a possible flow chart about how one can determine whether they are a U.S. citizen. The YES notations indicate possible derivative citizenship, if all other qualifications are met as outlined in Figure 7.3.

The flow chart on Figure 7.3 gives you some indication about who may qualify as a derivative citizen, but with the twelve or more Congressional amendments to the citizenship rules, it becomes a very complex issue. For example, it is conceivable one member of a family acquired U.S. citizenship on their day of birth, while a later born sibling is out of luck. After May

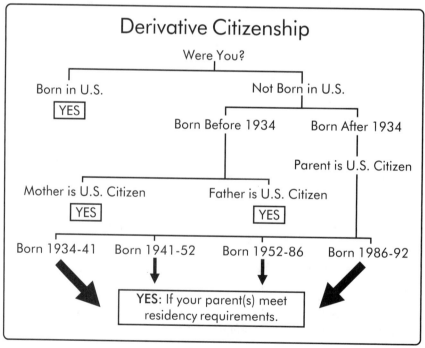

FIGURE 7.3

24, 1934, U.S. residency of the U.S. citizen ancestor becomes a vital ingredient in establishing American citizenship entitlement. In addition, during certain periods of time, Congress required the potential derivative citizen's parent(s) to have some residency requirements. Figure 7.3 is further explained in the following summary:

Born In The U.S. If you were born in the United States you have likely retained your U.S. citizenship, unless you have actively done something to renounce it. Prior to 1990, a United States born person taking up citizenship, or even just voting in another country, was considered to have renounced their U.S. citizenship. Since then, the State Department has published new guidelines to determine retention of U.S. citizenship: they now presume a person intends to retain U.S. citizenship, even though that person obtains naturalization in, or declares allegiance to another country. This new policy is retroactive. This means that it applies to people who think they may have lost their U.S. citizenship; even if the U.S. Consulate has already made a negative finding.

Both Parents are U.S. Citizens. If both your parents were U.S. citizens at the time of your birth, you will generally have a claim to U.S. citizenship if one or both of your parents ever "resided" in the United States. This applies even if you have never lived in the U.S.

One Parent is a U.S. Citizen. If only one of your parents was a U.S. citizen you may be a U.S. citizen if you and your parent have resided in the U.S. for the requisite time periods as summarized below.

Born before May 24, 1934. If you were born before this date and your father was a U.S. citizen, you are eligible for U.S. citizenship. The law was changed effective October 06, 1994 to give mothers the same rights as fathers in conferring citizenship on their children. This is particularly important to persons and descendants of persons born to U.S. citizen mothers before May 24, 1934.

Born May 25, 1934 to January 13, 1941. Canadians born in this time frame are subject to two conditions. First, the U.S. citizen parent must have had a prior U.S. residency. Second, the would-be derivative citizen must retain his citizenship through a two-year continuous presence (although not necessarily an uninterrupted stay) in the United States. The terms residency and presence have no clear definition, but are interpreted through facts and circumstances and prior case law.

Born January 13, 1941 to December 24, 1952. Similar to those Canadians in the prior category, the prospective derivative citizen and their U.S. parent are subject to residency requirements. Here, the U.S. parent must have ten years U.S. residency, at least five of which were after age 16. The two year continuous presence requirement for the potential derivative citizen is also in force.

Born December 24, 1952 to November 13, 1986. If you were born in this time period, your U.S. parent must have been physically present in the U.S. ten years, at least five of which were after age 14. After October 10, 1978, the retention through residency requirement for the potential derivative citizen was abolished.

Born After November 13, 1986. The U.S. parent must have five years of prior physical presence in the United States, at least two of which were after age fourteen in order to transmit citizenship. No residency is required of the prospective derivative citizen.

As of October 1994, a new law allows a person who was a citizen at birth, but who lost that citizenship by failing to meet the physical presence requirements of the time, may re-apply to regain their U.S. citizenship

Once you've established that you're eligible for derivative citizenship, the biggest and most rewarding challenge comes from documenting the facts of the U.S. parent's relationship and residency. Prospective derivative citizens often need to become ancestral detectives; searching through old family and government records to shed new light on their past. Family bibles, voter registrations, census records, sworn statements of family members, all have been used successfully to establish entitlement for U.S. citizenship status.

APPLYING FOR U.S. CITIZENSHIP

United States Citizenship is acquired through three methods:

- Birth

- Derivation

- Naturalization

Obtaining citizenship by birth and derivation were explained in the previous section on Derivative Citizenship. You may apply for, or confirm your citizenship status by either completing a Form N-600 with the INS or simply submitting an application for a passport to the United States State Department. Most people will find the passport route the quickest and most hassle-free method of confirming your United States citizenship status. The State Department is not nearly as bogged down as the INS in other immigration issues, and if you are turned down you will know about it much earlier, and you can begin the appeals process that much sooner, if you feel you have a legitimate claim.

Acquiring U.S. citizenship by naturalization is available to those who have a five-year continuous legal permanent residence in the United States. In other words, you must have had a green card and been physically present in the United States without any interruptions over six months for five years. There are a few exceptions. Those married to a U.S. citizen only have a three year continuous residency requirement. For naturalization, one needs to demonstrate physical presence for the required amount of time; good moral character; minimum knowledge of English, U.S. history and government.

Naturalization is a relatively simple process which begins with submitting application Form N-400 to the INS, along with a $95.00 fee, two colour photographs and a set of fingerprints. The most difficult question on Form N-400 is providing the details of every trip you took outside of the United States since you received your green card. There is an oral examination scheduled within four months after filing the N-400 to prove U.S. and English knowledge and verify eligibility for U.S. citizenship. Shortly after a successful examination, a U.S. District Court Judge or an immigration officer will confer citizenship at a swearing-in ceremony.

Whether American citizenship is acquired through birth, naturalization or derivation, it can provide the ease of U.S. access many Canadians seek. We remind those who are considering United States immigration or citizenship to use the services of a competent cross-border financial planner to address the tax consequences of such a move before they occur.

DUAL CITIZENSHIP - IS IT POSSIBLE?

There are few issues — outside of which way the Canadian dollar is going, that are more hotly debated by Canadians in the United States, than whether one is, or can become, a dual citizen of the U.S. and Canada.

To begin with, there is such a thing as dual citizenship, even though you will have a difficult time finding an immigration official in either Canada or the United States who will admit that it exists, let alone tell you anything about it. There is no formal procedure to apply for dual citizenship. You basically acquire it by applying for U.S. citizenship, and not relinquishing your Canadian citizenship.

Dual citizenship exists for Canadian citizens under two basic premises. First, there is the case where a Canadian green card holder — Lawful Permanent Resident of the U.S. becomes a naturalized U.S. citizen. Since February 15, 1977, Canada has not revoked its citizenship upon the U.S. naturalization of its citizens. Consequently, the Canadian holds citizenship status in both countries. Secondly, a Canadian born person who meets the criteria for a United States derivative citizenship status as outlined earlier in this Chapter can hold both a Canadian and United States passport at the same time. As a result, they are a dual citizens as well.

Dual citizenship does not come from any formal application for "dual citizenship" but by default. Consequently, individuals calling the United States Immigration and Naturalization Service Offices, or even Canadian Consulates in the United States inquiring about how they can apply for dual citizenship, get a series of blank stares and/or negative responses.

You can currently hold dual citizenship if you are a Canadian citizen who qualifies for U.S. citizenship, by simply applying for the United States citizenship and not formally renouncing your Canadian citizenship. Your new Canadian passport will indicate your dual status inside the passport. The United States basically ignores the fact that someone applying for American citizenship would want to remain citizens of another country at the same time, and does nothing to formally recognize or deny this dual status situation. The reluctance of the INS to accept dual citizenship may stem from fear of divided loyalties and citizenship by convenience.

The Canadian/U.S. dual citizen is envied for having the best of both worlds, and is in no way restricted from living, working or vacationing in either country for any reason for their entire lives. In addition these dual citizens can pass this on to their children.

THE GREEN CARD LOTTERY

From time to time, the United States Congress allows for an Immigrant Visa Lottery. This is a free lottery, which offers a large number of visas on a random determinant with no employment or family based qualifications required. Congress decides from which countries it will take entries based on which countries they feel have not gotten a fair stake in the immigrant categories through the normal visa process and other political reasons.

In 1992 and 1993 Congress held two separate lotteries of 50,000 applicants each. Canadians were eligible for these bulk lotteries but have been excluded from subsequent lotteries including 1997. However, if you are a citizen of some other country but are living in Canada or are also a Canadian citizen you may be eligible for the lottery under the non Canadian citizenship lottery quota. Typically, the entry process is made public several months before the drawings are made and each person is allowed only one application. Spouses however, may each file separate entries.

The entries are very simple to complete, and contrary to advertisements from immigration services, you do not need to pay, nor do you gain advantage, from having someone prepare and submit your application.

Those who are interested in future lotteries should keep their ear to the ground or contact INS periodically.

LEGAL RETIREMENT IN THE UNITED STATES

Even though statistics show large numbers of Canadians spending much of their retirement in the Sunbelt, there is no such thing as a retiree's visa. A separate visa category for retirees did exist, but it was closed down in the mid 1970s, due to some changes in U.S. immigration rules. There is a move afoot to bring back this retirement visa, because of the obvious economic benefits to the Sunbelt states. However, all immigration policy is a political football and it is difficult to predict how soon, if at all, any form of retirement visa will again be available. This surprises many Canadians who do not intend to create any burden whatsoever, upon the U.S. economy.

Canadians who retire in the U.S. not only find a bit of sunshine for themselves, they also help brighten the lives and economies in the communities where they make their home. That's why *The Border Guide* supports passage of a retiree immigration visa status. To make this kind of farsighted legislation happen, however, we need support from readers like you.

If you agree that the United States needs a retiree immigration visa status, share your thoughts with Uncle Sam. Write your favourite congressperson or any of the representatives in any state you winter or travel in.

Although immigration is now a hot issue, you can help diffuse some of the controversy by sharing some of your positive contributions. Remind Congress that Canadians support the U.S. economy with real estate purchases, retail sales, taxes and just by being nice folks! Each time an immigrant is bashed by some opportunistic politician, the chances of the retiree visa lessen. Make your voice count now!

See the sample letter below, which includes language of the proposed legislation. Please feel free to use this language or create your own, unique letter (you can get names and addresses of the senators or congressmen from any government office or local political party office). The important thing is to make your voice heard!

Since there is yet no retirement visa, how then, can you legally retire in the U.S.? In this chapter we have covered many immigration options, all of which apply to anyone, regardless of whether they are officially retired or not. In spite of this, most Canadian retirees or business persons probably travel to the U.S. as temporary visitors. Because of the relationship between Canada and the United States, entering each other's country as a visitor is free from any formalities, even though there are certain requirements which must be followed.

There are really two types of non-immigrant status for these people: visitors for business, and visitors for pleasure. Visitors for business are B-1 visitors. Visitors for pleasure are B-2 visitors. The INS normally allows Canadians six months when they enter on this temporary visitor status. The B-1 and B-2 visas for Canadians require no formal application or documentation. All that's required to be allowed into the United States on this status is a simple statement with respect to the time and purpose of your visit. Although B-1 and B-2 Visas only allow you to remain in the United States for six months, there is no prohibition against leaving the country and re-entering, even if it's only a day trip to Mexico. However, if you are entering the U.S. with the sole intention of remaining there as a resident, you will be entering under false pretences. You will be considered an illegal alien so leaving and re-entering will do you little good.

In Chapter 1, we discussed the differences between being a legal resident of the United States for tax purposes and immigration purposes. Consequently, leaving the United States after six months as a visitor, and then re-entering may work on a limited basis for immigration purposes, but subject you to a whole new set of tax rules as you become a U.S. tax payer on your

The Honorable Jon Kyl
328 Hart Senate Office Building
Washington, D.C. 20515

Re: Passage of a Retiree Visa

Dear Senator:

I believe that a retiree immigrant visa status would benefit the United States. I am in the position of retiring to this county. Presently, I own property and pay taxes to your state and country. In the winter, I help support the local economy.

Many people like me need your assistance to pass legislation and support bill H.R. 225 that would allow me to stay up to four years at a time, providing I can show continued self sustenance and adequate health care. The proposed legislation is as simply worded as its purpose:

(T) An alien and the spouse of the alien if accompanying or following to join, who

(i) seeks to enter the United States for a period not to exceed initially four years solely to retire from active business or employment; and

(ii) provides documentation of self support and health care.

(iii) Extensions of status to be granted in three year increments if provisions of (T) subsection (i) and (ii).

(iv) Volunteer and leisure employment is permissible by aliens establishing eligibility under the provisions of (T) set forth above.

We appreciate your help in this very important matter.

Sincerely,

I.M. Retired

world income. Refer back to Chapter 3, for more on the tax implications of remaining in the U.S. for more than six months a year.

As a temporary visitor, the retiree or business visitor must maintain a residence in Canada, because he or she cannot intend to reside permanently in the United States. To avoid problems in being refused entry to the United States when you enter as a visitor, carry a border kit proving you have a residence in Canada and are intending to return there, include the following items in your border kit:

- most recent phone and other utility bills;
- most recent property tax notice if you own, or rental agreement if you rent;
- most recent Canadian tax return;
- valid provincial drivers licence and medicare card;
- proof of employment if still employed (eg. latest pay stub);
- Canadian vehicle registrations if driving, or return plane tickets if flying.

CANADIAN RESIDENTS HOLDING GREEN CARDS

It is estimated that thousands of Canadians, who currently reside in Canada, also hold green card LPR status in the United States, because of previous employment, former more open immigration policies or the immigrant lottery. Often, these persons are not sure what they should do with their green cards — whether they should leave them in the drawer, move to the U.S., throw it away, or get in touch with the INS for direction.

The bottom line is that anyone holding a green card under these circumstances, needs to carefully consider their options before deciding whether to use it or lose it.

In strict technical terms, when a green card holder takes up permanent residency outside the United States, they have abandoned their LPR green card status. In actuality, they still are in possession of the green card, and could use it to take up full-time residency in the United States, as long as they appeared in all respects to be a United States resident. Some Canadians, have had their cards seized when entering the United States, because they gave immigration officials reason to believe that they were no longer a permanent resident of the United States.

Keeping your green card active entitles you to all its privileges such as being able to live and work year round in the United States. On the other hand, a green card comes with corresponding responsibilities like filing tax returns and maintaining a presence in the United States. The tax consequences of holding a green card are discussed in Chapter 3 and the tax advantages given in Chapter 8. Since it is very difficult for most people to obtain a green card, Canadian residents who have one should carefully consider all their options before making any decision. There is no real middle ground here, as the INS allows no lengthy stays outside the United States without having to meet admission criteria for re-entry. The only real way to keep your green card is to use it. The following guidelines should help guide those who wish to maintain their green card LPR:

- Use your green card every time you enter the U.S.

- Maintain clear evidence of residence. For example, file U.S. Income Tax Returns, use a U.S. drivers license and vehicle registration, keep U.S. bank and investment accounts — all with a United States address.

- Keep Alien Resident Card information current. You can update by filing Form I-90 if name changes or Form AR-11 for change of address.

- Ensure trips to Canada or abroad don't exceed one year from your last U.S. entry date. (If you anticipate an absence from the U.S. in excess of one year, obtain a Re-entry Permit (INS Form I-131) before leaving. Re-entry Permits are valid for a maximum of two years and cannot be renewed).

If, after weighing all the factors you are certain there will be no advantages to your keeping your green card, you should mail it to any United States Consulate office, or surrender it next time you cross the border. As noted in the section titled *New U.S. Tax Legislation concerning Expatriation from the U.S.* in Chapter 3, long term green card holders may be subject to some new 1996 U.S. tax rules when they give up their green card. Extreme caution and professional advice from a cross-border financial planner is recommended before you give up a green card or U.S. citizenship.

MARRIAGE TO A U.S. CITIZEN

There are probably thousands of Canadians who marry American citizens every year. Many of these are second marriages, where the respective spouses have been widowed by their previous partners.

These marriages will trigger several important decisions that cannot be ignored without some major tax problems or missed opportunities. Some of the issues facing these cross-border couples are:

- Where do they, as a couple, actually reside?

- Where and how do they file tax returns for their maximum advantage?

- How do they revise their estate plan to fit a cross-border situation that avoids double estate taxation, and takes advantage of all available deductions?

- How do they maximize government benefits like CPP, OAS, Social Security and U.S. or Canadian medicare?

- How do they merge the two separate families in the two countries into their own personal goals, financial or otherwise?

All of the these issues are covered indirectly through discussions in other chapters. This section will attempt to put them all into focus. Cross-border marriages may be a common occurrence, but there is little assistance available, and a great need for cross-border financial planning.

The first area of concern is which country to call home. As a married couple, it becomes largely a matter of choice. The Canadian citizen spouse can sponsor the U.S. citizen spouse for Landed Immigrant status in Canada, or the U.S. citizen spouse can sponsor the Canadian citizen spouse for a green card into the United States. The third option is for each spouse to remain a resident of their original country, and a non-resident of their spouse's country. This option presents some unique difficulties, and is recommended only in unusual circumstances, and only then, on a short term basis.

Many couples in similar situations make their decisions based on the economic realities of where they can get the best bottom line results from their combined financial resources. The major issues to consider here are income and estate taxes, medical coverage, and the cost of living.

The cost of living is generally accepted to be lower to substantially lower in the United States. Depending on lifestyle, large savings can be achieved by a couple spending the majority of their time in the United States.

Income taxes are covered in great detail in both Chapters 3 and 8. Estate tax issues are discussed in Chapters 4 and 8. Chapters 5 and 9 cover medicare, medical insurance, and the entitlements to government sponsored programs such as U.S. Social Security, Canada Pension Plan and Old Age Security.

Even after reviewing all the issues in the previous chapters, and making the appropriate calculations, it should be abundantly clear that there is no good answer as to where a Canadian — American couple should reside. It really depends on personal preference, along with a combination of all the other factors, as applied to your own personal situation. A complete cross-border financial planning analysis can help you determine the financial implications of either move. The assistance of a cross-border financial planner is recommended for couples in this situation and their guidance should result in a good return on the investment of time and money.

WHAT TO DO IF YOU ARE REFUSED ENTRY TO THE U.S.

A traveller's greatest fear crossing an international border is being hassled by some overly officious immigration officer. Many of you have heard stories about friends or relatives being detained, or turned away for no apparent reason. Perhaps their vacation plans were ruined because an immigration officer misinterpreted an innocent remark. Some of you may have even had this happen to you. Are you really defenseless against the onslaught of a border guard who is just having a bad day? Absolutely not! Here are some things you can do, to ease your exits and entries to and from the United States, and eliminate some of the stresses involved with dealing with immigration. When entering the United States:

- Have proper personal identification, we recommend Canadians have at least one of the following: A valid provincial drivers license, birth certificate and a passport.

- If you have a green card or other United States visa, produce them to the immigration official.

- If you are a visitor to the United States, be prepared to provide proof that you intend to return to Canada. You should always keep a border kit as noted in the section of this chapter entitled *Legal Retirement In The United States.*

- If you are refused entry to the United States, and can't see any quick resolution, ask for a deferred ruling to the nearest INS office in the United States where you will be staying. You may be allowed to enter the United

States until a hearing is set up, and you will get to present your case in a more favourable environment. You will also have the time to engage an immigration attorney.

CROSS-BORDER Q&A

Many of the issues covered in the preceding chapter of this book have been touched upon in the author's weekly column *Cross-border Q&A,* which appears in *The Sun Times of Canada,* published in Tampa, Florida and circulated throughout the U.S. Sunbelt for Canadians living or wintering there. The majority of these questions have been posed by readers of the Sun Times and/or readers of the previous editions of *The Border Guide.* Most were looking for advice relating to their own specific problems or situations. At the end of this chapter, we have included some typical reader questions, along with our response, to illustrate and broaden the concepts presented in the preceding chapter.

PLAN AHEAD FOR CROSS-BORDER MARRIAGE

We, my fiancee and I, are engaged to be married. We are both 65 plus and retired. This is a new and different venture for us because I am a citizen of the USA and she is a Canadian. We find so many unanswerable questions we would hope you could help us.

1. Would it be beneficial for each of us to apply for American and Canadian citizenship? I understand that I would have to sponsor her application to the INS for permanent resident alien status. Is the acceptance of this application a green card? And if you keep this green card for three years does this entitle you to U.S. Citizenship? What is the procedure? To apply for the green card is it acceptable to lives six months in Canada and six months in U.S.?

2. With regard to myself - how do I apply for Canadian citizenship?

3. Would it be advisable to apply for dual citizenship?

4. Taxes. When we are married will we continue to submit our income tax forms to our individual countries? Or because we will be married, does that mean we will both have to submit to both countries? My income is approximately $30,000; hers is about $21,000.

5. I own two condos in Florida; she owns one. If we rent two of these, the

rent about covers the cost of ownership. Would it be advisable to sell two of these condos and invest the money received? I presently have investments worth $25,000 in the U.S. She has about $85,000 invested in mutual funds in Canada. She owns a condo in Ontario and we plan on spending six months there and six months in Florida at this time. However, there may come a time when we might prefer to spend eight months in Florida and four months in Canada, hence the need for dual citizenship.

6. Is a living trust a good thing? My will has been prepared in Florida and hers in Ontario. Are these acceptable in each other's residence or must they be prepared in both places?

7. Upon death, will our estates be treated by Canadian, U.S. or both laws?

8. If there is anything else you can suggest to us, we would appreciate hearing from you.

—*J.T. Sanibel, Florida*

Your questions are very good and very relevant for anyone in your situation of a Canadian and American about to be married. However, most of the questions require lengthy detailed analysis and answers in order that you would be in position to take the correct action. I will, in the brief length of this column give you the key issues you need to resolve to obtain the answers to your questions.

There are several steps that you need to go through before or immediately after you are married to determine the best course of direction to take. The first step is to determine which country you are going to call your tax home. This will then, in turn determine what tax filings, estate planning documents, immigrations requirements, medical coverage and other forms of insurance you will require. If you attempt to be residents of both countries or if one spouse is to be a resident of Canada and the other a resident of the U.S. you will have an endless state of confusion as to what tax, estate and immigration requirements apply and which don't. Generally speaking you want to be in a position such that you file the least number of returns and pay the least amount of taxes but residency and/or U.S. citizenship all affect what returns you file.

To determine which country you should call your tax home a cross-border financial plan is definitely in order. This plan will determine such things as the amount of income tax you would pay according to which country and which scenario your are looking at and net out any potential increases or decreases in other costs such as medical coverage and estate taxes. The plan should come out with the answer as to which country is best for you economically as a family unit to call home. Once the country that gives the net best financial advantage surfaces, whether or not to become a dual citizen, what tax returns should you file, what changes have to be made to your wills or trusts, what changes have to be made to your investments and what Medicare and other government benefits can you obtain becomes substantially easier to determine.

Please note, just because you call one country or the other your tax home it does not prohibit you from spending time in both countries. The only thing you should remember is to spend the most time in the country that you are calling your tax home.

I realize I have not answered your questions directly but the issues go much deeper than you have anticipated and are not easily addressed until some cross-border financial planning is completed. A cross-border financial plan through an experienced cross-border financial planner is in order.

U.S. CITIZENSHIP A MATERNAL MATTER

I have a copy of your excellent book, "The Border Guide", and attended your Cross-Border Living workshop presented in Toronto last September. I am interested in pursuing the issue of becoming an American resident.

I retired eight years ago from a career in the Canadian Armed Forces and the Federal Government. My wife and I own a condominium in Canada where we live during the summer months. We also own a home in Florida near Tampa where we spend up to six months per year.

I was particularly interested in your comments on derivative citizenship. I was born in Walkerville, Ontario in 1931. My father was Canadian but my mother is American, born in Chicago, Illinois. You indicated that there was some U.S. legislation pending that would allow me to claim U.S. citizenship. I believe you referred to it as the "Equity in Citizenship Act". I have not been able to track any progress in this legislation and fear it may not be passed before the present session of U.S. congress ends. Perhaps you could inform me of its present and future status.

On the pessimistic assumption that the is no future for this legislation, I wonder what other avenues are available to me. Is there any possibility that a claim in court for American citizenship based on the inequities of the present legislation would prove successful?

—D. W., Mount Hope, Ontario

We have great news for those persons in your position. The Immigration Technical Corrections Bill was passed October 6, 1994. This means that those born before 1934 to U.S. citizen mothers, have derived U.S. citizenship from their mothers. Prior to this Technical Corrections Bill, citizenship could be derived only through a U.S. citizen father. Your best bet is to apply for a U.S. Passport to affirm your U.S. citizenship status. A strong note of caution: complete a comprehensive cross-border financial plan to ensure you are aware of the tax implications of being a U.S. citizen.

RETIREMENT VISA, A U.S. POSSIBILITY

I would like to say again how much I enjoy your more informative column Q & A in the Sun Times. In the April issue you mentioned a bill being considered by Congressman McCollum of Florida, regarding visas allowing people to retire in the United States.

In response to your suggestion, I wrote letters to: 3 U.S. senators, 1 congressman, 3 state senators, and 9 state representatives.

I would be interested to know (and I'm sure, many other Q&A readers) if there been any progress made on Congressman McCollum's bill?

—M.G., Ottawa, Ontario

Thank you for your comments on *Cross-border Q&A*. It is time to update every one on the question of retirement visas for those who wish to retire in the U.S. and have the visible financial means to support themselves. This visa would not allow a person to work in the U.S. but would allow year round residency for as many years as the visa holder wished. Retired Canadians who want to take advantage of both the warmth of the U.S. Sunbelt longer than six months and lower U.S. income tax rates, could do so without worrying about whether or not they have gone over their six month welcome.

This visa, called a Retirement Visa, has the support of several influential U.S. congressmen and senators. Congressman McCollum has now drafted and submitted to the Congress Immigration Committee, a Retirement Visa as bill H.R. 225 in January 1997. I urge all Border Guide readers to write their local Senators and Congressmen in support of this bill. You can get their addresses by calling any local federal government office or political party headquarters.

Rest assured that this matter will not be forgotten. There is a strong lobby spearheaded by American immigration attorneys to keep this initiative alive. Many other supporters see this visa as a potential source of economic improvement because of the jobs it would create. This issue should be a "no brainer" for most senators and congressmen, especially those in the Sunbelt states. The only opposition seems to be a few diehards who believe that affluent immigrants should take a back seat to refugees and illegals entering the United States.

KNOW U.S. RULES FOR RESIDENCY CHANGE

My husband and I are thinking about residing in Florida on a permanent basis about five years from now. We will be 75 & 76 respectively at that time and feel that the 1,300 mile trip from Northern Ontario will become too difficult. We need to know the following:

1. Health Insurance - how will it affect us?

2. What do we need to do to achieve resident status but keep our Canadian citizenship?

3. We both have government pensions and pensions set up by ourselves.

4. Income Tax -There would be no income from the U.S. except small amounts of interest income from bank accounts.

— A.C., Clearwater, FL

Health insurance in most U.S. states is difficult to obtain when you are over 65 since most U.S. residents are covered by U.S. Medicare starting at 65. U.S. insurance carriers generally provide only supplemental coverage to Medicare. You can buy into U.S. Medicare if you have been a legal permanent resident for five years, are a U.S. citizen or have worked in the U.S. for a minimum of ten years. There is limited coverage from insurance carriers outside the U.S. for those over 65, with policies like the Nomad Travel Insurance Plan II, which is being improved to provide coverage for up to $150,000 or more of benefits. This Plan II is limited to two years of coverage and covers pre-existing conditions on an 80-20% emergency basis only. Lloyd's of London or the Danish "Danmark" company may also be useful for your health insurance coverage in the U.S. Don't forget about long term nursing care insurance since U.S. Medicare and other health insurance policies don't cover extended care for long term disabilities or incapacity's. This coverage can be obtained at any age up to around 85 from numerous U.S. insurance companies.

To achieve residency you need either a family or a business to sponsor you for a visa or a green card (Legal Permanent Resident) status. This may be difficult under current law unless people such as yourself contact their local representatives to approve a retired persons' visa. This initiative is being sponsored by some congressional members in the Sunbelt states as means of bolstering local economies. This visa would provide legal residence for all those who could prove they are financially able to look after themselves without becoming a ward of the state. None of these visas or legal permanent resident status's require that you give up your Canadian citizenship.

Income tax would not likely be a problem for you since rates in Florida are much lower than in any Canadian province. You would have to file a return on your world income in the U.S. and you would cease to file any returns in Canada if you became a U.S. resident. Revenue Canada would withhold a non-resident withholding tax of 15% on all your non-governmental pensions and 10% on interest earned in Canada and you would receive credit for this tax when you file your returns in the U.S. Revenue Canada will withhold 25% of CPP and OAS payments for non-residents. You need to calculate the difference between your reduction in tax, food, clothing, and housing costs and the cost of your health insurance to see if you'll come out ahead. For more information on these topics I suggest you obtain advice from a cross-border financial planning professional.

RECLAIMING CANADIAN CITIZENSHIP IS A COMPLICATED, LENGTHY PROCESS

I became a U.S. citizen in 1974, three years before the new Canadian Citizenship law in 1977. I would like to reclaim my Canadian citizenship without jeopardizing my U.S. citizenship. Is that feasible without resorting to an application to a citizenship court? Are you aware of any challenges to claim dual citizenship on any basis for a case similar to mine?

— *Brian M., Kanata, Ontario*

Under the current set of rules the only way you could reclaim your Canadian citizenship is to become a landed immigrant in Canada. This would require your having some family member in Canada sponsor you and then once you have immigrated to Canada, you must reside there for at least five years. As a landed immigrant in Canada, you can apply for Canadian citizenship and the U.S. will not require you to give up U.S. citizenship just because you have taken this step. Although it may be a lengthy process, you can become a dual citizen. Those Canadians who became U.S. citizens after 1977, did not lose their Canadian citizenship and are therefore dual citizens who don't need to go through this lengthy, complicated process.

GREEN CARD GONE? START OVER AGAIN

This writer recently purchased your book on the recommendation of a friend and must congratulate you on the excellent information regarding U.S. investments, immigration and retirement planning.

My spouse and I are in good health and financially independent. We are aware that since the mid-70s, there has been no separate visa category for us due to changes in the U.S. immigration rules. On page 124 (3rd edition), you state that those who have had a five year continuous legal permanent residence in the U.S. and not had any interruptions over six months for five years are eligible for U.S. citizenship by naturalization.

Both of us had green cards from the 1950s, until we surrendered them to U.S. immigration in 1969 for family reasons. I would appreciate your comments on the following questions:

1. In respect of the fact we had a green card and were physically present in the U.S. without any interruptions over six months for five years, are we eligible for naturalization via application form N-400?

2. Regarding taxation, is the criteria residency or citizenship?

3. Where does dual citizenship fit into this situation?

4. Can you recommend a competent cross-border financial planner?

Thank you for your book and any answers you may be able to forward to us. We are currently at our summer residence and will be there until approximately the last week in October.

— *Hollis & Anne G., Gravenhurst, ON*

Sorry, when you turned in your green card in 1969, you gave up the qualifications you had to become a naturalized U.S. citizen. You could have become a naturalized U.S. citizen at that time in 1969, but since you are no longer a legal permanent resident of the U.S., you cannot use the INS Form 1-400. You, in effect, have to start over and get another green card for legal permanent residence and have it for five years before you apply again. If you had any children while you lived in the U.S. who are U.S. citizens they can sponsor you for the new green cards.

Contact my office again if you still need recommendations of a cross-border financial planner or help with any other issues.

BORN IN U.S., DUAL CITIZENSHIP NOT LOST

I believe our situation is just the reverse of one you covered in an issue of "The Sun Times of Canada" earlier this year. My husband and I had three children, all born in the U.S. and U.S. citizens until they became Canadian citizens in 1972. We had always assumed that by doing this we lost U.S. citizenship. Is this true?

— *Ethel M., Indian Harbour Beach, FL*

Your becoming Canadian citizens in 1972 no longer means you have lost your U.S. citizenship. Under new U.S. immigration rules introduced in 1992, you would not be considered as having given up your U.S. citizenship in 1972, unless it was specifically your intention to do so. If it was not your intent or you are not sure whether it was your intent, you can likely reinstate your U.S. citizenship by contacting the U.S. State Department for a passport or the U.S. Immigration and Naturalization Service.

OBTAINING A GREEN CARD

We are retired and financially independent Canadians and we want to retire in Arizona. What are our chances of immigrating to the U.S.? What is a "green card" and how do we get one? Does it help that I have a brother who is a green card holder and living in Florida?

— *Axel R., Phoenix, AZ*

There are two basic ways of immigrating to the United States. One is to achieve permanent resident status through a job, and the other, is through a relative. There are other ways as well, but these can involve lengthy immigration proceedings. In your case, since your brother already has a green card, immigration through a relative seems like the better possibility. However, a lawful permanent resident (or green card holder), cannot petition for his siblings. He must become a United States citizen to do so. Citizenship normally requires five years of permanent residence, unless the permanent residence was acquired through a United States citizen spouse, in which case the permanent resident need only wait three years before filing his application for U.S. citizenship.

Once sworn in as a United States citizen, your brother may immediately file a visa petition for you in the category of "fourth preference." The date of filing becomes your "priority date" as far as the wait associated with most preference visa categories. At the current time, the "quota wait" for fourth preference for Canada is ten years. If this seems out of the question, we recommend to try the business routes to immigration.

DERIVATIVE CITIZENSHIP

My parents were both U.S. citizens, but I was born in Canada and have lived there all my life. I am now 65. Could I obtain U.S. citizenship easily if I wanted to? Similarly, my wife, who is 61, also had U.S. citizens as parents. Would it be any easier for her to get U.S. citizenship?

— Donald E., Scottsdale, AZ

One or both of you may already be United States citizens. You must prove your derivative citizenship by filing Form N-600, "Application for Certificate of Citizenship," along with supporting documentation with the Immigration and Naturalization Service (INS) or apply for a U.S. passport from the State Department.

Since you both were born before 1934, citizenship could only have been transmitted through either or both of your respective parents. This means that you must discover if your parents ever knowingly abandoned their United States citizenships prior to your birth, by taking an oath of allegiance to the government of Canada, and forswearing allegiances to all other nations.

In the event documentary evidence is lacking for one of your derivative citizenship claims, all is not lost. It would only be necessary for one of you to prove U.S. citizenship. The other could immigrate as the immediate relative of the U.S. citizen, a category for which there is no quota wait.

HIRING AN IMMIGRATION ATTORNEY

When should I use an attorney to help me immigrate to the U.S.? What would it cost relative to my status? How long does it take?

— Alice C., Tucson, AZ

There is no law that says immigration documents may not be filed by an individual. However, there may be alternatives available to you that you may only find out about through a consultation with an attorney. Certainly, if you become involved in a problem with the Immigration Service, you would be well advised to get professional assistance immediately. Most immigration attorneys work on an hourly basis.

IMMIGRATION STRATEGIES AND THE NEED FOR FINANCIAL PLANNING

I read your articles in the Sun Times of Canada, and have the following questions regarding cross-border financial planning and immigration. My husband and I wish to immigrate to the U.S. My husband is a civil technologist currently employed by a road construction firm. I run my own advertising/promotions firm, registered as an Ontario Corporation.

1. How can we immigrate with a minimum of fuss and expense? (I have heard rumours about bringing in $100,000 and hiring one employee.) What are the costs involved? Also, my husband's sister has lived and worked in Michigan for the last 15 years. If she becomes an American citizen, could she sponsor us and could we both get jobs and work? How long would it take for her to get U.S. citizenship and sponsor us?

2. Would it be to our greater advantage to procure jobs in order to immigrate? Or, is it a disadvantage to me, especially since I have an existing corporation?

3. If we are no longer Canadian residents, I assume there are tax advantages, but does this lack of residency affect our current investments i.e. our family home (must we sell), our RRSP's held in a Canadian brokerage house, our life insurance held by Canadian firms, etc.

— Laura P., Toronto, ON

1. From what you have told us, the best alternative for you to immigrate to the U.S., would likely be through your business of advertising/promo-

tion. By forming a similar business in the U.S., this business would then be the means for you to qualify for a Visa under Treaty Investor Route (E-2) or a regular inter-company transfer (L-1), or even the new green card category (E-IC) for established businesses similar to the L-1.

The E-2 is likely the quickest and easiest to achieve. Many good immigration attorneys recommend you invest $100,000 or more in the U.S. business to qualify for this type of visa. However, Arizona immigration attorneys working for our clients in non-capital intensive service industries similar to your business, have gotten E-2 visas for investments of less than $10,000. Even though there is no requirement to hire U.S. workers, the more employment you can create, and the more capital you have to back up your business, the better off you are.

The best long term route if you can swing it, is the green card route through a transfer from your established Canadian Company to your U.S. affiliated company which you would set up. The green card is a permanent residency status, whereas all the other visas may be subject to continuing requirements and/or have expiration dates. In addition, the green card is the only route that will give your husband the ability to work in the U.S., without separately qualifying for a visa under the same rules as yourself.

Your husband's sister can become a naturalized U.S. citizen if she has had her green card for 5 years or more. It is currently taking 3-8 months, from date of application, to complete this process. Once she is a citizen she can sponsor your husband for permanent resident status (or green card). However, there is a waiting list in this category of nearly ten years. It wouldn't hurt to get on this waiting list as sometimes quotas are changed, and the waiting list can disappear, or at least be shortened.

As you can see, the maze of rules and regulations can be overwhelming and I recommend you use a good immigration attorney located in the area where you are likely to relocate to in the U.S. Be prepared to spend $2,000 - $4,000 on legal fees to get the job done for you and your husband. If you are well organized and can do a lot of the necessary work yourself, the legal fees could be lower, but they will increase if you do not have a concrete plan of action, that you can outline to the attorney.

2. You will not legally be able to procure employment in the U.S. unless you have a visa or have some special skills/education that allows you a work

visa, based on these exceptional qualifications. If you have a Ph.D. or other post secondary degree(s) or equivalent experience, your immigration attorney will direct you to these special categories.

3. As far as taxes and other financial matters are concerned, there are some good planning opportunities and there are some pitfalls. These are difficult to condense and require a great deal of factual analysis. To assure you maximize the opportunities and avoid the pitfalls, I recommend you complete a comprehensive financial plan, with the assistance of a professional planner that is knowledgeable in both Canadian and U.S. tax, investment, estate and insurance requirements.

IS U.S. CITIZENSHIP REQUIRED FOR ESTATE TAX EXEMPTIONS?

You mentioned in a previous article that dual citizenship exists, and that Canada does not revoke citizenship if one chooses to become a U.S. citizen. Does the U.S. also allow a U.S. citizen to remain a citizen of Canada?

My husband and I are both Canadian citizens by birth who became permanent U.S. residents and green card holders in 1977. We live permanently in Florida. Our problem is whether to become U.S. citizens to take advantage of the $600,000 exemption from estate tax, since you mentioned that only U.S. citizens can take full advantage of this exemption.

— *M. S., North Miami, FL*

It is Canada's choice, whether or not you keep your Canadian citizenship. Only the country conferring citizenship can require that person to relinquish prior citizenship. For the time being Canada allows individuals to retain Canadian citizenship after becoming a U.S. citizen.

Since you are a green card holder domiciled in the U.S. you already qualify for the $600,000 estate tax exemption and so does your husband. You do not have to become U.S. citizens to qualify for these exemptions.

As a U.S. citizen you gain the ability to defer estate tax on estates over $600,000 to the second spouse's death by using the unlimited marital deduction. You may use a Qualified Domestic Trust to take advantage of the unlimited marital deduction as an alternative to becoming a citizen.

If you or your husband's estate(s) are over $600,000, you need to consider your options with the help of a professional estate planner. If you still have assets in Canada you'll need a cross-border estate planner.

THE REAL DEAL ON DUAL CITIZENSHIP

I am confused about your statement regarding dual citizenship in the Sun Times. I have it on good authority that dual citizenship is only possible under some very unusual circumstances in the United States. Would you kindly tell me the real facts on this issue.

— Ray Y., Venice, FL

There are few issues outside of the state of the Canadian dollar, more hotly debated by Canadians in the United States, than whether one is or can become a dual citizen of Canada and the United States.

To start off, there is such a thing as dual citizenship. I am a Canadian citizen myself and have become a United States citizen. Since Canada does not require that I give up my Canadian citizenship, I am a dual citizen. In my practice, I have recommended and assisted several clients to become dual citizens and personally know many others.

Dual citizenship comes not from any formal application for "dual citizenship" but by default. Consequently, individuals calling the United States Immigration and Naturalization Service Offices, in particular, or even Canadian Consulates in the United States inquiring on how they can qualify for or apply for dual citizenship, get a series of blank stares and/or negative responses.

Since 1977, Canada has stopped demanding that Canadians who emigrate and who take up foreign citizenship, to give up their Canadian citizenship. There are only a few other countries in the world that have the same policy such as the United Kingdom and Israel. Even the United States now allows its citizens to hold United States citizenship if they become citizens of another country.

So you can currently achieve dual citizenship if you are a Canadian citizen by simply applying for United States citizenship and not formally doing anything to renounce your Canadian citizenship. Your new Canadian passport will indicate your dual status. The United States does nothing to formally recognize a dual status situation, and ignores the fact that someone applying for U.S. citizenship is retaining the citizenship of the other country.

RECOVERING CANADIAN NON RESIDENT WITHHOLDING TAX

We are Canadians. My husband is working with a green card. I am not working. Early this year, I cashed a RRSP and tax was withheld. How do I get this tax back?

— *Kaye K., Duluth, Georgia*

In the brief summary that was provided in your letter, there was no mention of the amount of your RRSP withdrawal. The amount will determine whether you can get back any or all of the 25% non-resident withholding tax Revenue Canada collected.

If the withdrawal was less than $7,000 CDN, a Section 217 can be filed with Revenue Canada to receive a full refund of the withholding. On a withdrawal amount of $7,000 to $20,000, you may be eligible for a partial refund through the Section 217 filing. However, over the $20,000 withdrawal amount, there is no significant refund available from Revenue Canada. On the larger withdrawal amounts, your only hope of getting a benefit from the non-resident withholding tax paid is through foreign tax credit planning to use the credits from the Canada withholding on your U.S. return as best you can over a six (6) year period. To accomplish this, you would need a combination of a good cross-border tax advisor and investment advisor.

MOVING BACK TO CANADA AS A PERMANENT RESIDENT

I am a Canadian citizen with green card who lives in Florida six months of the year. I have a residence in Ontario where I reside for the other six months and want to return to Canada as a full-time resident. What is the procedure?

Should I sell my house here as I would no longer get the Homestead and Widow's Exemption? What should I do with the green card? I would appreciate any information you can give me.

— *Donyale S., Boynton Beach, Florida*

Since you are already a Canadian citizen, the procedure for becoming a Canadian resident, is simply moving back to Canada and reestablishing your residential ties, such as applying for OHIP, a driver's license and filing a Canadian tax return. You will need to effectively give up your green card by mailing it to the Immigration and Naturalization Service (INS) or surrendering it at the border. Make sure you are prepared for possible higher Canadian income taxes before you give up U.S. residence.

If keeping your Florida Homestead Exemption is the only reason for your keeping this property, you should sell it as you will lose your exemption if you are no longer a resident of Florida. It is not necessary to sell this residence if you still want to visit Florida during the winters and need a place to stay.

MOVING BACK TO CANADA — THE SEQUEL

In 1982 we were transferred to the U.S. by a subsidiary of a large Canadian company. My husband worked there until retiring in 1992.

We applied for and received our resident alien status in June 1987. In 1992 we returned and resumed Canadian residency in order to take advantage of OHIP. We did not apply for or receive Medicare. Our ages are 68 & 69.

We own a home in the U.S. where we spend 6 months every year. My husband has a small company pension, social security, stock, investments and IRA's. Our total U.S. assets amount to approximately $400,000 and we file a 1040NR & 8840. Our assets in Canada exceed this amount and include our home, property, company stock, investments, RRSPs, GICs, company pension, OAS and CPP.

We regret our decision to return to Canada and we wish to reinstate our U.S. resident alien status. We still have our green cards and since purchasing the Border Guide, we are now aware of the implications. Would you advise us or inform us as to where we can obtain information on the following:

1. Re-activating our NR status.

2. Can Medicare be secured prior to re-establishing residency?

3. The need of an estate planner and legal counsel.

4. Should we begin using our green cards upon entry to the U.S. & reinstate residency?

— *Sid & Nancy V., Holiday, Florida*

Since you have been living 6 months every year in the U.S. and still have your green cards, you are probably permanent legal residents in the U.S.

and have likely not abandoned your green card status. However, you have been filing the wrong returns with the IRS for a resident and should go back and refile 1992 through 1994 returns. You need to file Form 1040 not 1040NR returns and no Form 8840. This should get you in compliance with both IRS and INS and may also get you some tax benefits to top it off.

2. Medicare can be applied for January 1 through March 31 every year and will become effective July 1 the year in which you apply, so you may have to cover the gap from January to July with alternative coverage.

3. You definitely do need professional help but not just for estate planning as you have several other financial, tax, investment and insurance issues to address. A good cross-border financial plan can save you a lot of money and aggravation in these areas.

4. I need to answer this one with a conditional yes after you have covered all the other issues discussed above.

DOES CANADIAN SPOUSE RECEIVE MEDICARE

I live on the Maine-New Brunswick border. My friend lives on the New Brunswick side. We spend most of our time together and winter in Florida. We would like to get married and live in the U.S.

However my fiancee has MS and depends on the New Brunswick government for medication and medical services. Would she receive medicare help here in the U.S. if we were to get married? Could she use the same hospital/doctors if medicare were to help? I'm 59, disabled and on medicare.

— Joe C., St. Agatha, ME

Your fiancee can become eligible for U.S. Medicare, however, the following items need to take place first. (1) she must be age 65, and (2) you should have celebrated at least your first year's wedding anniversary together. This assumes you would also be over 65 and on U.S. Medicare at the time you apply for your fiancee's coverage. Your fiancee would need a good Medicare supplement to ensure complete coverage of hospital, doctors and medicine. It is unlikely she will be able to use the same doctors she has now if she is on U.S. Medicare. Except in the case of an emergency, this coverage is generally only for the U.S., so she would need to establish new relationships with U.S. doctors near your Florida home.

163

STAYING ON BOTH SIDES OF THE BORDER

My husband and I have both lived and worked in Canada since 1965. I retired in 1993 but my husband is still working and would like to continue until he is eligible for Canada pension. We are both 57 years old.

We applied for and received our resident alien status in February 1993 sooner than we expected and are not ready to move to the U.S. yet. We plan on moving permanently when my husband retires. In June 1993, we bought a retirement home in Florida.

I have been living in Florida for 6 months and 6 months in Canada since we received our green cards in May 1993, thinking I was within the bounds of immigration laws of both countries this way. We file both U.S. and Canadian income taxes and opted out of the homestead tax deduction offered for first time home buyers in Florida.

On my recent trip to the U.S., I was questioned at length by U.S. immigration officials in Toronto. I was told I should either give up my green card or OHIP card. My questions are the following:

1. Can U.S. Immigration confiscate either my green card or OHIP card? Is there a law that entitles them to do this?

2. Does 6 months in the U.S. constitute legal permanent resident status? Does it have to be 6 consecutive months and only in one particular state?

3. If I were to give up my green card, will U.S. Immigration issue me one easily later on when my husband retires? Will it take very long?

4. I am covered by my husband's company health plan. If I move ahead and live permanently in Florida, will I still get free medical health coverage without my OHIP card?

5. We own properties and all our investments are in Canada. In the light of the continuing decline of the Canadian dollar, the increasing high cost of health care in the U.S. and the new non-resident tax deduction in effect on CPP and OAS, would we be better off to forget about residing permanently in the U.S. and just spend 6 months in Canada and go for 6 months to Florida in the winter as Canadian tourists?

— *Elaine F. Toronto, ON*

1. U.S. immigration has authority to take your green card if they can determine you are not living permanently in the U.S., a requirement to keep your green card. They cannot take your OHIP card, only OHIP can do that and they will do just that once they discover an OHIP member has a green card.

2. You should not reside outside the U.S. longer than six months at any stretch and maintain full U.S. residency ties at all times to maintain your green card.

3. Whether or not you could get another green card once you give this one up depends on how you got it. If you got it in the lottery you would have to wait for another lottery and hope you are lucky. If some close family member sponsored you then you would have to reapply, that is taking anywhere from six months to three years depending on performance status.

4. You would have to check with your husband's company benefits department, they should be able to answer this easily. Most plans require you to be a member of OHIP to get full health insurance coverage. OHIP requires you to live at least six months a year in Ontario and not be in possession of a green card to ensure full coverage. I recommend you shop for U.S. coverage as soon as possible. If you need help locating a stable carrier call or write my office.

5. These kinds of questions require you to have a knowledgeable cross-border financial planner do a detailed cross border financial analysis. Your planner can compare all the tax, immigration and insurance issues and provide you with the information you need to make an educated choice. Only you can decide which country will be best for you.

Please note that your husband does not have to work until age 60 to receive CPP. He only needs to wait until age 60 (the earliest age at which he can apply) to start receiving CPP payments.

REASONS FOR BEING REFUSED ENTRY AT THE BORDER

An immigration officer refused us entry into the U.S. last November because we rented our house in Canada for 6 months while we are away. Why? When I mentioned I was born in North Dakota he said if I hadn't renounced my U.S. citizenship I can hold dual citizenship. Can I do this?

— *E. W., Arizona City, AZ*

It sounds like the immigration official at the border was being a bit over zealous but if he was concerned you were living in the U.S. permanently he had every right to refuse you entry as a visitor. Remember, that whenever you enter the U.S. you are presumed to be coming here permanently unless you can prove otherwise. It is this proof you must supply, if asked. We recommend you carry a border crossing kit showing property tax notices, recent utility bills, proof of Canadian Medicare, vehicle and drivers registration, pay stubs, bank and investment account records all to prove you are remaining as residents of Canada.

In response to your concern regarding citizenship, it is relatively easy for you to confirm if you are still a U.S. citizen by simply applying for your U.S. passport at the nearest passport office. However, with U.S. citizenship there may come tax obligations that you will need to address before you proceed any farther. I suggest you contact a knowledgeable cross-border financial planner to analyse your specific situation.

MANAGING A RRIF FROM OUTSIDE CANADA

My experience, as a U.S. resident was similar to your advice with respect to problems arising from U.S. residents dealing with Canadian brokers, even when they were former residents of Canada. I transferred my brokerage accounts to the U.S., so far not too satisfactorily.

However, my real problem is with a self-directed RRIF held by a Canadian broker. I can't buy any funds, even money market, or stocks. As far as I know, if I transfer it to the U.S., I lose deferred taxation status. Are you aware of any solution?

— Holden. W., Ocala, FL

With respect to problems arising for Canadian brokers dealing with former Canadian residents, your solution may be to transfer your self-directed RRIF to a trustee who has a broker and brokerage company licensed in your state of residence (try TD GreenLine). This will allow them to trade your securities without breaking any U.S. securities laws. Also some Canadian brokerages will trade RRIF and RRSP accounts as there is some claim to special exemptions.

The Grass is Always Greener

CANADIAN VS. U.S.
TAXATION POLICIES

O ne of the major considerations for anyone considering a move to the United States is how much income tax they may be able to save. Many Canadians are frustrated by the seemingly endless spiral of federal and provincial taxes, PST, GST and property taxes. Most Canadians accept higher taxes as the price of Canada's superior social welfare system, but recent tax increases seem to have come with commensurate decreases in government services. Have Canadians lost confidence in the politicians who have created this monster, and who now seem incapable of stopping it? Some Canadians have voted with their feet, by moving to the United States, and voting themselves a major tax cut.

This chapter will address those tax saving opportunities, and will provide a good guideline for those Canadians who may be derivative citizens of the United States, or have other immigration possibilities. It is for those who may be looking for some financial advantage, by becoming a resident of the United States for tax purposes. Chapter 9 will discuss the opportunities in investments, medical coverage, insurance and U.S. Social Security benefits.

In Chapter 3, under the heading of *Canada — United States Income Tax Comparison,* we outlined some of the basic tax rates and tax deduction comparisons between the United States and Canada. We will now incorporate these comparisons into a cross-border financial plan from the perspective of someone who is actually moving or contemplating a move to the United States. We will use real life examples showing how some Canadians have effectively utilized cross-border financial planning, to maximize the benefits while minimizing the pitfalls of moving south.

First, our discussion will look at a line by line analysis of each type of taxable income and deduction, and then we will tie it all together using full comprehensive case studies of Canadians who have gone through professional cross-border financial planning.

KEEP MORE OF YOUR CPP & OAS

A popular misconception among Canadians, is that they lose CPP and/ or OAS benefits after exiting Canada. In fact, the opposite is true and they will actually receive more of their benefits on an after tax basis. The new 1994 Canada — United States Tax Treaty, effective January 1, 1996, provides for some very interesting tax advantages for those Canadians who are collecting or are eligible for CPP and Old Age Security.

Because of provisions contained in the treaty, neither your CPP and OAS are taxable, when you file tax returns in the United States as a resident. Revenue Canada, under the previous treaty did not withhold any tax on CPP or OAS, but under the new treaty a non-resident withholding of 25% will apply to all payments to non-residents.

Since July 1996, Canadian residents in the U.S. are subject to the same OAS clawback rules as residents of Canada. The prior clawback exemption no long applies and now, all U.S. resident recipients of OAS must file Revenue Canada Form 1136(E) each year reporting their world income or risk having their OAS payments stopped altogether. Form 1136(E) should be filed by all non-residents of Canada who have a world income of less than $84,400 CDN. Those over this amount should not bother with this form at all since once the $84,400 threshold is reached the 100% clawback applies and filing the form is a waste of time.

For those in the income range of $53,215 CDN (the income level in which the OAS starts) and $84,400 CDN, you will find your OAS payments now reduced by the calculated clawback amount. Then the non-resident withholding of 25% would apply on the reduced OAS payment. Couples who are U.S. residents with significant investment income and who also receive OAS should shift the investment income to the highest income spouse to ensure the lower income spouse receives the entire amount of their OAS.

For those under age 60 before the March 1996 Canadian Federal budget, or those opting to be included in the budget's new Income Security plan to be in effect in the year 2000, both spouses' world income will be combined when determining the application of the OAS clawback with a combined income threshold of $74,000. In the near future, many more Canadians — residents or non-residents alike — will be subject to the OAS clawback. In addition, the March 1996 budget decreased the age at which RRSP withdrawals must begin to age 69. This will move many more Canadians residents and those non-residents not following the RRSP withdrawal strategies outlined later in this Chapter into the OAS clawback much sooner. We expect Revenue Canada to lower this age for the start of RRSP withdrawal in steps from 69 to 65 to fit more closely with the new Income Security rules in 2000.

Let's look at a real example of what this one item can mean to George and Susan, who moved from Ottawa to the United States with $8,000 of CPP and $4,700 of OAS benefits. This couple are both retired in the maximum Canadian tax bracket and are subject to the OAS clawback. (All dollar amounts in Figure 8.1 through 8.8 are in Canadian funds, and we have used the tax rates from Figure 3.2)

As you can see from Figure 8.1, with the new treaty and new clawback rules for non-residents, George would see a drop in his average tax rate from 70%, to a maximum of 53%. This is on his combination of CPP and OAS income. The resulting tax saving of $2,160 is significant, especially when

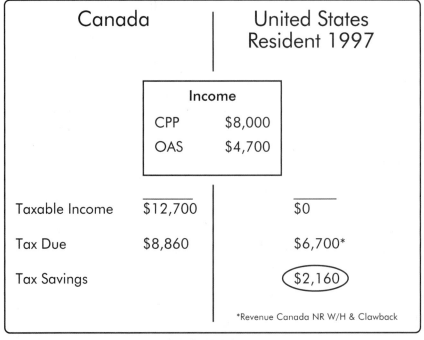

FIGURE 8.1

you consider George's wife is in a similar situation. Their combined savings would double to $4,320. So, before George and Susan even consider any potential tax reductions on investment and other pension income, they are in line for a raise of nearly $400 a month! Since 1997, when they would be subject to the full OAS clawback, either as residents or non-residents, their total annual savings would be about $4,320 per year based on CPP alone. Figure 8.7 shows George and Susan's complete sources of income. Revenue Canada's rules of attribution of investment income cease if they become non residents of Canada. If they were to shift all this investment income from one spouse to another, say from George to Susan, George would receive almost all of his OAS, even with a nearly $300 a month raise. This transfer would not be possible if they remain Canadian residents, since under the rules, the income would attribute back to the transferring spouse.

INTEREST INCOME - TAX-FREE IF YOU WISH

In the United States, Municipal Bonds are a form of local government bonds that pay interest without attracting income tax at either the federal or state levels. These are the bonds cities use to fund public buildings, roads, airports and hospitals. As a result, someone earning a great deal of interest income can in effect, zero out the tax liability on any amount of interest they earn, by holding these municipal bonds. Some types of these bonds may be subject to U.S. alternative minimum tax. But, when you consider interest in Canada is taxed at rates of up to 54% or more in some provinces, a zero tax rate looks pretty attractive. From the investment planning aspect (see Chapter 9) you already know it's not wise to place the majority of your investment portfolio into municipal bonds or any other asset class for that matter. Municipal bonds are currently paying higher rates of interest than most Canadian bank deposits. These bonds are currently paying around 5% compared to about 4% on Canadian term deposits or GICs. If you're in a 54% income tax bracket, you will keep less than 2% of the 4% you earn on a GIC. A 5% rate on a tax-free bond would still yield 150% more after tax. In fact, at maximum Canadian tax rates, you would have to earn 10% or better on a GIC, to net the same amount, on an after tax basis, as a 5% tax-free municipal bond.

In various federal budgets over the past dozen years, Canada's Parliament has gradually eliminated the ability to defer income taxes on Canada Savings Bonds, annuities and long term GICs. This means all interest earned on any investment must be paid on a current annual basis and cannot be deferred to a later date when the interest is actually received. For anyone saving for future retirement, the ability to defer income tax to a future date, particularly when they may be in a lower tax bracket, can dramatically increase their total return. For example, if you had $100,000, earning 10% interest over 15 years and were in a 50% tax bracket, you could net $158,850 of earnings after tax, if you could defer paying tax until the fifteenth year. You would net only $107,900 if you paid the tax on a current or accrual basis under present Canadian tax rules. This amounts to over a 47% increase in income from a basic investment. That's why RRSPs work so well over the long haul. In addition to receiving a deduction for your RRSP contribution, the interest and other income accumulates tax-free. This ability to defer tax on interest in the United States is not limited to RRSP-like investments. Taxpayers can deposit unlimited sums into investment vehicles that allow for tax-free compounding and deferral of interest, dividends and capital gains for periods of years. Even so, it's still not prudent to place all your investments into tax-free or tax deferred

Canada	United States
Interest Income	
$10,500	$3,000
	$3,500
	$3,500
	$10,000
Current Tax Due	
$5,565	$1,085
Amount Left After Tax	
$4,935	$8,915
Taxes Saved	
	$4,480

FIGURE 8.2

investments from an investment or an estate planning stand point.

Let's call on George and Susan again, to look at the interest income portion of their tax picture, and then compare this with their tax savings potential of moving to the United States. In the example used in Figure 8.2, we assume they have $150,000 of investments in interest bearing vehicles such as bonds and GICs, earning an average rate of interest of 7% for a total of $10,500. After moving to the United States, they split their portfolio into 1/3 tax-free municipal bonds earning 6% or $3,000, 1/3 tax deferred annuities earning 7% or $3,500 and leave the remaining 1/3 in investments similar to their Canadian portfolio earning 7% or $3,500. Amounts in Figure 8.2 (and through Figure 8.8) are shown in Canadian funds.

In the Figure 8.2 example, George and Susan's interest income, after taxes are paid, is more than 81% higher. It should be noted that 1/3 of the investment portfolio is in tax deferred annuity and will be subject to tax if withdrawn at some future date. But as we have mentioned, tax deferred can be tax saved. In the 31% tax bracket, you only have to defer the tax for approximately six years, before you can save the entire amount.

There is a common misconception that moving to the United States, means accepting lower rates of interest on savings. In fact, U.S. interest rates are now higher than in Canada. You can always earn exactly the same rate of interest by leaving your GICs and term deposits in Canada, but own them as a non-resident. This may not be the best alternative from an investment strategy or estate planning perspective, but it is possible to have and hold Canadian certificates and bank accounts, while you are a non-resident. See Chapter 6 and 9 for more details on investment strategies that reduce risk and increase income.

PENSIONS - PARTIALLY TAX-FREE

There are major differences between the United States and Canada in the way pensions are taxed. Revenue Canada taxes all pensions by including 100% as taxable income, minus an equivalent exemption of $1,000 each year. This exemption is slated to disappear in the year 2000. The IRS allows pensioners to receive the portion of the pension resulting from the taxpayer contribution to be tax-free. If an individual made 50% of the annual contributions to their company pension, roughly half of their pension at retirement would be tax free. The actual amount received tax-free, depends on current interest rates and the life expectancy of the employee at the time they start receiving their pension. The IRS considers a pension annuity created from an RRSP, and fully taxable in Canada, to be just a regular annuity. Only the annual interest earned is considered taxable. As a result, a significant portion of the monthly payments from your RRSP created pension would be tax-free.

Finally, for those Canadians who have held United States employment during their career and qualify for U.S. Social Security, the IRS provides for more tax favoured treatment, depending on total current income from all sources; anywhere from 100% of U.S. Social Security, to a minimum of 15% can be received free from tax.

Let's look at George again. He's receiving $50,000 a year from a company pension that he contributed to over his 30 year employment. His numbers work out such that the IRS will consider 20% of his pension to be excluded from taxation in the United States. Susan did not have a company pension but purchased a 20 year RRSP term annuity. She receives $20,000 a year from this and her return of principal from the annuity, would be approxi-

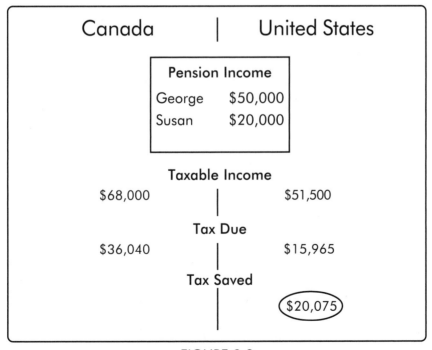

FIGURE 8.3

mately $8,500 per year. In her case approximately 43% of her annuity would be excluded from U.S. taxes. Figure 8.3 shows the net effect on taxes on George and Susan's pensions, by moving to the United States.

George and Susan would effectively cut their tax on the pension portion of their income by 66%. Obviously, this is a major raise for them, allowing them to keep $54,035 of their pension after tax, instead of only $33,960.

EMPLOYMENT INCOME

Earned income in the United States, is taxed in a similar manner to the same type of income in Canada — it is added to taxable income. Earned income is taxed at your marginal tax rates in both countries. This makes tax comparisons between Canada and the United States very simple.

Although Susan is retired, she still does some management consulting for her former employer. She receives a fee of $25,000 a year and Figure 8.4 compares the taxation of this income between the two countries.

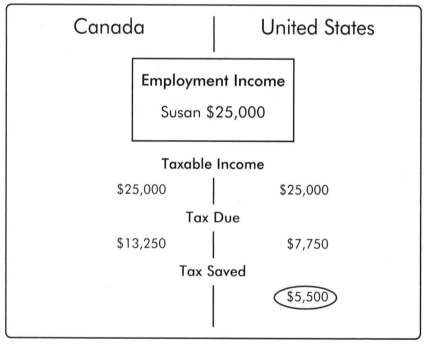

FIGURE 8.4

We discover that Susan is entitled to a whopping 42% tax reduction. This amounts to an effective 47% after tax pay raise without even having to talk to her boss. The tax savings simply results from the fact that the maximum tax rate is 53% for Ontario and 31% in Florida on this amount of income. Other provincial or state tax comparisons would of course, be different.

CAPITAL GAINS

Capital gains receive some favourable treatment in both Canada and the United States. Since the lifetime $100,000 capital gains exemption in Canada was eliminated in the February 22, 1994, federal budget, gains are taxed at a maximum of 40% depending on your province of residence. In the United States, the maximum federal tax rate on long term capital gains is 28%. There is strong move afoot in the Republican congress to lower it to 20%. Since there is generally considerable risk in the types of investments that produce capital gains, most prudent people do not have a large

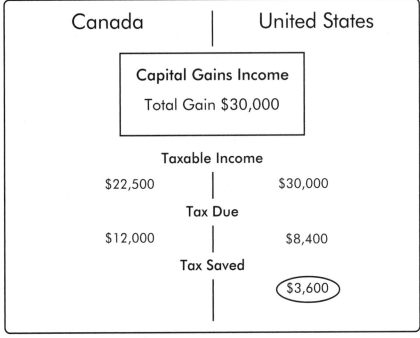

FIGURE 8.5

percentage of their assets tied up in this area of investment. Consequently, the tax savings on capital gains are generally not enough to create any significant advantages either way when contemplating a move to the United States. That is unless you have a small or closely held business which is highly appreciated (see Chapter 10).

Those who buy and sell real estate for investment purposes, or as their occupation, will find the ability to roll the gain tax-free from one property to another in the United States, an excellent tax saving device in those instances where it is applicable. There is also no deemed disposition tax at death on appreciated assets in the United States, as there is in Canada. This means a surviving spouse, or other beneficiaries who inherit highly appreciated property, can sell it free from capital gains tax. Some U.S. estate tax may apply for non spousal beneficiaries for estates over $600,000 U.S.

Let's turn again to George and Susan who would like to trade in some growth mutual funds, and a bit of real estate. For the current year, they have received capital gains distributions and other trading profits from their mutual funds of $8,000. They also sold a piece of property that netted them a gain of $22,000. Figure 8.5 displays the results. The tax reduction on capital gains is over 30% in the United States, even though only 75% of the gain is taxable in Canada. George and Susan discover they can realize greater tax savings on their capital gains by setting up the mutual funds as a variable annuity. These funds provide for the unlimited deferral of capital gains, interest and dividends income until the deferred income is actually withdrawn.

DIVIDENDS - SMALL SAVINGS

Dividends are taxed very differently in Canada than in the United States. In the U.S. they are taxed the same way as employment income or regular interest. In Canada dividends are multiplied or grossed up by 125% when calculating taxable income. An offsetting tax credit equal to 13.3% on the federal tax calculation of the grossed up amount is allowed. This makes the maximum tax rate of 35.4% on dividends in Ontario, compared to 31% in Florida at this income level.

George and Susan have $10,000 of dividend income. Figure 8.6 compares the net result of being in the maximum tax rates and earning dividends in either country. Even after taking the Canadian dividend tax credit, they will realize a tax reduction by 12% on their dividends by moving to the United States. As noted in the *Capital Gains* section of this chapter, they can use mutual funds in the form of variable annuities, to defer income on dividends in the United States and pay no current tax.

In both United States and Canada, dividends are taxed twice, once at the corporate level and again at the individual shareholder's level. If you own a dividend paying corporation, both levels of tax must be considered to do a fair comparison. For someone with a Canadian controlled small business qualified for the small business tax rate, the total tax paid on dividends at both the corporate and individual shareholder levels, will be less on the Canadian side of the border on income under $200,000. In the United States it is generally better to pay salary and bonus to owner shareholders, or use flow-through companies that pay no tax at the corporate level than it is to pay a dividend. Salaries can only be taxed once at a maximum federal individual rate of 40% for salaries above $271,000 U.S. or $370,000 CDN.

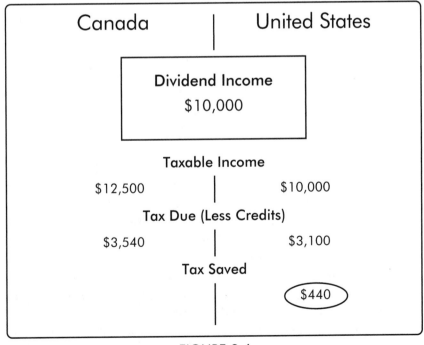

FIGURE 8.6

TOTAL INCOME - THE REAL COMPARISON

The examples used in Figures 8.1 through 8.6 are a good way to compare taxes on major incomes sources on a line by line basis. It does not however, provide the complete picture, since it does not take into consideration personal deductions, the progressive tax rates and the different filing options available in the two respective countries. The best way to do a realistic tax comparison, is to take the total world income with deductions, and simultaneously calculate the Canadian and U.S. tax as if the individuals were residents of either country, and then net out the final tax figures.

Since we are already somewhat familiar with George and Susan, we will first do their total tax comparison in Figure 8.7. George and Susan are both retired, so we will also take a look at Bill and Mary who are medical doctors, still working, with dependent children in college, in Figure 8.8.

George and Susan are both over 65, and own a summer cottage near Ottawa and a single family dwelling in Naples, Florida. They pay property taxes totalling $6,000 CDN per year, have no mortgages and donate $5,000 CDN a year to their church. They have two cars and pay $500 CDN per year to license them. They have no sources of income, other than those detailed in Figures 8.1 to 8.6.

George and Susan have cut their tax bill by 64% by moving to the United States and have increased their after tax income by over $3,000 per month. If we were to assume that their joint life expectancy is 20 years and that they could invest this annual tax savings to earn an after tax return of 6%, they would accumulate a total of $1,423,713 in additional net worth over their lifetimes.

The tax reduction experienced by George and Susan is quite typical of someone who retires in the Sunbelt. Larger savings can be achieved with more comprehensive cross-border planning. Persons whose income comes primarily from RRSPs or RRIFs and other investments, can realize even greater savings than George and Susan did with proper planning

Now let's take a look at Bill and Mary, in their late forties, with two children in college. Bill is an anesthesiologist who earns $200,000 net annually from his practice. Mary is also a doctor who works in a medical clinic as a general practitioner, with a salary of $90,000. They have a large mortgage on their home in Winnipeg with payments of $4,500 per month and both make the maximum contribution to their RRSPs each year. Their

Income

	George	Susan	Combined
CPP	8,000	8,000	16,000
OAS	4,700	4,700	9,400
Pension	50,000	20,000	70,000
Interest	5,250	5,250	10,500
Dividends	5,000	5,000	10,000
Employment	0	25,000	25,000
Capital Gains	15,000	15,000	30,000
	----------	----------	-------------
Total Income	$87,950	$82,950	$170,900

Canada | United States

Adjustments to Total Income

Canada		United States	
Dividends	+$2,500	Tax Free Interest	-$5,500
Capital Gains	-$7,500	Tax Defer Interest	-$3,500
OAS Repayment	-$8,785	George's Pension	-$10,000
		Susan's Pension	-$8,500
		Pers Exemptions	-$6,892
		Church	-$5,000
		Prop/Veh Taxes	-$6,500
		OAS/CPP	-$25,400

Taxable Income

$157,115 $101,608

Federal Tax Credits

$6775

Net Tax Due

$60,103 $21,400

Tax Savings

$38,703

FIGURE 8.7

property taxes are $5,000, vehicle licence is $1,000 and their two children, still live at home. They have some joint term deposits that earn about $10,000 per year interest, making their total income $300,000. Both have job offers in Arizona, at the same income level and want to compare after tax income between Manitoba and Arizona. Figure 8.8 shows the results of that comparison.

Even though their circumstances are quite different, Bill and Mary achieve nearly the same level of tax reduction, about 54%. They would realize an after tax raise in monthly income of over $5,000. This tax savings is due to not only lower Arizona tax rates, but also because they deduct their large mortgage interest payments, property tax, and state income tax. They make a large contribution to their Simplified Employee Pension, rather than an RRSP. Bill and Mary would also have to pay Social Security taxes in the U.S. Although Social Security benefits are larger than CPP so are their contributions. To keep the tax comparisons simple we have not included any CPP, UIC or Social Security payments in the net taxes due.

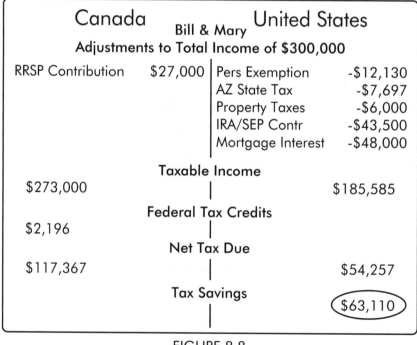

Canada		Bill & Mary	United States
Adjustments to Total Income of $300,000			
RRSP Contribution	$27,000	Pers Exemption	-$12,130
		AZ State Tax	-$7,697
		Property Taxes	-$6,000
		IRA/SEP Contr	-$43,500
		Mortgage Interest	-$48,000
		Taxable Income	
$273,000			$185,585
		Federal Tax Credits	
$2,196			
		Net Tax Due	
$117,367			$54,257
		Tax Savings	
			$63,110

FIGURE 8.8

Our two couples, George and Susan, and Bill and Mary, both have high incomes. Those in lower income brackets will generally experience proportionate tax cuts ranging from a 1/3 to 2/3 reduction in overall tax, on the same amount of income. If you and your spouse are paying a total of $10,000 or less in Canadian taxes, a move to the U.S. will not likely be of much benefit unless you have access to low cost medical coverage from U.S. Medicare, your employer's group retirement health plan, or a bridge insurance carrier until you can get on U.S. Medicare.

CANADIAN NON-RESIDENT WITHHOLDING TAX

Canadians who leave Canada but still receive Canadian income, have to look at the Canada — United States Tax Treaty for the rules governing taxation of the income sourced in Canada. The treaty, as described in Chapter 1, was created to prevent citizens and residents from being taxed twice on the same income, while at the same time allowing both countries

---

Canadian Non-Resident Withholding Rates 1997

- Interest 10%
- CSB's, Treasury Bonds 0%
- Dividends 15%
- CPP and OAS 25%
- Pensions 15%
- Lump Sum RRSP's 25%
- Rental Income 25%
- Management Fees................................. 15%
- Capital Gains .... Variable%

FIGURE 8.9

some limited power of taxation according to the income source and type.

In Figures 8.1 to 8.7, George and Susan provide us with a typical example of a situation where the treaty comes into play. They have a number of income sources which cannot be changed, their CPP, OAS, and pensions. This means that Revenue Canada, under the tax treaty, will be able to levy some tax on this income as non-residents, since it is sourced in Canada. At the same time, the IRS will have taxation rights on the income, because they are United States residents. The treaty however, ensures that George and Susan will not be double taxed on any of this income, by specifying how the income will be taxed and allowing for tax credits in one country, for taxes paid to the other. The table in Figure 8.9, lists the withholding tax rates between Canada and the United States, on major forms of income, a Canadian is likely to encounter when moving to the United States.

The rates in Figure 8.9 are withheld at the source, such as at the bank that pays the interest, or the company that pays the pension. It is the responsibility of the payer to withhold the correct treaty rate from the non-resident's income and forward that amount to Revenue Canada. It is the responsibility of the non-resident to notify any applicable payer, that they are, or are becoming residents of the United States. If the improper amount has been withheld, Revenue Canada will send a bill to the non-resident and expect payment. If they cannot locate the non-resident, and the payer was at fault for under withholding, they can be held liable for any taxes due.

If the correct non-resident withholding has been taken, the non-resident is not required to file a tax return with Revenue Canada. However, there are special filing options for those non-residents with rental income or pension income, if the withholding rate is higher than the actual tax would have been, if that person had been a resident of Canada. For example, if a non-resident has rental property which earns no net profit, they could elect to file a non-resident return under Section 216 of the Income Tax Act netting out income and expenses and pay no tax rather than a 25% withholding on the gross rental receipts. Similarly, under Section 217 of the Income Tax Act, someone receiving a Canadian pension whose tax rate would have been less than the 15% withholding, had they been a Canadian resident with that pension income only, can file a special return and claim a refund (see restrictions for a Section 217 following later in this chapter in the *Withdraw Your RRSP Tax-free* section). In addition, they could apply to Revenue Canada for a reduced withholding rate on future payments on Revenue Canada Form NR5.

On capital gains income, non-residents must either face withholding rates of up to 50%, or file for a clearance certificate, form T2062, prior to the sale of the capital property, from Revenue Canada. When Revenue Canada issues the clearance certificate, it will determine what portion of the gain is taxable, and authorize the buyer to withhold at a rate that assures total tax payment. The seller must file a Canadian return as a final reconciliation of the transaction, in the year in which the sale occurred.

Payments from RRSPs and RRIFs are considered pension payments subject to the 15% withholding rate as long as they are periodic. Periodic means the RRSP must be in the form of an annuity with payments to at least age ninety. Periodic payments from a RRIF must not exceed twice the annual minimum payment, to qualify for the 15% withholding rate, rather than the lump sum rate of 25%. See the section *Withdraw Your RRSP Tax-free* later in this chapter!

Income	George	Susan	W/H Tax
CPP	8,000	8,000	4,000
OAS (Clawed-back)	0	0	0
Pension	50,000	20,000	10,500
Interest	6,750	6,750	0
Dividends	5,000	5,000	1,500
Employment	0	25,000	3,750
Capital Gains	15,000	15,000	10,000
Total Non Resident Withholding Tax			$29,850
Total U.S. Tax Due			$21,400
Credit for Cdn W/H Tax			$21,400
Net Tax Payable to U.S.			$0

FIGURE 8.10

To more clearly illustrate how this system of withholding taxes and credits works, let's go back to George and Susan again, and see what actually happened when they exited Canada for the United States. For this example, we assume that they converted all of their interest bearing bank deposits in Canada to the United States, just as their cross-border financial planner recommended. Revenue Canada agreed that a 30% withholding tax on their capital gains was suitable. You can refer back to Figure 8.7 if you wish to review George and Susan's income sources and taxes due, as Figure 8.10 only summarizes these numbers.

Figure 8.10 indicates that George and Susan would owe no additional taxes to the United States, because Canadian non-resident withholding tax was allowed as a foreign tax credit on their U.S. return. The credit from the Canadian withholding tax in fact, wiped out any tax they would have paid to the IRS, had the income been generated in the United States. Since there was more Canadian withholding than U.S. taxes due, the excess unused credits can be carried forward for up to five years to be used in a year when the withholding tax would be insufficient to provide a full credit against the U.S. taxes due on the foreign income earned.

The foreign tax credit in the United States is subject to some special rules that can affect the amount of credit actually allowed by the IRS. George and Susan's case has been simplified somewhat, to show the overall effect of the withholding and credit system under the Canada — United States Tax Treaty. On an actual return, their results would likely be slightly different. Had the IRS under any of its own rules, disallowed any of the Canadian tax withheld as a foreign tax credit, it could have been carried forward for up to five years, to be used against future foreign income earned.

WITHDRAW YOUR RRSP TAX-FREE!

Many Canadians have small fortunes sitting in their RRSPs, but are reluctant to withdraw any money from them, because they face such high rates of taxation on the withdrawals. This section will deal with some of the cross-border financial planning techniques that can help you withdraw even large sums from your RRSP and effectively pay no or very little net taxes. In many cases, these cross-border financial planning techniques can provide a major incentive for becoming a United States resident, as the savings, especially on the larger accounts, can be thousands of dollars!

The issue of what to do with RRSPs when Canadians exit Canada to take up residency in the United States is more often than not overlooked, especially for those who fail to complete a cross-border financial plan. When taking up residency in the United States, RRSPs can be a great source of tax savings, if they are planned for correctly. Without proper planning, RRSPs can create unnecessary United States taxes, and can potentially be double taxed by both the United States and Canada. Most people either ignore planning for their RRSPs, think there is nothing they need to do, or that they can let their RRSPs sit and accumulate interest, as if they were still a resident of Canada.

How Canadian RRSPs are viewed by the United States Internal Revenue Service, will help explain some of the problems surrounding them, and how you can plan around them. We touched briefly upon this issue earlier in this chapter, in Figure 8.3 with respect to Susan's RRSP annuity pension. The IRS considers your RRSP to be an ordinary investment looking right through the RRSP trusteeship. As a resident of the United States, whatever the underlying investment is in the RRSP, is how the IRS will treat it. For example, the IRS will consider the contributions you made and the accumulated interest or dividends in a RRSP, as tax paid principal prior to becoming a U.S. resident. (Please note this IRS treatment for interest and dividends does not apply to unrealized capital gains at your entrance date into the U.S., nor does it apply to U.S. citizens or green card holders who have been resident in Canada.) But as a U.S. resident, citizen or green card holder, the IRS will tax interest earned and paid during the year, in the same way as if you had earned the interest in a standard U.S. bank account. Similarly, dividends and capital gains on your RRSP account are subject to U.S. tax, as they are paid or realized, without the deferral of tax provided for by Revenue Canada.

As a U.S. resident, if you were to leave your RRSPs in Canada, or if you are a U.S. citizen or green card holder with RRSPs, the IRS will tax you on all interest, dividends and capital gains earned on your account, even though you may not have actually received them. When you are taxed on income that you do not actually receive, it is called phantom income. Many Canadians with RRSPs have been in the United States for years, and never realized that they have a United States tax liability on this phantom income. The Canada — United States Tax Treaty which came into effect in 1996, allows you to make an election annually on your United States return, to defer the payment of United States tax on the RRSP phantom income until such time as it is actually withdrawn. Please note that if you live in a state that has a state income tax — state income tax may be due on the phantom income every year, as states are not party to the treaty or its elections. Withdrawals of your principal contributions to the RRSP are not taxed by the Internal Revenue Service at any time.

What then, is the best thing to do with your RRSPs upon leaving Canada? There are no provisions between Canada and the United States for a direct transfer of your RRSP to the U.S. equivalent, an Individual Retirement Account (IRA). You only have two options — withdraw the RRSPs, or make the annual elections under the treaty to defer federal tax on the income. We recommend the former solution for ten key reasons indicated below:

1. If you leave your RRSP in Canada, not only are you subject to the tax rules of both Canada and the United States, but you are subject to any future Canadian tax legislation that could restrict future withdrawals more than they are now. As recently as December 20, 1991, Revenue Canada made several changes to the Income Tax Conventions Interpretation Act, restricting the definition of what qualifies as a periodic RRIF withdrawal, forcing RRIF holders to pay a 25% withholding rate instead of a 15% rate on withdrawals larger than twice the annual minimum. The March 1996 Canadian Federal budget reduced the age of which RRSP withdrawals must start from 71 to 69.

   In addition to these tax risks, expect Revenue Canada to continue tightening these restrictions, as they are constantly looking for more revenue. Just like the old sayings "make hay while the sun shines" or "get out while the getting is good," you can cash in your RRSPs now, and pay as little as zero tax once you leave Canada. Why wait for future legislation to come along that will restrict your options?

2. Persons with estates over $600,000 may face a double taxation in a similar manner to the potential double indemnity on capital gains tax at death discussed in Chapter 4. The double tax arises because Canada will withhold 25% from your RRSP at your death, and this amount will not be allowed as a credit against United States estate tax due. The most recent Canadian —U.S. Tax Treaty does not provide for a credit of the RRSP withholding at death against the estate taxes in the U.S., so a double tax will likely occur on any larger U.S. estates with Canadian RRSPs. Similarly for those taxable under U.S. estate tax rules, having significant assets in a foreign country locked into the special rules that

apply to RRSPs, make it very difficult to use standard estate tax reduction planning techniques available to most U.S. residents.

3. Another reason to cash in your RRSPs after becoming a United States resident is to avoid unnecessary currency speculation. We have already covered the hazards of unknowingly becoming a currency speculator in Chapter 2. Keeping an RRSP in Canadian dollars when you are likely to need U.S. dollars for retirement is exposing yourself to unnecessary risk.

4. Canadian investment restrictions dictate that a maximum of 20% of your RRSP can be invested outside of Canada. From an investment management perspective this places the RRSP portfolio into additional investment risk or missed investment opportunities. Since Canada is only 3% of the world economy, the 80% Canadian content rule makes it very difficult to obtain proper worldwide diversification at a time when we live in a global economy more than ever in the past.

5. As noted earlier in this section, the individual U.S. states are not party to a Federal treaty like the Canada—U.S. Treaty. In states with a state income tax, an additional level of tax may apply each year even though you may have elected a deferral of the IRS tax under the Treaty. For example, if the Canadian with RRSPs takes up residence in the state of California and has elected the deferral of the RRSP income at the federal level under the Treaty, they will pay up to 11% state tax annually on the RRSP phantom income. This tax would not be recoverable in the US. under California state tax rules so would in effect be an unnecessary or a double tax.

6. Income deferred on RRSPs under the Treaty election as a U.S. resident, is Income In Respect to the Decedent (IRD) under U.S. rules at death. IRD results in double tax generally whenever it occurs particularly where there may be non-resident beneficiaries.

7. From an investment standpoint, getting your RRSP out of Canada early in your U.S. residence can be to your advantage for two key reasons, cost and investment selection. In a practical investment sense, competition favours an investor in the U.S. through lower commission on securities, transactions and lower management fees on mutual funds. Mutual Fund Management fees and expense ratios are generally 2-3% in Canada, while in the U.S. around 1% or generally less than half the cost for a similar Mutual Fund. In addition, the larger selection of U.S. mutual

funds allows you to choose index funds with expense ratios as low as .25% or one-tenth the cost. This cost savings over a number of years compared to leaving your mutual funds in Canada can be substantial, amounting to many thousand of dollars in unnecessary fees.

8. The U.S. Security Exchange Commission requires that your Canadian broker and his Canadian brokerage firm holding your RRSP funds be licensed in your state of residence before they can legally transact security trades for you in the U.S. As a result, you may be stuck with all the stocks, bonds and mutual funds you own in your RRSP without being able to change investments to react to changing market conditions after you leave Canada, not a good situation.

9. For those individuals who have total post 65 retirement income around the $50,000 CDN range with an RRSP, will find even the minimum RRSP/RRIF withdrawal as required by Revenue Canada will result in your OAS clawback kicking in. If, as a U.S. resident, you have been able to withdraw your RRSP as outlined in this chapter before your forced withdrawal at age 69, the clawback may be avoided altogether adding $4,700 of OAS income for you to spend each year in your retirement.

10.   There is something to be said for simplicity in one's financial life. Consequently, leaving your RRSP in Canada when you are a U.S. resident, complicates your tax and investment management life substantially. You need to constantly find U.S. tax and investment advisors who understand RRSP reporting procedures, a difficult job at the best of times, when most of them are struggling just to keep current on the usual IRS rules and regulations. The cost of these advisors, particularly if you get the wrong advice, can often outweigh the benefits of any tax deferral you might obtain by leaving the RRSP in Canada and electing the Treaty deferral.

In spite of all these reasons to get your RRSP out of Canada once you become a U. S. resident there are circumstances, when considering the factors below, that we recommend leaving some or all of your or your spouse's RRSPs in Canada for limited periods to obtain maximum tax or investment advantage.

Making withdrawals from your RRSP that maximize benefits and minimize taxes, is no simple task and should not be done without the supervision of a qualified cross-border financial planner. This is one area of cross-border planning where a simple error can be costly and irreversible. Using a knowledgeable professional can pay big dividends.

The timing of the withdrawals is critical. You need to match Canadian withholding taxes with U.S. taxability of foreign income. This correct matching of taxes paid to Canada and available foreign tax credits in the United States, can mean the difference between paying 25% or 0% tax on a net basis on your RRSP balance. When calculating the usable foreign tax credits on a U.S. tax return, all sources of foreign income must be considered, not just the RRSP income.

I have been inundated with hundreds of requests from Border Guide readers asking me to include more specific examples on withdrawing RRSPs at the lowest possible rate. Many would like to attempt withdrawing their RRSPs tax-free on a net basis on their own and I would strongly advise using a knowledgeable professional. I am reluctant to provide these examples because this is one area that is far too complex and dependent on too many factors to even attempt presenting it in any condensed written format. Any RRSP withdrawal planning for non-residents of Canada is affected by this partial list of factors:

- Your age and marital status.

- Your spouse's age.

- Type, amounts and sources of your current and future income.

- Type, amounts and sources of your spouse's current and future income.

- Amounts of past, current and future non-resident tax paid or to be paid to Revenue Canada by you and your spouse.

- Your need for current or future cash flow.

- You and your spouse's net worth.

- Location and tax basis of non-RRSP assets.

- Size of you and your spouse's RRSPs.

- The types of investments in your RRSPs.

- Whether or not any of your RRSPs are "locked in" by provincial legislation.

- Whether you are still a Canadian resident for tax purposes.

- How long you've been a resident in the U.S.

- Your immigration status in the U.S.

- Whether you have previous U.S. tax returns in which you reported RRSP income correctly.

As you can see, the many factors affecting RRSP withdrawal planning can be mind boggling particularly when you consider the number of combinations and permutations so many factors create. Consequently, if one is not careful, or fails to use competent professional advice with their RRSP withdrawals, as a non-resident of Canada, opportunities can be missed to reduce taxes significantly. Worse yet, taxes and penalties can wipe out savings entirely.

For smaller RRSPs, namely those with less than $100,000 in value, staged withdrawals can be controlled to match the foreign tax credits available. Section 217 of the Income Tax Act allows persons who withdraw between $7,000 and $25,000 from their RRSP, and who have no other taxable Canadian income, to file a return, and obtain either a full or partial refund of the withholding tax. Revenue Canada amended Section 217 filing requirements in 1992, eliminating filers who do not derive 50% of their world income from Canada. Consequently, this option is no longer viable for those with substantial U.S. or world income. You need to consider the interest rates on RRSPs, foreign income, amounts withdrawn, and available U.S. tax credits, in order to withdraw your RRSP out of Canada in the shortest time, and at the lowest possible tax rate.

Other than the non-resident withholding tax, you have no further Canadian obligations with respect to your RRSPs, and no need to file a return when making withdrawals, unless you qualify for a refund under Section 217.

TAX ON EXITING CANADA

If a Canadian resident moves to the United States, Revenue Canada requires that they file an exit tax return in the year of their departure.

On October 2, 1996, Revenue Canada announced major changes to the income tax rules as they relate to those exiting Canada to take up residence elsewhere. The new rules came about as a result of the Auditor General revealing that under the old rules, Revenue Canada had allowed two

Bronfman family Trusts to move $2 billion of capital assets out of Canada without paying a dime in capital gains tax. Since the new rules do not effect a single penny of the controversial $2 billion, they really amount to closing the barn door after the horses are gone. The net result is that the average tax payer has a new set of Canada departure tax rules to contend with.

Under the old rules, when a Canadian resident ceased being a resident, there was a deemed disposition at fair market value of all of the individual's property other than certain taxable Canadian property. Taxable Canadian property includes such items as Canadian real estate, shares in Canadian private companies and RRSPs. Therefore, capital gains tax was payable on the accrued gains on such items as publicly traded securities, U.S. real estate and personal property, regardless of where it was located. This tax is known as the departure tax or exit tax.

However, you could elect out of the departure tax for any property subject to the tax, provided that you posted adequate security with Revenue Canada . In such cases, you would be taxed when you sold the property if any tax remained due at that time.

The October 2, 1996 rules impose the departure tax on all your property with some exceptions noted below. Therefore, all accrued gains are subject to an immediate capital gains tax when the individual ceases to be resident of Canada. You are no longer allowed to elect out of the departure tax and the departure tax now applies to taxable Canadian property as well as other property. The only exceptions from the departure tax are Canadian real estate, capital property used in a business carried on in Canada, and certain pension and employee stock options.

Instead of paying the departure tax up front, Revenue Canada will allow you to post security for the tax due which then can be paid at a later date without accruing interest on the tax.

There is also a new reporting requirement for those exiting Canada after January 1, 1996 whose total property holdings exceed $25,000. They will be required to report all of their property on a Revenue Canada form with their exit returns for the year of departure.

If you did not sell your Canadian principal residence prior to departing Canada, you need to be aware of some special rules under the Canada — United States Tax Treaty that can help you reduce future capital gains tax on the ultimate sale of the Canadian home while you are a United States resident. In Chapter 3, when we compared the basic differences in taxation between the United States and Canada, we saw that Canada does not tax capital gains on the sale of a principal residence while the United States will tax those gains, if they are not rolled over into a new residence of equal or greater value (those over 55 in the United States have up to a $125,000 lifetime exemption). The treaty helps you around this problem by making it appear, for tax purposes, that you purchased the Canadian home at its fair market value the day you entered the United States. As a result, you are responsible to the IRS only for gains on this property from the date you became an official resident. Note that this step up in basis, applies only to your principal residence, no other capital property receives this special treatment. It is highly recommended that Canadians who keep their principal residence when moving to he United States get a fair market appraisal just prior to leaving Canada and keep it for future tax reference.

Upon your exit from Canada, you either need to elect a deemed disposition of your principal residence on your exit tax return, or convert it to rental property. This will step up your Canadian cost basis to further reduce possible capital gains on the ultimate sale of the property.

CANADIAN DEPARTURE CHECKLIST

If you're departing Canada for the U.S. or other treaty country the Treaty will generally provide clear rules as to what income can be taxed, at what rate and by which country. Your exit from Canada should be as clean as possible to avoid Revenue Canada attacks on your residency or non-residency status. There are several key actions you should follow when exiting Canada and if you follow these rules you will likely have little problem with Revenue Canada attempting to tax your world income in Canada. Some items are not covered by Treaty provisions and to avoid paying full Canadian tax rates we've developed a checklist. These can assist you in establishing Canadian non-resident status after your departure, thereby avoiding future controversy with Revenue Canada. The items are listed in no particular order, but the first five are considered key. Remember that there is no single thing you do, but rather the combination of facts and circumstances that determines residency.

A. Sell your Canadian principal residence or rent it out on a long term (6 months or more) on or about your date of departure, preferably before your exit date. Having unrestricted access to a year-round accommodation in Canada, regardless of whether you own it, is considered as having principal residence in Canada. A cottage or other seasonal type residence generally would not be considered a principal Canadian residence.

B. Make sure you spend as much time out of Canada after your exit date as possible, particularly in the first two years after your departure. Under no circumstance spend more than six months a year in Canada after your departure. In general, keep your visits to Canada relatively short in duration (4-6 weeks) and as infrequent as possible.

C. If you have a business in Canada or Canadian employment income develop proof you are not required to be in Canada on a continuous basis to operate the business. Other employment or business income should be earned in the same manner as a U.S. person who has never resided in Canada would do. Try to do all your work from the U.S. side of the border. You are allowed to earn up to $10,000 in Canada without being subject to Canadian tax under the Canada-US Tax Treaty. If you go over this amount you must file Canadian tax returns and pay full Canadian tax rates on your income earned in Canada, even though you may be a non-resident.

D. Close all your Canadian bank and brokerage accounts and move them to the U.S. Maintaining a chequing and/or savings account at a Canadian bank generally is okay providing it is clearly set up as a non-resident account.

E. Notify any Canadian payers of Canadian sourced income such as banks, brokers, pension payers and government agencies in writing that you have departed Canada and are to be considered a non-resident for all purposes as of your exit date. Give them your U.S. address for all future payments and statements to be forwarded to.

F. Cancel your Canadian Medicare coverage before your exit date or within the provincially allowed grace period after your departure. Make sure you have U.S. health insurance in place.

G. You must be a legal resident in the U.S. before you can exit Canada for tax purposes. Ensure that proper U.S. immigration documentation is in place before you depart Canada.

H. Cancel all church, clubs or equivalent memberships in Canada. All churches and most clubs will allow you to visit or use the facilities as a non-resident.

I. Cancel all of your Canadian credit cards, drivers license and vehicle registration. Do the reverse and establish all of these in the U.S.

J. Accept no mail deliveries at any address in Canada. Have all mail forwarded to the U.S. Do not have personal mail sent to a Canadian relative or business address.

K. Change wills and other legal documents to reflect U.S. residence.

In general, always think and act as a visitor to Canada in all respects. It is sometimes good to just think of yourself as entering Canada as a visitor for the first time and act accordingly.

TRANSFERRING YOUR CREDIT RATING TO THE U.S.

Many Canadians moving to the U.S. are shocked to discover their hard earned good credit rating in Canada cannot even get them a simple Visa card in the U.S. This problem can usually be overcome by knowing what to tell a credit card company, or whoever you are borrowing from, what they need to do to verify your credit history. The people doing the credit check will normally feed your social security number into various credit bureaus and see what comes back. Since you are a new resident with a new social security number, usually nothing will come up. No credit will be advanced, since lenders usually consider someone with no credit history to be a poor risk. The trick is to give them your Canadian social insurance number and explain that credit bureaus in Canada operate on a very similar basis. If they call a Canadian reporting agency with your social insurance number, they can access your complete credit history. Without some direction from you, clerks at most lending institutions will simply reject you because their rule books don't tell them what to do in this situation.

U.S. ESTATE PLANNING

Necessity is often the mother of invention. Since there is a greater need for comprehensive estate planning in the United States, a number of very good and proven techniques have been developed to help make management of your estate easier while you are alive, and then provide for a smooth transition to your heirs. Many of these techniques will work equally well for

Canadians who become residents of the United States and can be used to cover assets still remaining in Canada.

When someone is moving or contemplating a move to the United States, cross-border estate planning needs to be a top priority, as there are many complex issues which if not addressed before taking up residence, could cause unnecessary estate settlement costs and death taxes.

Normally the first issue of cross-border estate planning is doing a comparison of what your estate costs and taxes are in Canada, and then in the United States, to see if there is any advantage in either country. It is not very often in this book that we can state a general rule that applies in almost every case, but couples with estates under $1,200,000 U.S. or $1,600,000 CDN at current exchange rates, have an unquestionable tax advantage as residents of the United States. Since there are Spousal Trusts in Canada, and Qualified Domestic-Marital Deduction Trusts in the United States to transfer assets tax-free between spouses, we will concentrate on estate tax and settlement costs at the death of the second spouse, to measure the full

Assets		Amount Subject to Canadian Death Tax
RRSP/RRIF	$400,000	$400,000
Cdn Residence	$250,000	$0
Mutual Funds	$150,000	$56,250
	(Cost $75,000)	
U.S. Residence	$250,000	$112,500*
	(Cost $100,000)	
Land	$150,000	$75,000
	(Cost $50,000)	
Term Deposit	$100,000	$0
Personal	$80,000	$0
Total	$1,380,000 CDN	
Canadian Resident Death Taxes		$412,289
U.S. Resident Death Taxes		$0

* Subject to a U.S. Non Resident Estate Tax in addition to the Canadian Death

FIGURE 8.11

impact of these costs and make a proper Canadian — U.S. comparison. Figure 8.11 give us an example of this situation, using a reasonably well off couple with an estate of $1,380,000 CDN.

The Canadian death taxes in Figure 8.11, are calculated by taking the amount subject to deemed disposition tax at death of the surviving spouse, and adding in the U.S. non-resident tax on their United States vacation home and the probate fee.

The total deemed disposition tax is $341,189; U.S. non-resident estate tax is $50,400 and the probate fee for an estate of this size in Ontario, would be $20,700. Thus, a total death tax of $412,289 would be payable by this couple's estate if they were Canadian residents at the time of their deaths. If this couple, or at the very least, the surviving spouse, does not undertake some preventive planning, their heirs will pay what amounts to a total of $412,289 Canadian inheritance tax, after the second spouse's death. These taxes will be due right away, within six months of death. The new U.S. — Canada Tax Treaty will now provide this couple with a tax credit for the U.S. non-resident estate tax paid so their total inheritance tax at the second spouse's death would be reduced by $30,400 to $381,889.

However, if this couple took up residence in the United States and had a similar asset mix at the time of death, they would have no estate taxes due, since the size of their estate would be only $1,033,400 U.S., less than their total of $1,200,000 U.S. estate tax exemptions. In Chapter 4, we listed some of the double tax consequences of having assets in both Canada and the U.S., and earlier in this chapter we listed things to look out for when leaving Canada under the heading *Tax on Exiting Canada*. The complexity of these issues underscores the necessity of consulting with a cross-border financial planner, to ensure you maximize the opportunities and minimize the pitfalls.

For estates over $1,200,000 U.S. per couple, or $600,000 U.S. for individuals, other estate planning techniques can be used to deal economically with almost any estate tax (see the table in Figure 4.2 for the estate tax rates). Substantial United States residents with estates over their personal estate tax exemptions, and who are concerned about their estate depletion as discussed in Chapter 4, will use one or more trusts set aside and funded with income tax savings, to pay any potential estate taxes, even when they total into the millions of dollars. In addition, there are many other effective estate tax planning techniques for larger estates, which go beyond the general scope of this cross-border guide.

Under *The Living Trust - The Simple Solution to the Problems of Wills* section of Chapter 4, we outlined a number of benefits of using a Living Trust in an estate plan. These trusts are used in the United States for estates of any size, to assist in minimizing probate costs and delays. These trusts, combined with wills that are designed to place assets outside trusts into them at death, Powers of Attorney and living wills round off a cross-border estate plan. Powers of Attorney were explained earlier in Chapter 4. A living will is a separate document that deals with the possibility of you becoming incapacitated, connected to life support systems with no hope of recovery. The living will tells your family and medical professionals your wishes, under this set of circumstances.

CROSS-BORDER Q&A

Many of the issues covered in the preceding chapter of this book have been touched upon in the author's weekly column *Cross-border Q&A,* which appears in *The Sun Times of Canada,* published in Tampa, Florida and circulated throughout the U.S. Sunbelt for Canadians living or wintering there. The majority of these questions have been posed by readers of the Sun Times and/or readers of the previous editions of *The Border Guide.* Most were looking for advice relating to their own specific problems or situations. At the end of this chapter, we have included some typical reader questions, along with our response, to illustrate and broaden the concepts presented in the preceding chapter.

DEFER TAX ON RRSP UNDER TREATY

I have the following questions: If under the "Closer Connection Rule" I would elect to file a U.S. income tax return:

A. Would I have to report interest income earned within my Canadian RRSP?

B. Would I be able to claim mortgage interest for a house bought in the U.S.A.?

C. How would earnings and expenses from a Canadian partnership be treated?

— *Robert V., Myrtle Beach, South Carolina*

In answer to your questions:

A. Yes - interest income on an RRSP is treated for U.S. tax purposes the same as any other interest earned on any investments. You could also elect, under the Canada/U.S. Tax Treaty, to defer any U.S. federal tax, on the income until withdrawal, giving you the same deferral of income that an RRSP may provide.

B. Also affirmative — mortgage interest and property taxes on up to two homes are itemized deductions on a U.S. tax return.

C. The partnership expenses from Canada have to be re-stated and translated to U.S. depreciation schedules and deductions to determine the U.S. net taxable income, which could be either higher or lower than the net taxable Canadian net taxable income depending on the type of property in the partnership.

You should note that simply electing to be taxed as a U.S. resident does not mean you are going to be taxed as a non-resident of Canada at the same time. You need to be a legal resident of the U.S. before you can exit Canada. Without exiting Canada for tax purposes being able to deduct mortgage interest and pay lower taxes in the U.S. will be negated by having to file a Canadian return and paying full taxes to Canada.

CONVERTING E2 VISA STATUS AND HOLDING CANADIAN RRSPS

In August of 1990, after obtaining an E2 visa, I moved to the United States and purchased a business and a home. I am a Canadian citizen, residing in the U.S. with my wife and children and would like to establish permanent immigrant status. I own a rental property in Florida under a numbered Ontario corporation. My income is derived from the business in the United States and from dividends received from less than arms length Canadian corporations. As of 1991, I have elected to be taxed in the United States. I still hold an RRSP in Canada and own a private Canadian corporation. I realize these are rather complex issues, but I would like to hear from you.

1. In who's name should any United States assets be held?

2. What should I do with my Canadian assets?

3. What should I do with my Canadian RRSP?

4. What should I do with my United States rental property?

5. What can be done to convert my E2 non-immigrant status to immigrant status? My sister is a U.S. resident and holds a green card.

— *Jimi H., Wilmington, NC*

You are absolutely right! Your questions cover some very complicated issues. Consequently, the answers will also be complex, depending on your ultimate objectives, and other extenuating circumstances.

1. The titling of your United States assets generally would follow the same procedures that you would use in Canada. Business assets would likely best be owned by the business itself, depending on whether you are operating under a sole proprietorship, or are incorporated. Personal assets would be in your and/or your spouse's name. You should also look into using a Family Living Trust with provisions for a Qualified Domestic Trust to own all your assets. This trust would help organize your estate to help avoid probate in Florida, North Carolina and Ontario, and make better use of the United States estate tax exemptions.

2. Unless your Canadian assets are of a nature that there is no comparable asset available in the United States that can produce a similar return on your investment, your life will be greatly simplified if you liquidate all your Canadian assets. Maintaining a Canadian corporation, when your intentions are to permanently reside in the United States, can create double income and estate tax, subject you to possibly a higher rate of income tax, and force you into special Internal Revenue Service reporting on your Canadian personal holding companies.

3. RRSPs, and what to do with them when you move to the United States will be explained in the next two *Q&A* questions.

4. Your United States rental property in the Ontario company should be moved out of the Ontario company into either your own name, or possibly a United States corporation similar in purpose to the Ontario one. On the United States side of the border, there is no advantage to holding small rental properties in holding companies. In fact, you would likely be at a tax disadvantage by using a United States holding company, not to mention all the extra costs involved with corporations. There are both Canadian and United States tax implications in taking this rental property out of the Ontario corporation, which are too complex to be discussed here. I recommend you seek professional help with this and any other changes you are contemplating, as mistakes can be costly.

5. If your sister has been married to a U.S. citizen and has resided in the United States for more than three years, she can become a United States citizen and sponsor your "green card" immigrant status. The waiting time for this type of sibling sponsorship of the "green card" is around ten years from application, so you would need to keep renewing your E2 visa until that time. You have some other options to obtaining immigrant status through your company, which may require a somewhat difficult labour certification. A consultation with a good immigration attorney would be advised.

MAKING RRSP CONTRIBUTIONS FOR THE YEAR LEAVING CANADA

My husband and I are moving from Toronto, to take up new positions in Florida and will be leaving Canada on what appears to be a permanent basis. Do you have any recommendations as to what to do with our RRSPs before we leave Canada? Is it to our advantage to make RRSP contributions in the year we leave? What will happen once we leave Canada if we keep our RRSPs in Canada? Can they be transferred to a retirement plan in the United States, or should we cash them in before we leave?

— *Lucetta S., Safety Harbor, FL*

You didn't mention how much, or what types of investments you had in your husband's RRSPs, so I will explore most of the options with you, since this is a very common problem.

First, let's deal with the question of what to do with your RRSP before you leave Canada. Assuming you both have employment income in the same year you are leaving, cashing in your RRSPs will add greatly to your total income for the year, and likely be taxed at your maximum marginal tax rates of 53% in Ontario. Unless you want to lose half of all your accumulated RRSPs savings to Revenue Canada, you should explore other alternatives to cashing them in before you leave Canada.

There are some alternatives which may allow you to withdraw the full balance of your RRSPs at no or very low Canadian taxes.

If your RRSP consists of mutual funds, stocks or other appreciated assets, we recommend you realize these gains prior to becoming a United States resident. You would realize the gains by either liquidating all the investments and transferring the proceeds directly into a new RRSP savings account or short term deposits. If you have mutual funds, this transaction can be accomplished generally at no cost by merely switching from one fund to another, within the same family of mutual funds. This exercise to realize your gains does not affect your Canadian tax one bit, because your investments remain sheltered under your RRSP. However, for American tax purposes, should you liquidate them while a United States resident, you will pay more U.S. tax unless you complete this gain realization process. The United States can tax capital gains on your investments, so by realizing these gains before you take up residency, you are establishing a higher cost basis and hence less United States capital gains, when the investments are eventually sold.

Before you leave Canada, we recommend you make your maximum contribution to your RRSPs for the current year. With Canada's new RRSP rules, which base this year's contributions on last year's income, you can take advantage of some great tax savings. For example, if you and your husband each earned up to $17,500 from your Canadian employment in the current year before you left the country, and could make the maximum RRSP contributions of $13,500 each, based on last year's earnings, you could eliminate any tax on your income in Canada during your year of exit. Your RRSP contributions and your personal credits, should qualify you for a full refund of any tax withheld. At these levels of income, we would estimate a refund of over $8,000 in the short year of your exit.

After taking up residency in the U.S., withdrawals from your RRSPs, if planned correctly can be a great source of tax savings. Without proper planning, they can create unnecessary United States taxes, and could be taxed by both the U.S. and Canada.

There are no provisions between Canada and the United States for a direct transfer of your RRSP to the U.S. equivalent, an Individual Retirement Account (IRA). However, you can cash out of your RRSPs and pay as little as zero taxes, once you leave Canada, and use the net proceeds to contribute your maximum to your IRA's or other tax deductible qualified plans in the United States.

The background of how Canadian RRSPs are looked at by the United States Internal Revenue Service will help explain the problem and how to plan around it. The Internal Revenue Service (IRS) considers your RRSP to be an ordinary investment, without the deferral of tax that Revenue Canada provides. Consequently, as a U.S. resident, if you were to leave your RRSPs in Canada, the IRS will tax you on all interest, dividends and capital gains on your account, even though you may not have actually received them. When you are taxed on income that you do not actually receive, it is called phantom income. The Canada —United States Tax Treaty that came into effect in 1985, allows you to make an election annually on your United States return, to defer the payment of United States federal tax (individual states generally do not and are not required to follow tax treaties) on the RRSP phantom income, until it is actually withdrawn. Withdrawals of your principal contributions to the RRSP are not taxed by the Internal Revenue Service, at any time.

You should know that Revenue Canada will tax all lump sum RRSP withdrawals by non-residents at a flat 25% withholding rate, and periodic withdrawals at a 15% rate. On December 20, 1991, Revenue Canada made several changes to the Income Tax Conventions Interpretation Act restricting the definition of what qualifies as a periodic RRSP withdrawal, forcing planners to use some alternate methods to qualify clients for the 15% withholding rate instead of the 25% rate.

The question of what to do now should be somewhat easier to explain, now that you have some background. Since Revenue Canada has made it next to impossible for younger RRSP holders to have their withdrawals classified as periodic payment, a series of lump sum withdrawals at the 25% withholding rate is probably the best alternative. If you arrange for a series of annual lump sum withdrawals, and the total of these withdrawals is less than $7,000, you can file, as a non-resident, under Section 217 of the Canada Income Tax Act, to get a full refund of the withholding tax each year. To qualify for the Section 217 filing the RRSP withdrawal and other Canadian reportable income on this must equate to at least 50% of your world income so if you are working or have significant investment income this option would not be a useful one for you. If the payouts are more than $7,000 but less than $25,000, you could receive a partial refund of the withholding tax under Section 217.

Other than the withholding tax, you have no further Canadian obligations with respect to your RRSPs. However, you are going to have to reconcile the income earned on this RRSP, with the Internal Revenue Service, by adding it to your U.S. taxable income. You will receive foreign tax credits for the tax withheld by Canada on your United States return. There are a number of alternatives to consider when reporting the income on your United States return, but without knowing your United States tax information, it is difficult to speculate which alternative will be best. You will likely need some professional help in this area.

MOVING BACK TO CANADA

Relocation between Canada and the U.S. is not just a one way street to the South. There are also a lot of Canadians who return to Canada after years of living and working in Florida as U.S. residents. These people would love to hear something about their tax planning opportunities as well, such as Deferred U.S. Annuities. Florida tax planners are in general, not really knowledgeable about Canadian tax law and changes in the past.

— *Enocho B., Naples, FL*

Great question. It is true that movement between Canada and the U.S. is not a one way street. We often deal with Canadians and Americans moving back and forth in both directions.

Since we live in such a ever-changing society, good cross-border planning will generally keep all doors open so persons moving out of Canada may move back without adverse tax or other consequences.

Tax planning opportunities and concerns arising when moving from the U.S. back to Canada are numerous, and not necessarily the reversal of the planning procedure of the original move to the U.S.

Unrealized gains on stocks, bonds and investment real estate are best realized prior to exiting the U.S. for Canada. The maximum capital gains rate in most provinces is 40% whereas the U.S. maximum is now 28%. If you don't realize the gains prior to your entrance into Canada you will have a Canadian cost basis equal to the value of the properties or securities on the date of your return to Canada.

If you have a large capital gain built up in the personal residence you own in the U.S., you should take advantage of the lifetime $125,000 tax exemption, by selling the residence prior to leaving the U.S., or you could lose it. Canada will not recognize this U.S. lifetime exemption, nor will the U.S. recognize the Canadian principal residence capital gain exemption.

If you have acquired IRA's in the U.S., which are equivalent to Canada RRSPs, you may get some good tax breaks when you head back to Canada, providing you cash them in before exiting the U.S. Canada will tax you on the principal, interest and dividends you earn on these accounts, once you become a resident. If you still own IRAs or other U.S. qualified plans when you return to Canada, you will pay higher Canadian tax rates on all your withdrawals.

If you own deferred annuities of any type when you move back to Canada, they will lose their ability to shelter income build up from current Canadian taxation. Canada requires you to report all interest, dividend and realized capital gains on deferred annuities on a current basis, and will not allow you to accrue this income, to defer the payment of tax. Annuities are best cashed in, and invested in term deposits or similar Canadian investments, or converted to annuity payout options.

If you are collecting U.S. Social Security, under the Canada —United States Tax Treaty, you will be allowed to exclude 100% of this income from Canadian taxation. If you are a U.S. green card holder when you take up permanent residency back in Canada, you will be required to surrender it. If you don't, not only are you going against U.S. Immigration regulations but the Internal Revenue Service will continue to tax you as a resident. If you have become a U.S. citizen or a dual Canadian/U.S. citizen, much of what I have indicated here as planning opportunities, will apply differently to you, unless you directly and formally surrender your U.S. citizenship. If you are a dual citizen, and are a resident of Canada, you will need to be filing full returns in both Canada and the U.S. on your world income and taking allowable credits back and forth to avoid being double taxed on that income.

When you re-enter Canada, be prepared for a tax shocker. There is no tax-free or tax deferred income available in Canada. There are fewer deductions and the marginal tax rates are much higher and the amount of income required to reach the highest rates is much lower. If your primary sources of income are interest and pensions, you can expect your income tax bill to nearly double. You will of course, be the beneficiary of Canada's comprehensive, although deteriorating, medical care system and more generous social welfare systems. So what you give up in taxes, you may well recover in security.

In any case, when you are moving cross-border in either direction, you need a detailed plan with the assistance of a professional, fully knowledgeable on both sides of the border, to direct you through the maze of opportunities and pitfalls.

RECOVERING WITHHOLDING TAX ON CANADIAN INCOME

My two brothers and I own a family farm in Saskatchewan, rented out since 1952. One brother lives in Ottawa, the other in San Diego. We all depend on the on the income from the wheat sales.

My 1994 U.S. taxes gave me no tax relief on my Canadian income and I got no relief from my Canadian taxes. Did the U.S. — Canada Tax Treaty change that much in 1994? What about 1995? I am a widow living on Social Security plus a small income, so I feel I should have got some refund.

— *Freda M. Tampa, Florida*

While you have a unique situation, it should not be difficult to resolve. You may file a short form Canadian tax return to get back some of the withholding tax from Revenue Canada. On this return, you should include only the portion of income from the Saskatchewan farm allocated to you, deduct any expenses you have related to this income, and then collect any refund due. The deadline for filing such returns are July 1 following the year end, so you may be out of luck for 1994, but will likely benefit for 1995.

SHOULD YOU COLLAPSE YOUR CANADIAN RRSP

I read an article in *Globe and Mail* entitled "Don't Collapse Your RRSP If You Move To The US." The article stated that I would lose money if I moved my RRSP and it would be to my advantage to leave my RRSP in Canada as a U.S. resident. I have been a U.S. resident green card holder for two years and my wife and I have $350,000 in RRSP mutual funds in Canada. We are unlikely to return to Canada in the foreseeable future.

As you can see, due to the size of our RRSP, this is an important issue and the advice in the article appears to conflict with the advice you and others have given us in the past, which is to cash my RRSPs in 1997. Is this something new or is there some other reason for the advice given in this article? My wife's U.S. income is about $20,000 and mine is about $90,000. Would a Section 217 filing apply to us and could we get a refund of the non-resident withholding from Revenue Canada?

— *Kurt K., Seattle, Washington*

There are some good reasons why this strategy will not work for the majority of Canadians moving to the U.S. with RRSPs.

Stepping up the basis in your RRSP by buying the assets from your own RRSP would be considered a non-event by the IRS. This kind of transaction would be similar to changing brokerage firms by transferring your RRSP from one firm to another. To qualify for a step-up in basis in your RRSP prior to your U.S. entrance, the securities must be sold to a third party (your spouse doesn't count either). You can switch mutual funds to other funds in the same family to get a step up in your cost basis prior to a US residency without transaction cost. Since you are already in the U.S. this would not apply to you.

In addition, a Section 217 filing won't help obtain refunds of the non-resident withholding tax for those with incomes over $25,000. This is generally only practical for those with incomes around $15,000, not the $30,000 mentioned in the article. For those with incomes over $15,000, it becomes more practical to use Foreign Tax Credits in the U.S. rather then looking for a refund from Revenue Canada. The article overlooked several other key issues that I believe, would lead most people to conclude that they should take their RRSPs out of Canada soon after departing for the United States.

1. Leaving your RRSP in Canada exposes you to significant Government risk. In other words, you are at the mercy of Revenue Canada or the IRS' ability to change the rules on these investments and greatly increasing your tax. The withholding tax on RRSP lump sum withdrawals used to be 15%, now it is 25% and we expect it to continue to go even higher. Make hay while the sun is shining! The current 25% withholding on lump sum RRSP withdrawals may be the lowest you'll ever get.

2. Getting your RRSP out of Canada greatly simplifies your financial life. You will only be subject to U.S. tax rules and you won't need the specialized tax and investment advice that comes with maintaining an RRSP as a U.S. resident. This specialized advice is not only expensive, but hard to find since most U.S. advisors don't have any experience with RRSPs and don't have the time required to get up to speed.

3. The article failed to address the complications of state income tax rules, which vary somewhat from state to state. American states are

not bound by any federal tax treaties, so the election to defer U.S. taxes on income in the RRSP at the federal level, would have no effect at the state level in many states. This would result in an unnecessary and added level of tax.

4. Once your RRSPs are withdrawn, you can invest the net proceeds in the U.S. in a very broad range of tax-free or tax-deferred investments without all the restrictions of an RRSP.

5. On average mutual funds in Canada charge about double what they do in the United States. Management expense ratios average 2-3% in Canada, while in the U.S. you have a large selection of no load mutual funds with expense ratios as low as .25%. Based on the size of your RRSPs, the savings in expenses alone could be close to $10,000 a year.

6. The *Globe and Mail* article also did not mention the potential double estate tax that occurs at your death with RRSPs in Canada. The Canada — U.S. Treaty does not provide for a credit offsetting the tax on RRSPs at death and U.S. estate taxes. This deferral election on taxation of the income from U.S. taxation would result in 'Income in Respect to the Decedent' (IRD). IRD creates double taxation just about any time it appears, particularly with non-resident beneficiaries.

There are other reasons why you should not leave your RRSPs in Canada once you are a U.S. resident, but these should be sufficient to convince you.

Give My Regards to Wall Street

INVESTING AS A U.S. RESIDENT

9

A sound investment strategy should be built around the basic concepts of asset allocation, risk allocation, risk control and performance tracking. Risk control and performance tracking are easily understood. Due to the cyclical nature of our economy, attention to asset allocation is necessary. A country's economy changes from periods of prosperity and low interest rates, to times of recession and high rates. Proper asset allocation strategies allow portfolios to contain different types of investments that will perform well in various economic environments. Regardless of which way the economy of the United States or Canada is headed, you have a relatively steady return with good safety of principal.

In Chapter 6 we spoke a great deal about investment types, investment risk, and currency fluctuations mainly from the perspective of the non-resident Canadian. Canadians who take up residency in the United States, need to consider all these factors, make some necessary adjustments and position their investments in such a way that the proper balance between assets is achieved to realize their financial goals. Most people find this is a difficult task, because not only are they treading new ground in the United States, but there are interlocking factors that need to be addressed simultaneously among the financial planning areas of taxation, estate, cash flow and investments. In other words, changes in one segment of your financial plan, may require modification to several other areas as well. There are also cross-border considerations, since most Canadians moving to the United States leave several investments in Canada. These investments need to be integrated with their United States investment program in order to derive maximum benefit.

The first step is determining what your actual objectives and needs are, from your investment portfolio. This may be restating the obvious, but our experience in financial planning has proven that many people neglect doing even a basic analysis of what exactly they want or need from their

208

investment portfolio. Consequently, their current investments do not match their needs. Figure 9.1 is a quick exercise designed to help you determine your priorities.

The investment characteristics listed in Figure 9.1, are the main attributes one should consider when looking at investments. In the boxes on the right, priortize these characteristics by assigning a numerical value from 1 to 9; one being the most important to you, and nine the least. Use the same number only once, so when you are finished, you will have a list of the nine main characteristics, in order of their importance. Now you will have a guide from which you can measure how well your investments meet your priorities.

For example, if liquidity and inflation protection are the two most important characteristics, and you have most of your money locked into term deposits or GIC's of one form or another, your investments are mismatched to your own needs, since those investments will provide neither inflation protection or liquidity.

Investment Priority Checklist

Inflation ☐

Tax Advantages ☐

Safety ☐

Diversification ☐

Professional Management ☐

Growth ☐

Liquidity ☐

Income Now ☐

Income Later ☐

FIGURE 9.1

There are some sophisticated computerized asset allocation programs used by professional money managers, which can compare your current portfolio with twenty or more years of historical data, to determine the overall level of risk or variability your investments have, and the expected rate of return, assuming you leave the investments as they are. These programs can also recommend changes or "optimize" a portfolio, to achieve greater returns at reduced levels of risk. Of course, historical data cannot guarantee future results, but this sort of analysis is very useful in quantifying levels of risk, determining the relationship of one investment to another, and looking at how changes to an individual portfolio can affect the risk and return parameters. When setting up your United States investment program, this type of analysis should be routine, and can provide you with greater security and increased return.

The next step in developing your portfolio is to determine your overall objectives. There are four key objectives or modes, that can be realistically achieved by an investment portfolio:

INCOME

Who Should Consider this Objective:

- Investors whose primary concern is current income.

- Investors who will tolerate only minor erosions of principal in any given year.

- Investors who are not concerned with the long term effects of inflation on their purchasing power.

Typical Investors:

- Retired individuals looking to enhance their income in order to live more comfortably.

- Conservative investors willing to accept a relatively small degree of principal fluctuation.

- Families who need to supplement their income.

Objective:

The Income and Preservation of Principal objective seeks a high level of current income with liquidity and relatively low annual principal fluctuation. It does not seek to maintain purchasing power against inflation.

Management Technique:

Use mutual funds that invest in U.S. or foreign government securities, investment grade corporate debt securities, high quality mortgage securities, investment grade and/or insured municipal bonds. Equity exposure is limited to 30% of the total portfolio.

GROWTH AND INCOME

Who Should Consider this Objective:

- Investors with long investment horizons (3+ years).

- .Investors who want some long-term growth along with stability of principal.

- Investors who want current income that could increase each year to offset inflation.

- Investors who can live with the possibility of some losses as well as gains in any given year.

Typical Investors:

- Retired individuals concerned about the effects of inflation on their retirement income.

- Conservative working individuals looking to build a nest-egg.

Objective:

The Income With Growth objective seeks to provide an income stream that on the average, increases annually to compensate for the loss of purchasing power, due to rising inflation. This objective also strives to maintain portfolio purchasing power. This objective will entail some year to year volatility in portfolio values.

Management Technique:

Use mutual funds that invest in large capitalization stocks and investment grade debt securities. Investments in cash/short-term debt and fixed income funds will comprise at least 20% of the portfolio for each category. Thus, maximum exposure to equity markets will be 60%.

GROWTH

Who Should Consider this Objective:

- Investors with long-term investment horizons (5+ years).

- Investors who can live with the possibility of large losses as well as gains in any given year.

- Investors who do not have to live on all of the income generated from their investments.

Typical Investors:

- Working individuals who are looking to aggressively build an asset base.

- Retired individuals who at present require little or no investment income to live on.

- Bank savers who realize that by keeping their investments solely in bank accounts they may be sacrificing opportunities for superior long-term investment returns.

Objective:

The Growth objective is to seek capital appreciation over the long run (3-10 years). Current income is not a consideration.

Management Technique:

Use mutual funds that will not be limited by size or type of company. Investments in cash and fixed income funds will usually be minimal, but must comprise at least 10% of the portfolio. Thus, maximum exposure to equity markets will be 90%.

AGGRESSIVE GROWTH

Who Should Consider this Objective:

- Investors with long-term investment horizons (3-10 years).

- Investors who want a chance to maximize long-term growth.

- Investors who can tolerate potentially large year to year volatility in the value of their investment.

Typical Investors:

- Aggressive retirees not needing investment income to live on.

- Aggressive middle-aged investors working to build a retirement nest egg.

- Young investors not "now" oriented.

Objective:

The Aggressive Growth strategy offers potentially high long-term returns (5-10 years) at the cost of year to year volatility. This offers the highest potential for growth over the long run, but will probably be the most volatile of all the objectives in any given year.

Management Technique:

Use mutual funds that will not be limited by size or type of company. Investments in cash and fixed income funds will usually be minimal. Equity exposure can range as high as 100%. It is anticipated that this objective will make use of small company funds in both developed countries and emerging markets to a greater degree than the Growth objective.

Once you have determined your own objectives, you are probably 90% of the way toward developing your investment portfolio. The final 10% is important — the actual investment selection. A professional money manager can select and maintain the investments that match your objectives, making future modifications as your objectives change. Refer back to the section in Chapter 6 *Choosing an International Investment Manager,* which will assist in locating the best management firm to meet your needs.

The U.S. provides a wide variety of investments to achieve any investment objective, many of which are tax advantaged. These investments allow investors to achieve greater tax savings without sacrificing liquidity, diversification or increased risk.

PENSIONS AND SOCIAL BENEFITS

Retired or not, a major objective in cross-border financial planning is to position yourself to qualify for both Canadian and U.S. government social programs; CPP and OAS in Canada and Social Security in the United States. Qualifying for these benefits requires careful long term planning. Canada Pension Plan benefits are earned by being employed in Canada for ten years or longer. Once you have exited Canada, the benefit goes with you. You can apply at age sixty or wait longer, in order to qualify for increased benefits. But the longer you wait, the more zero income years you will have reducing your average monthly earnings, offsetting potential increases by delaying the payment of benefits. Widows can qualify for a reduced benefit based on their spouses earnings record.

To qualify for full Old Age Security benefits, you need to be a resident of Canada for forty years past the age of 18. Anything less will result in a proportionate reduction in benefits. For example, if you had only thirty years in Canada past age 18 you would receive 75% of the maximum monthly benefit.

Those receiving CPP and OAS may recall from Chapter 8 under the section *Keep More of Your CPP & OAS,* that there are great tax savings while receiving these benefits while a resident of the United States.

Before we explain how to qualify for U.S. Social Security, we want to make you aware of another, sometimes very beneficial, treaty between Canada and the U.S., the Canada — United States Social Security Agreement. This provides for a coordination of benefits between the two countries, so that citizens spending time in both countries are not disadvantaged by any loss of benefits.

As a result, a Canadian moving to the United States can qualify for a minimal U.S. monthly benefit as early as age 62, by working as little as 18 months and earning as little as $200 per month. The normal qualifying time is ten years of earnings. With United States Social Security, the spouse of the qualifying person also automatically qualifies to receive approximately 50% of the amount of the spouse, even though they may have never contributed to the system. A Canadian who marries a United States resident who is receiving or who qualifies for Social Security from their U.S. employment can, after one year of marriage, receive 50% of their spouses monthly amount and U.S. Medicare for life indexed for inflation.

Even retired Canadians who become U.S. residents at age 70 or less, should attempt to put in the minimum amount of qualifying time for Social Security and Medicare. This can be accomplished by earning about $2,800 a year, working part-time, doing some consulting work, or by holding a seat on a board of directors. You need 18 months of work to qualify for benefits, and up to 120 months to qualify for free United States Medicare as well.

The universal coverage plan currently being debated is expected to dramatically change the U.S. health care system. The impact of these proposed changes may take many years to materialize, but the ultimate goal is to improve access to health coverage for all legal residents and citizens of the U.S. Canadians often tend to downplay the fact that they've worked in the United States, or for an American company. If you worked in the U.S. anytime after 1933 when Social Security began, you will have accumulated useful quarters towards a monthly benefit or Medicare.

United States Social Security benefits are entirely tax free for a married couple with less than $32,000 total income, 50% of the benefits tax free if total income more than $32,000 but less than $44,000 and after that up to 85% of the benefits must be included in taxable income.

Canadians who have made contributions to a company pension plan, will be able to claim a portion of their pension as tax free return of principal, while a resident in the United States. The exact amount of tax free pension is determined by using the size of the pension annuity purchased, your age and the IRS tables.

U.S. MEDICAL COVERAGE

Canadians routinely hear about Americans being denied medical treatment because they have no money or insurance. Americans hear about the evils of Canada's socialist medical system; patients dying from inadequate care or long waiting lists for surgery. In reality, things are seldom as grim as the media portrays them, and many of these horror stories have been exaggerated or taken out of context by special interest groups and advocates of one particular system. The most important thing to remember about the U.S. medical system is that it is not inherently more or less humane than the Canadian system; it is just different.

American hospitals and health care providers usually operate on a profit making basis. They compete for patients and this competition results in improved access to the most sophisticated medical technology. A medium-sized American city often has more specialized diagnostic equipment such MRI scanners, than are available in all of Canada. The down-side of the equation, is that patients under 65 must either pay for the services out of their own pockets, or buy health insurance to cover medical expenses. Those without either, generally have access to free medical care through a system of county hospitals, which operate in much the same way as Canadian hospitals. Available U.S. medical care can vary greatly from state to state, just like in Canada, where there are numerous inter-provincial differences in applying federal medicare guidelines.

For a new Canadian resident to the United States, we recommend you purchase private health insurance. Those under age 65 with no pre-existing conditions, will find many insurance companies that will provide coverage at reasonable cost. The cost will vary from state to state, with California and Florida tending to be more expensive. The best value by far, is what is known as catastrophic coverage — insurance that only pays when a claim exceeds a specified dollar amount like $2,500, $5,000, $10,000 or even $25,000. Coverage can cost from $50 to $300 per month, depending on age and the deductible level chosen. I cover my entire family of six with $2,000,000 of individual insurance coverage with a highly rated company, on a preferred provider network. We pay $25 for each doctors visit and the first $18 of each prescription, for a $250 premium per month.

Some Canadian retirees may find their pension plans will provide full or partial U.S. coverage. Retired federal government employees are eligible through their group plan, called PSHCP, for supplemental coverage, that will pay all reasonable doctor and prescription drug costs as well as a small amount toward daily hospital expenses in the United States.

For those over age 65, the choices are more limited, since most Americans at that age go onto U.S. Medicare. Because of this, there is little demand for individual plans other than Medicare supplements. Consequently, the key cross-border financial planning strategy is to ensure the Canadian resident of the United States becomes eligible for American Medicare. Figure 9.2 outlines the key means to qualify for U.S. Medicare.

There are insurers who will provide supplements to fill in gaps left by Medicare coverage. These medigap policies currently cost up to about $75 a month, depending on the level and type of medigap chosen. Canadians who have not contributed the minimum forty quarters (120 months) to U.S. Social Security through employment, or who are not married to a U.S. resident or citizen who has made the necessary contributions, can expect to pay around $300 per month for U.S. Medicare coverage.

For those Canadians over 65 who do not yet meet the five year residency requirement for Medicare, there are few options. Chapter 5 referred to one insurance product, Ingle Health's International Plan, that provides coverage to Canadians who are not on provincial medicare. Premiums run around $150 to $300 per month depending on age, for $1,000,000 in coverage with a $250 deductible. Another solution is to self-insure by setting aside all, or a portion of the annual tax savings into a highly liquid investment account. In Chapter 8, Figure 8.7, our couple saved nearly $36,000 a year in taxes. If they set aside these tax savings in a money market account, they would build a self insurance fund sufficient to cover most major hospital stays, within a few years.

U.S. health insurance and Medicare does not cover extended care in nursing homes or similar facilities and a separate policy is needed to cover these expenses. A large number of insurance companies offer this coverage, but great caution is advised. Premiums can vary as much as 200% to 300%, for the identical coverage. The minimum recommended coverage is $125 per day for up to four years with an inflation rider. Those over age 75 could eliminate the inflation rider which tends to nearly double premiums. Premiums from a good A+ rated insurance company can range between $50 to $200 per month, depending on your age at the time the policy is taken out. This coverage can be applied for at any time, beginning at about age 50.

U.S. Medicare Eligibility

- Age 65 or older, and one or more of the following:

- Five years or more as a legal U.S. resident or Green Card holder; or

- U.S. Citizen (including derivative citizen); or

- Married to a U.S. citizen or resident on Social Security who qualified through their own employment.

FIGURE 9.2

Insurance premiums paid for any of the medical coverage referred to in this section are deductible, as an itemized medical expense on your U.S. tax return. However, total monthly premiums can be substantial, especially for those who do not qualify for free U.S. Medicare. This added cost must be weighed against the potential income tax and other savings of becoming a United States resident. In George and Susan's example in Chapter 8, they are able to save enough in taxes just from their CPP and OAS clawback, to pay for good medical insurance coverage in the United States.

CROSS-BORDER Q&A

Many of the issues covered in the preceding chapter of this book have been touched upon in the author's weekly column *Cross-border Q&A*, which appears in *The Sun Times of Canada*, published in Tampa, Florida and circulated throughout the U.S. Sunbelt for Canadians living or wintering there. The majority of these questions have been posed by readers of the Sun Times and/or readers of the previous editions of *The Border Guide*. Most were looking for advice relating to their own specific problems or situations. At the end of this chapter, we have included some typical reader questions, along with our response, to illustrate and broaden the concepts presented in the preceding chapter.

CROSS-BORDER LIVING CAN GET COMPLICATED

I am a Canadian of seventy-eight. Almost two years ago I married an American and I wish to live in the U.S. Things get very complicated as my family lives in Canada and I have a few assets there. Do I need a green card? We hope to go to Canada to visit a couple of months in the summer. I do not have assets in the U.S. but will have to pay income tax here for 1995 as I now get a small amount of Social Security. I pay income tax in Canada.

Any information you could send me would be greatly appreciated. So few people seem to have answers.

— *Mark H., Mesa, AZ*

Things do get complicated for those Canadians in your situation. You have numerous sets of tax, medical, and immigration rules that apply to you from both Canada and the U.S., and complicating things further, some rules conflict with each other. Consequently, accurate advice is hard to come by since you need someone who will help you through all the applicable rules and at the same time resolving any potential conflicts amongst the rules themselves.

You have no problem living in the U.S. and visiting Canada providing your wife sponsors you for a green card. Without a green card you are in the U.S. illegally. In other words, you are an illegal alien and you may not be admitted back into the U.S. from one of your visits back to Canada if the border officer picks up on it. Obtaining your green card requires a simple application to the Immigration and Naturalization Service in Phoenix, a process that usually takes 4-6 months to complete at a cost of about $95.

As a non-resident of Canada you no longer have to file a return there even though you may still have income there. All you need to do is to ensure your banks etc. withhold non-resident withholding tax at the rate specified under the Canada — U.S. Tax Treaty, usually 10%. As a U.S. resident, illegal or not, you must file a U.S. tax return reporting your world income — either as married filing separate returns, or married filing joint returns — depending on which method results in the least amount of tax.

You didn't say whether you had U.S. Medicare, but if you don't you will qualify for it along with possibly a higher Social Security benefit if your wife has her own employment record with Social Security.

U.S. MOVE NEEDS FORETHOUGHT

My wife and I are both 74 years of age and are enjoying second marriages after losing our respective spouses some years ago. We are both Canadian citizens.

My wife has a daughter aged 52 who married a American approximately 25 years ago and is now an American citizen herself. It is the daughter that we hope can sponsor my wife and I to obtain green cards.

I would be very much obliged if you would answer the following questions to enable my wife and I to make a judgment on whether we should move permanently to the USA. We presently spend six months in Florida each year in a condominium that we own.

1. Would my wife's daughter be permitted to sponsor us to obtain green cards to enable us to permanently live in our Florida residence?

2. Assuming this is possible would we both qualify for Medicare?

3. Would we qualify for a Homestead Exemption when paying Florida real estate taxes?

4. I understand that a physical examination is required for green card. I have had diabetes for years but have it well controlled. Would the fact I have diabetes disqualify me?

My wife and I both have adequate pension and investment income and would have no need to supplement this income by seeking employment. I look forward to receiving your reply.

— *Arthur H., Clearwater, FL*

Your wife's daughter may indeed sponsor your wife into the U.S. as a legal permanent resident or more commonly called green card status. Your wife could then in turn sponsor you for your green card.

You would not qualify for U.S. Medicare under the current Medicare rules until you both have had your green cards for at least five years. After five years you may apply for the Medicare coverage but you would be required to pay the full premium since you have never worked in the U.S. Currently the premiums would be about $300 per month each. In the mean time if you are going to obtain your green cards you will need private major medical insurance from one of the companies I have mentioned in previous Q&A columns but you need to hurry as the better coverage becomes difficult for new customers over age 75. You should obtain this medical coverage now rather than waiting until you actually get your green cards.

Once you have your green cards and are full time residents of Florida you will be able to obtain all the residential privileges afforded any other Florida resident including the Homestead exemption.

You need only worry about the medical exam you must complete to obtain your green card if you have one of the highly contagious communicable diseases such as AIDS or TB. Diabetes will not disqualify you but may make it more difficult to obtain the private health coverage.

If you decide to go ahead and become full time U.S. residents, there are many other issues that you need to address, other than the ones in your questions. These would include taxation, estate planning, risk management and investment planning. We recommend you complete a cross-border financial plan through an experienced professional cross-border financial planner addressing these issues as well as assisting you to get proper medical coverage. Cross-border financial planning is one area where the investment in planning results in huge returns.

KNOW SOCIAL SECURITY RULES

I worked for three years as a professor in the U.S. The U.S. Social Security office tells me I have 12 quarters of qualifying time towards a U.S. monthly Social Security pension but I must have a minimum of 40 quarters of employment history before I may receive any benefits. I also have nearly $70,000 U.S. accumulated in a TIAA/CREF (this is similar to a Canadian Registered Retirement Savings Plan) that I contributed to while I was in the U.S. to take a deduction against my teaching salary. The questions I would like to ask are as follows:

1. As a Canadian resident, can I continue to pay into social security so my wife and I can collect Social Security benefits in our retirement years?

2. If not, how can I get my money back from them?

3. Do you have any other suggestions? What should I do about my TIAA/CREFF?

Looking forward to hearing from you in the near future.

— *Walter J., Saint John, NB*

1. Yes, you can continue to pay into Social Security but only if you earn $2,800 or more per year of qualifying employment type income sourced and taxable in the U.S. The $2,800 of earnings will give you four quarters of Social Security credit per year. Once you have your total of 40 quarters of benefits of credits, or 28 more than you currently do, both you and your wife can receive U.S. Social Security and Medicare at age 65 even if you don't wish to become U.S. residents in the future. You will need some form of legal immigration status in the U.S. before you can earn employment type income in the U.S.

2. You can get the Social Security money back by applying for a reduced monthly benefit under the Canada/US Social Security Agreement through any U.S. Social Security office once you reach age 62 or older even if you do not contribute any more to the U.S. Social Security system.

3. The tax treatment of TIAA-CREF and other RRSP type U.S. qualified plans in Canada has recently been changed retroactively. The new Canadian rules, as outlined in Section 243(1), reg S.6803 of the Canada Income Tax Act, state the income earned on these U.S. accounts is not taxable on a current basis until actual withdrawals are made from the plan. At the time of withdrawal, both income and principal are taxed at the current Canadian rates as income. As a result, withdrawals should be made at times when income is lower, such as retirement in a similar manner to your Canadian RRSP's. You are also subject to U.S. rules and taxes on the withdrawals from your TIAA-CREF. You must commence your withdrawals before the year in which you become age 70 1/2. Any tax that you may pay to the IRS would be a credit to you on your Canadian return so you should not be double taxed on this income.

WORK FOR U.S. SOCIAL SECURITY

I am in the process of obtaining my "green card." I shall be sponsored by my son who is an American citizen and will work for him for three or more years. My questions concerns Medicare and health insurance at the age of 65. Does the "agreement on Social Security between the U.S. and Canada" offer any credits toward Medicare coverage?

— *F. W., Orillia, Ontario*

In order to qualify for U.S. Medicare paid by Social Security at age 65 or later you need to have forty quarters or ten years of contributions to Social Security through employment income in the U.S. You would be eligible to belong to U.S. Medicare after you have had your green card for five years and have reached age 65. However, if you do not have the required forty quarters of contributions to Social Security you will have to pay approximately $300 premium per month for the coverage instead of $40. If you are married, your wife will qualify for Medicare at age 65 as well as a monthly Social Security payment based on your employment contributions to the plan. Consequently, making the effort to earn $2,800 each year, the minimum amount to get four quarters of qualification during a year, for the total of ten years can give you both a total of over $7,000 of benefits per years for life. This is quite a return on you investment considering that the Social Security tax on $2,800 of earnings is only about $215 ($430 if self-employed.

You can make contributions to Social Security through your earnings at any age so the sooner you get started the sooner you will qualify. If you work only three years, the agreement on Social Security between the U.S. and Canada will assist you to receive a reduced monthly Social Security pension but since U.S. Medicare is not part of this agreement you will get none of your Medicare premiums paid by the Social Security.

If you are not married and find a U.S. citizen spouse (one who has qualified for Social Security based on her own earnings), after one year of marriage, not only will you get a spouses Social Security pension equal to about 50% of her monthly benefit but you will also get U.S. Medicare.

MARRIAGE AND LIVING IN THE U.S.

I am a Canadian who 2 1/2 years ago married an American. We have a condo in Canada and a condo in Florida. We spend six months here and six months in Canada. It now appears that it is ridiculous to go back and forth every six months. I would like to know what is involved if I choose to stay in the U.S. full-time and sell our condo in Canada. The following are the questions I have:

1. I don't want to give up my Canadian citizenship.

2. We plan to live here 12 months of the year and visit my children in Canada in the summer.

3. I am retired and do not want to work in the U.S. We have enough income to live comfortably and do not require employment in the U.S.

4. Do I have to pay income tax in the U.S.?

5. I understand I would have to pay withholding tax in Canada.

6. I have heard I would be eligible for Medicare being married to an American? Also, I could buy a supplement and give up my OHIP.

7. What forms are required and who would I have to see about doing this?

— *Doug H., Redington Shores, FL*

You have all good questions that are very relevant to anyone in your situation. I will answer your questions in the same order you listed them.

1. You do not have to give up your Canadian citizenship at all. Your American spouse will have to sponsor you for a green card to allow you to live year around in the U.S.

223

2. No problems visiting your children. Keep your total stays in Canada to less than 6 months per year if you want to avoid paying Canadian income tax on your full world income.

3. You do not have to work in order to live in the U.S. under the circumstances as you have outlined.

4 & 5. You do have to pay income tax on your world income in the U.S. and you will have no Canadian return to file once you have officially exited Canada. Revenue Canada will require non-resident withholding tax on any of your Canadian sources of income. Generally you will receive a credit for the non-resident withholding paid to Canada on your U.S. returns , which will normally offset all or most of any U.S. taxes due on the same income. Your total tax paid will likely show a net decrease by your filing returns only in the U.S.

6. At age 65 you would qualify for U.S. Medicare under your American spouse's Social Security spousal benefits. You should get a U.S. Medicare supplement and you will be required to give up OHIP when you officially move from Ontario.

7. Most of the forms you would need would be from Immigration and Naturalization Services for immigration and the Internal Revenue Service for taxes. You should see a good cross-border financial planner before you do any of this.

Taking Care of Business

How Small Business Owners
Can Reap Huge Rewards

10

There is no other area of cross-border financial planning that offers owners of small, closely-held businesses more income tax saving potential than moving to the U.S. Consequently, a good cross-border financial plan can save a business owner between several thousand to several millions of dollars, depending on the size or the nature of their business. Most of these planning opportunities arise solely because a cross-border move is contemplated. They would not be available to the business owner if they were not in the process of moving.

The major considerations that small business owners need to be aware are outlined in the next five sections.

A CANADIAN CORPORATION CAN ASSIST WITH U.S. IMMIGRATION

Many a successful entrepreneur has worked long and hard to establish a business. Later, when they want to retire, or just sell the business to try something new, they apply the same amount of diligence to disposing of the business. When the money from the sale is sitting in the bank and all the income taxes are paid, they start thinking about retiring to the American Sunbelt. Unfortunately, our hypothetical business owner may have just sold off his simplest and best means of U.S. immigration.

As you may recall, the U.S. immigration procedures outlined in Chapter 7, all require some form of business or a family connection for U.S. Immigration. So, if there are no close family members in the U.S. or you have sold your principal business, you may need to establish a new business, in order to complete your immigration. A better route for business owners would be to complete a cross-border plan before the sale of the business has been completed. A sale could either be delayed for a short period of time, or structured in such a way to incorporate the necessary means to acquire a visa or green card. This forward planning could save the business owner a great deal of time and money. In addition, the failure to complete a cross-border plan before a business is sold, could mean that the vendor may have paid a great deal more income tax on the sale than necessary, as outlined in the next section of this chapter.

HOW TO TAKE A CAPITAL GAINS TAX HOLIDAY

Canadian small business owners are currently limited to a once in a lifetime tax-free capital gains exemption of $500,000. If the proper planning has been undertaken, then this exemption may be effectively doubled by including a spouse as a co-owner of the business(es). What happens if you have no exemption remaining, or your capital gains exceed the $500,000 or $1,000,000 limitations? A tax rate, which is currently 40% in most provinces, is applied to the amount of capital gains not eligible for the exemption.

So how much can you save doing it the other way? A properly drafted cross-border financial plan can reduce this tax liability to just 15%, using certain provisions included in the Canada-U.S. Tax Treaty. The 15% tax may then be recovered in the U.S. through foreign tax credits on income generated by a properly designed investment portfolio. The net result is that a successful business owner can sell their business and effectively pay no net tax. This no net tax scenario can apply even if the proceeds from the business are $500,000, $5,000,000, or more!

The means to accomplish these potentially enormous tax savings are based on sound legal precedents, but are much too complex to even attempt to explain within the context of a general guide such as this book. This complex plan has been made substantially more difficult and some savings reduced by Revenue Canada's change in the departure tax rules in response to the Bronfman's $2 billion tax maneuver discussed in the Tax on Exiting Canada section in Chapter 8. The key point that business owners should be aware of, is that these tax savings are possible and available to you. To use them to their maximum advantage, you need to seek the services of a qualified cross-border financial planing specialist, early in the selling process.

TAX RAMIFICATIONS OF MAINTAINING A CANADIAN CORPORATION

If a Canadian business owner wishes to maintain a Canadian corporation after becoming a resident of the U.S., they must deal with a number of issues. First of all, under the new departure tax rules of October 2, 1996, there is now a deemed disposition of the corporation shares on exit and tax either has to be paid at that time or other arrangements, including collateral, need to be made with Revenue Canada to defer the tax to when the shares are actually sold. Consequently, the sale of the corporate shares after becoming a U.S. resident, may be subject to both Canadian and U.S. capital gains tax, as calculated by the increase in share value since their original acquisition, or creation of the corporation.

The Canada — U.S. Tax Treaty does however, make some provision for sufficient tax credits to prevent outright double taxation on this gain. However, the new Bronfman departure tax rules make the planning before the business owner exits Canada extremely critical to ensure there is no double tax due to the timing of any foreign tax credits created in the liquidation of the corporate shares and departure from Canada. If the owner were to die in the U.S, they may still be subject to the double Estate Tax, a syndrome outlined in Chapter 4. Proper planning can help eliminate or at least greatly reduce any capital gains tax or estate tax due on the sale or wind up of a business, or the death of the business owner.

Another issue that a Canadian business owner living in the U.S. needs to address, is that if the Canadian company is largely a passive one earning income from rentals and investments, it will likely be considered a Foreign Personal Holding Company by the IRS and be subject to a myriad of reporting and other requirements. For example, if the company's fiscal year is not Dec. 31, calendar year reporting of the corporate income must be provided, and tax paid as if the shareholder(s) personally owned the corporate assets. This tax must be paid whether or not it is actually distributed to the shareholders during that year. Considering all of the IRS reporting requirements on Foreign Holding Companies, there is little or no advantage to maintaining a Canadian company of this type.

Canadian companies reporting active business income are also subject to special rules on reporting income. The income from an active Canadian company will generally be deferred until withdrawn. There is usually a current tax liability on the income from the holding company, the U.S. reporting and filing requirements for most companies. With an active Canadian company, and to a lesser extent a holding company, one very good method to reduce corporate income from the operation is to collect a reasonable management fee. The Canadian corporation would be able to deduct the management fee in full, and under the Canada — U.S. Tax Treaty, management fees are only subject to a flat 15% withholding tax. The 15% withholding tax is fully recoverable in the U.S., through the Foreign Tax credit.

If the actual management work is done on the U.S. side of the border, then the Canadian company can pay a reasonable management fee to the owner, or to a related U.S. company exempt from Canadian withholding. The net result is that income can be removed from the Canadian company without Canadian tax and taxed at the lower U.S. rates. The final tax rate paid will be determined by the owners marginal tax rate and his state of resident in the U.S. If Canadian salaries are taken by U.S. resident shareholders, then the shareholders would have to file non-resident Canadian returns and pay tax on the Canadian salary. The Canada — U.S. Tax Treaty states that if the salary remains under $10,000 no Canadian return need be filed.

What are the estate planning considerations of a Canadian corporation owned by a U.S. resident? As we have seen in Chapter 8, U.S. residents are taxed at death, on their world-wide assets. A Canadian who becomes a resident of the U.S. without proper planning, could subject all his Canadian holdings to the U.S. estate tax. In addition, he may face double taxation from the Canadian deemed disposition tax at death.

A proper cross-border plan would use one or more living and /or spousal trusts, to eliminate or greatly reduce both levels of tax by either Canada and the United States. Again, this kind of planning needs to be completed prior to a business owner immigrating to the U.S. Once you become a U.S. resident, the number of planning choices for a business owner to avoid unnecessary estate taxes is significantly reduced.

I ndividuals in Canada or the United States, with financial interests in only the country they reside, face a single set of rules, making it relatively easy to obtain the services of a competent financial planner, accountant or lawyer who can provide the necessary expertise and advice when required. As soon as a Canadian begins spending time or purchases real estate or a business in the United States, there are two new sets of tax rules, the Canada — United States Tax Treaty and the Internal Revenue Code, that need to be considered.

There are myriad other cross-border financial issues that must dealt with. These rules and considerations are complex, contradictory and are often in conflict with one another. Even a knowledgeable individual may have difficulty grasping all the implications and potentially costly mistakes are easily made. To make things more difficult, cross-border rules are so complex and highly specialized, that adequate professional advice is not easy to find. It can be an arduous job for most professionals, just learning and keeping current with a single country's rules, let alone make the time and effort to learn both Canadian and U.S. rules. Consequently, there are few professionals who have undertaken the task of becoming proficient in both American and Canadian immigration, financial and estate planning matters.

THE TEAM APPROACH

Any Canadian with assets in the United States, and certainly anyone who moves to the United States, will require the assistance of one or more professionals from either Canada or the United States. Because there are so many separate areas of expertise required to complete a valid cross-border financial plan, no one professional can successfully cover all areas of implementation. Consequently, our recommendation is that you opt for a team approach to cross-border financial planning.

The cross-border financial planning team may consist of two or more professionals from either country, depending on the complexity of your situation. Picking the right members of your team is critical and should be done in a similar manner to choosing a doctor or medical team. You would go first to a general practitioner or family doctor, who would assess your total health, provide the treatment that is within their scope of care and then, recommend or refer you to a specialist. The general practitioner monitors and coordinates all the other medical services, to ensure that treatments are not being duplicated, or conflict with one another. They will ensure that everyone is focusing on the same objective. Once your medical condition has been treated, the general practitioner will probably monitor your condition, to watch out for any future complications.

Your first step toward obtaining prudent cross-border financial planning, should be to find a good general practitioner. The cross-border financial planner can draw up a written cross-border plan for you, refer you to the individual experts you may require, and then implement the plan by acting as your team leader. Your planner can coordinate other team members to

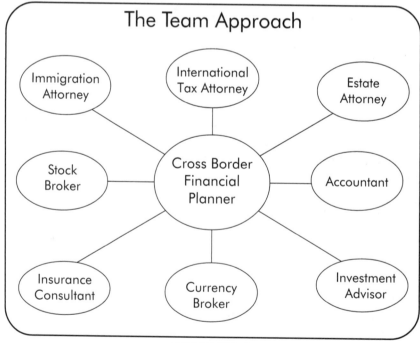

FIGURE 11.1

complete your plan in a timely and effective manner. Figure 11.1 displays one possible organizational chart for a typical cross-border financial planning team.

Not everyone is going to need all the advisors listed in Figure 11.1. Some may require more or less. For example, a winter visitor may only require a cross-border financial planner to find a U.S. estate attorney or provide investment advice for their assets, while someone moving to the United States might require the assistance of both a Canadian and an American accountant, in addition to all the other advisors. Even though Figure 11.1 indicates separate advisors for eight different services, several of them may be obtained from the same person or firm. For example, an experienced cross-border financial planner would likely have the necessary level of expertise in the areas of investment, tax and insurance, to eliminate the need for separate advisors in these areas.

LOCATING A GOOD CROSS-BORDER PROFESSIONAL

For those moving to the United States, it may be best to choose your financial planning team on the U.S. side of the border, particularly the cross-border financial planner who is your team leader. Once you have a team leader in place, they should be given the names of all your existing advisors, so they can assess the situation, and determine what other team members, if any, are required.

The best way to find the right cross-border financial planner to lead your team is by referral. If you have a friend or relative, or know of someone who has used a cross-border financial planner in a similar situation, ask them for a referral. If not, check with professional organizations such as the Canadian Association of Financial Planners (CAFP), in Toronto, or the Institute for Certified Financial Planners (ICFP), in Denver. These are the key professional associations that educate and license financial planning professionals in Canada and the United States. CAFP has local chapters in most major Canadian cities, and the ICFP in major American cities. They can be located by using the business listings in the telephone book.

The CAFP in Canada controls the use of Chartered Financial Planner (CFP) and Registered Financial Planner (RFP) professional designations in Canada. They are responsible for establishing standards and conducting courses and examinations for individuals wishing to make financial planning their career. To become an RFP, one must first pass the three year, six course CFP program, or an equivalent professional program, have at least two years experience in financial planning, write a very comprehensive examination, and be an active member of the CAFP. To maintain full membership in CAFP, the Registered Financial Planner must meet continuing educational requirements, have errors and omissions insurance, follow the association's code of ethics, and pay membership dues. We recommend that any Canadian planner you engage have a minimum RFP designation.

In 1996, several existing Canadian institutions, including the CAFP and Chartered Accountants, got together and agreed that the Certified Financial Planner, because of its international recognition, would be adopted as Canada's financial planning designation of choice. A Canadian CFP Board was set up as a licensee under the founding and current licenser, the U.S. IBCFP. The IBCFP, as noted below, licenses all U.S. CFPs and has licensed the use of the CFP designation in five separate countries. Canada's adoption of the Certified Financial Planner designation is a great start toward creating more uniform and higher standards, as well as better public confidence in and recognition of the financial planning profession. The RFP will still be the key designation of the CAFP for planners who can meet the special requirements over and above the basic CFP.

The ICFP in the United States works closely with the College for Financial Planning in Denver, establishing standards and requirements for those wishing to become Certified Financial Planners (CFP) in the U.S. Once the CFP educational and experience requirements have been met, there is a separate board, the IBCFP, that licenses individuals to use and maintain the CFP designation in the United States. A Canadian CFP cannot use their Canadian CFP designation in the United States, unless they have spent another two or three years completing the educational and licensing standards of the IBCFP. The College for Financial Planning has also developed a post graduate Masters of Science degree, in Financial Planning, for those who wish to further their studies in the United States. We recommend that any planner you engage in the United States have a CFP designation, and preferably hold a Masters Degree in Financial Planning, or possess the equivalent experience.

The cross-border financial planner selected to be your team leader should have a minimum RFP designation in Canada, or a CFP in the United States. Although rare, the ideal cross-border financial planner would have both a Canadian CFP/RFP and an American CFP, with financial planning experience in both countries.

When interviewing a prospective cross-border financial planner, do not hesitate to ask for references of other Canadians for whom they have successfully completed a cross-border financial plan, or developed a United States non-resident estate plan. Figure 11.2 provides a summary checklist to use, when you are interviewing potential candidates.

WHAT ABOUT USING AN ACCOUNTANT?

Many people are under the assumption that Charted Accountants (CA) in Canada, and Certified Public Accountants (CPA) in the United States, are qualified to do financial planning, whether it be for a cross-border situation or not. While CA's and CPA's are skilled in preparing financial statements and are generally qualified to give tax advice in their own country, problems arise when it comes to investment selection, insurance counselling and estate planning. Professional accountants, by training and

---

Choosing a Cross Border Financial Planner

Designations Held: CFP (Canada) ☐
                                    CFP (U.S.) ☐
                                    RFP (Canada) ☐
                                    Other ☐

Education: Degrees ☐
                                    Post Grad. ☐
                                    Other ☐

Experience: ___ yrs Canada; ___ yrs U.S.

Professional Association Member: CAFP ☐
                                    ICFP ☐
                                    Other ☐

Can Provide References: Yes ☐   No ☐
Provides Written Fee Agreement: Yes ☐   No ☐

FIGURE 11.2

temperament are neither investment counsellors or estate planners, nor do they generally have a good working knowledge of insurance matters.

Professional accountants make excellent cross-border financial planning team members, but because of their narrow focus, are not always suitable as team leaders, particularly in the area of plan implementation.

WHAT TO EXPECT FROM CROSS-BORDER FINANCIAL PLANNERS

Many people have never heard of cross-border financial planning. As a result, they have no solid concept of what it entails or what they should expect. By reading this far in this book, you should now have a pretty good grasp of the number and complexity of problems you'll encounter preparing any good cross-border financial plan. The sheer number of possibilities can be overwhelming.

A professional cross-border financial planner can very quickly sort through this myriad of rules and regulations, and very expeditiously tell you which rules apply to your situation, and how to incorporate them into your planning objectives. Expect a written plan which will address all of your concerns, along with a detailed analysis with specific recommendations. For a Canadian moving to the United States, the cross-border plan should:

- Tell you how each of your assets will be taxed by either country before and after exiting Canada.

- Provide a Canadian and U.S. net worth and cash flow statement.

- It should provide detailed tax projections on all the tax options available to you.

- Provide a risk management plan to safeguard you from any financial disasters in medical or liability expenses.

- Provide a complete cross-border estate plan, that looks after all your assets, whether they are located in Canada or the United States, and takes into account who your beneficiaries are, where they are located, and what are your personal desires.

- Provide a complete investment program taking into consideration your income needs, your tax bracket, your risk tolerance, the location and liquidity of your assets, and the size of your estate.

- Provide a retirement and benefit plan to maximize CPP, OAS and Social Security benefits, and ensure your income and assets are not depleted during you and your spouse's lifetimes.

Clear and easy to understand verbal and written communications are imperative from any cross-border financial planner you choose. Nothing is more frustrating than hiring a technically competent professional, and then not being able to understand their directions. Developing a good rapport with any professional you hire is critical, in order that a fair and open exchange of ideas takes place between you and your planner. If you do not feel comfortable with the person you are considering as your planner, either address it up front or seek another person for the job. The last section of this chapter, *The Consumer Bill Of Rights for Financial Planning,* provides more detailed information about what to look for, and how to work with a financial planning professional.

Don't be intimidated by any cross-border financial planner, no matter what their reputation or how expensive their fees. Remember he or she is only a person hired by you, to perform a service.

WHAT DOES A CROSS-BORDER FINANCIAL PLAN COST?

Financial planners are compensated by three key methods; by fee only, commission only, or by a combination of fee and commission. If you are dealing with a professional financial planner, they should provide you with a full written disclosure of fees and the method by which they are compensated for their services. If they do not, make certain you ask for the full disclosure or avoid using them all together.

Which method of compensation is best for the client is the subject of much debate. In cross-border financial planning, we have found that most clients prefer a fee only basis. They find it reassuring to know that they do not have to buy any financial products to get the necessary advice and that there are no hidden costs or motives. Since other cross-border financial planning team members such as accountants and attorneys are usually compensated by fees, there is usually a better rapport between the team members, if the financial planner/team leader is paid the same way.

Regardless of how you pay for your cross-border financial plan, a good general rule is, you get what you pay for. A budget plan could get you budget results, and may end up costing you thousands of dollars more in lost benefits, higher than necessary taxes and poor investment results. Cross-border financial planning is much too complex an endeavour, to take chances by cutting corners. Consider the fee you are paying as an investment and expect a return of and a return on your investment. You should find that a good cross-border plan has many more opportunities to provide you a much greater return on your investment than do basic planners on either side of the border.

You can expect a cross-border financial plan from an experienced fee only planner, to cost a minimum of $2,000 or more depending on the experience and credentials of the cross-border planner. Depending on the size and complexity of your estate, some plans can cost upwards to $50,000 and be worth every penny of it. A complete cross-border financial plan takes from 50 to 100 man-hours or more to complete, and can be comprised of 50 to 100 pages of analysis and recommendations.

Some cross-border financial planners will guarantee that their work will achieve tax or other savings in excess of their fees, or their fees will be partially or fully refundable. Ask for this type of a commitment from your chosen cross-border financial planner.

The highest paid member of the financial planning team should be the one that can save you the most money, and in most cases that will be the team leader/cross-border financial planner.

A CONSUMER BILL OF RIGHTS FOR FINANCIAL PLANNING*

As a consumer, you have a right to know. Whether you are just investigating your options, or have already engaged a financial planner, knowing your rights will help ensure that you have a successful working relationship with a competent, trustworthy financial planner, who can help you achieve financial independence.

Article I

You have the right to receive competent financial advice from a qualified, knowledgeable professional, with financial training, education and experience. Look for a person who has at least one of the following educational credentials:

- A designation in the U.S. such as Certified Financial Planner (CFP), Chartered Financial Consultant (ChFC), Certified Public Accountant (CPA), Personal Financial Specialist (PFS) or Chartered Financial Analyst (CFA). In Canada look for the Certified Financial Planner (CFP), Registered Financial (RFP) or Chartered Accountant (CA).

- A law degree (JD) in the U.S. or (LL.B. or LL.M.) in Canada.

- A bachelor's or graduate degree in financial planning, money management or related business from an accredited institution.

- Ask about a planner's continuing education activities. Ensure that financial planning is their primary — not part-time job.

Article II

You have the right to work with a planner who is registered as an investment advisor with the Securities and Exchange Commission (SEC), or an equivalent state registration.

It is important to know if the planner is registered in the U.S. as an investment advisor, because that is the minimum step a planner can take to comply with regulatory requirements. A planner must be licensed with the National Association of Securities Dealers (NASD) and appropriate state insurance departments to sell investments and insurance. In Canada, provincial registration and licensing is required to sell these products. A fee only planner does not need to be licensed to sell investment or insurance products since he has nothing to sell you but his services.

Article III

You have the right to receive references from the planner. Ask for names and phone numbers of clients whom the planner has worked with, as well as other financial service professionals. There are very strict rules in the U.S. on giving investment performance results, so referrals based on past investment results of an investment advisor are not legally available in most circumstances.

Article IV

You have the right to receive financial planning advice that is tailored to your financial needs. Look for a planner who prepares a financial plan based on the six-step process:

1. Information gathering.

2. Goal setting.

3. Identification of financial problems.

4. Preparation of written recommendations.

5. Implementation of recommendations.

6. Review and revision of the plan.

Ask to see a sample plan to ensure all six steps are included.

Article V

You have the right to receive a financial plan that is cost-effective. The cost to implement the plan should be within your financial means. You also have the right to obtain an estimate of the total costs involved in financial planning from your planner, and to know exactly what services the planner will provide.

Article VI

You have the right to receive from the planner, sufficient information on the risks and benefits of each investment recommended to implement the financial plan.

Make sure the planner explains everything thoroughly, including the "worst-case" and "middle of the road" investment scenarios. You should reject high pressure tactics, and be wary of promises of very high rates of return.

Article VII

You have the right to receive full disclosure about how the planner will be compensated. Inquire about the following four methods of compensation: fee-only, fee-and-commission, commission-only and salary. If you are concerned about conflict of interest in the planner's method of compensation, do not hesitate to ask the planner to explain.

Article VIII

You have the right to receive a full explanation about how the final plan is to be implemented. Ask whether the recommended investments come from one company, or from several different companies. Find out if the planner sells only those products on which they make a commission. And, ask whether the plan can be implemented by buying financial products from other sources.

Article IX

You have the right to receive assurances that the planner has the resources to serve your needs for the next year or more. Find out whether the planner has a network of related professionals — such as tax accountants, attorneys and/or brokers — to consult with you on any special needs that you may have. A good financial planner will pinpoint areas of potential financial difficulty (such as an out dated will) and relate the financial consequences back to you.

Article X

You have the right to receive regular written and verbal updates on the status of your financial plan, and the investments you have made to implement it.

Work with your planner to keep track of your investments on a regular basis. Make sure you understand how your investments are performing. If you are in doubt, keep asking questions.

*Reprinted with permission from the Consumer Bill of Rights for Financial Planning, published by the International Association for Financial Planning (IAFP), Atlanta, GA, 1-800-945-IAFP. You can also visit the IAFP website at http://www.IAFP.com

KEEPING IN TOUCH

One of the best ways we have found in keeping our readers current on changing issues and planning ideas is through our newsletter *The Sunbelt Canadian* published 3-4 times a year. We will be glad to mail *Border Guide* readers a sample copy of the Sunbelt Canadian for their examination at no charge. A subscription can obtained for $10.00 U.S. per year, if you wish to continue receiving them.

Numerous *Border Guide* readers have requested additional information regarding specific cross-border services, referrals to health insurance providers, or other professionals and for updates on matters that are pending at the time of publication. In response to these requests, we are making the toll free number of *Keats, Connelly & Associates, Inc.* available to readers.

You can use it to request information about the materials presented in this book. There will be no charge, provided of course, that you do not expect us to offer in depth planning advice.

We are a fee only planning firm who do not sell commission paying products of any kind. Providing free cross-border planning information would make it impossible for us to remain in business. So if you need specific advice or services we will be happy to forward our fee schedule. You can also get some free advice through our *Cross Border Q&A Column* in *The Sun Times of Canada,* provided you don't mind having your question appear in the paper. We would also appreciate hearing your comments and suggestions about the book, so we can make future editions of *The Border Guide* more informative and valuable.

You can call or write to us at:

Keats, Connelly & Associates, Inc.
4645 N. 32 Street, Suite A125
Phoenix, AZ 85018

Call toll-free from Canada or the United States:

1-800-678-5007

Our e-mail address is:

keatscon@sprynet.com

You can also visit the Keats, Connelly & Associates website at:

www.keatscon.com

Appendix

UNITED STATES

All of the following IRS publications are available free of charge at any IRS office, U.S. Embassy, or by calling toll free 1-800-TAX-FORM anywhere in U.S.

#54 Tax Guide for U.S. Citizens and Resident Aliens Abroad

This publication discusses tax situations for U.S. citizens and resident aliens who live and work abroad. In particular, it explains the rules for excluding income and deduction of certain housing costs. Answers are provided to the questions that taxpayers abroad most often ask.

Forms 2555, 1116 and 1040, Schedule SE (Form 1040).

#513 Tax Information for Visitors to the United States

This publication briefly reviews the general requirements of U.S. income tax laws for foreign visitors. You may have to file a U.S. tax return during your visit. Most visitors who come to the United States are not allowed to work in the United States. Check with the Immigration and Naturalization Service before you take a job.

Forms 1040C, 1040NR, 2063, and 1040-ES(NR).

#514 Foreign Tax Credit for Individuals

This publication may help you if you paid foreign income tax. You may be able to take a foreign tax credit or deduction to avoid the burden of double taxation. The publication explains which foreign taxes qualify, and how to figure your credit or deduction.

Form 1116

#515 Withholding of Tax on Non-Resident Aliens & Foreign Corp.

This publication provides information for withholding agents, who are required to withhold and report tax on payments to non-resident aliens and foreign corporations. Included are three tables listing U.S. tax treaties, and some of the treaty provisions that provide for certain types of income.

Forms 1042 and 1042S, 1001, 4224, 8233, 1078, 8288, 8288-A, 8288-B, 8804, 8805, and W-8, 8813, and 8709.

#519 U.S. Tax Guide for Aliens

This publication gives guidelines on determining your U.S. tax status, and calculating your U.S. tax. Resident aliens, like U.S. citizens, are generally taxed on income from all sources. Non-resident aliens are generally taxed only on income from U.S. sources. The income may be from investments, or from business activities, such as performing personal services in the United States. An income tax treaty may reduce the standard 30% tax rate on non-resident aliens' investment income. Their business income is taxed at the same graduated rates that apply to U.S. citizens or residents.

Aliens admitted to the United States with permanent immigrant visas are resident aliens, while temporary visitors generally are non-resident aliens. Aliens with other types of visas, may be resident aliens or non-resident aliens, depending on the length and nature of their stay.

Forms 1040, 1040C, 1040NR, 2063, and Schedule A (Form 1040).

#593 Tax Highlights for U.S. Citizens & Residents Going Abroad

This publication briefly reviews various U.S. tax provisions that apply to U.S. citizens or resident aliens, who live or work abroad and expect to receive income from foreign sources.

#1581 Foreign Investment in U.S. Real Property

This publication explains the tax consequences of a sale of U.S. property by a non-resident alien owner.

Form 1040NR, Schedule D (Form 1040), 4797, 6251, 8228, and 8288B.

FREE TAX PUBLICATIONS
AVAILABLE FROM REVENUE CANADA

- Capital Gains Tax Guide
- Pension and RRSP Tax Guide
- Tax Guide for Canadians Living in other Countries
- Tax Guide for Emigrants

REVENUE CANADA INTERPRETATION BULLETINS

IT-29	United States social security tax and benefits
IT-31	Foreign exchange profits and losses
IT-76R2	Exempt portion of pension when employee has been a non-resident
IT-161R3	Non-residents — Exemption from tax deductions at source on employment income
IT-163R2	Election by non-resident individuals on Certain Canadian source income
IT-171R	Non-resident individuals - Taxable income earned in Canada
IT-181	Foreign-tax credit — Foreign-tax carry over
IT-194	Foreign tax credit — Part-time residents
IT-221R2	Determination of an individual's residence status
IT-262R	Losses of non-residents and part-year residents
IT-270R2	Foreign tax credit
IT-298	Canada-U.S. Tax Convention — Number of days "present" in Canada
IT-370	Trusts - Capital property owned on December 31, 1971
IT-372R	Trusts - Flow-through of taxable dividends and interest to a beneficiary (1987 and prior taxation years)
IT-395R	Foreign tax credit — Foreign-source capital gains and losses
IT-399	Principal residence — Rental non-resident owner
IT-420R2	Non-residents — Income earned in Canada
IT-465R	Non-resident beneficiaries of trusts
IT-506	Foreign income taxes as a deduction from income
IT-520	Unused foreign tax credits — Carry forward and carry back

Appendix

PROVINCIAL AND STATE TAX RATES

B

1997 CANADIAN PROVINCIAL TAX RATES

In the wake of recent provincial budgets, new tax rates are now in effect. Here is what you pay if you are in the highest marginal income tax bracket, federal and provincial taxes combined. The table includes the provincial surtaxes that are applied to higher incomes in some provinces.

Newfoundland	53.3%
Prince Edward Island	50.3%
Nova Scotia	50.0%
New Brunswick	51.1%
Quebec	52.9%
Ontario	51.8%
Manitoba	50.4%
Saskatchewan	52.0%
Alberta	46.1%
British Columbia	54.2%
Northwest Territories	44.4%
Yukon	46.6%

SUNBELT STATE INDIVIDUAL INCOME TAXES

The following is a summary of state income taxes in popular Sunbelt states, to which individuals may be subject. It is not our intention to provide detailed information with respect to the taxation system of each particular state. The state income tax laws summarized herein are those in effect for the 1996 taxation year.

ARIZONA - INDIVIDUALS LIABLE TO TAXATION

Residents of Arizona are taxed on all income, whereas non-residents are taxed only on Arizona-source income. A non-resident's taxable income does not include income from intangibles (interest, dividends, etc.) unless derived from a trade or business carried on in the state.

Allowable Deductions:

Taxpayers are allowed the standard deduction. In lieu of the standard deduction, taxpayers can elect to use the revised itemized deductions. Deductions allowable under Arizona law are similar to those allowable for federal tax purposes. You must itemize on the federal return (Form 1040 only) to itemize for Arizona purposes.

Rates for Married Filing Jointly or Head of Household:

From	To	Tax Rate
0	20,000	3.0%
20,001	50,000	3.5%
50,001	100,000	4.2%
100,001	300,000	5.2%
300,001	Over	5.6%

All taxpayers are allowed credits for net taxes paid to other states or Canada.

CALIFORNIA - INDIVIDUALS LIABLE TO TAXATION

Residents of California are taxed on taxable income (AGI minus either the itemized or standard deduction). Non-residents and part-year residents are also taxed on taxable income, but their California tax liability is determined based on the ratio of California AGI to worldwide AGI, multiplied by the California tax on worldwide income. A non-resident's AGI does not include income from intangibles (interest, dividends, gains from sales of securities etc.) unless property has a business situs in the state.

California is a community property state. If a married couple is domiciled in California, one half of the community income earned by one spouse is legally owned by, and taxable to the other spouse.

Allowable Deductions:

Deductions allowable under California law are similar to the allowable for federal purposes, except that state income taxes are not deductible. Federal income tax is also not deductible. In lieu of itemized deductions, single and married taxpayers may claim standard deductions of $2,431 and $4,862 respectively.

Rates for Married Filing Jointly:

From	To	Tax Rate
$0	$9,444	1.0%
9,444	22,384	2.0%
22,384	35,324	4.0%
35,324	49,038	6.0%
49,038	61,974	8.0%
61,974	214,928	9.3%
214,928	429,858	10.0%
429,858	Over	11.0%

Rates for heads of households range from 1% on the first $9,445 to 11 percent on income over $292,550. For others, the rate on the first $4,722 is 1%, and on income over $214,929 it is 11 per cent. California has an 8.5 per cent alternative minimum tax (AMT). All taxpayers are allowed credit for taxes paid to other states.

FLORIDA - INDIVIDUALS LIABLE TO TAXATION

No individual income tax is imposed by Florida.

HAWAII - INDIVIDUALS LIABLE TO TAXATION

Residents of Hawaii are taxed on their gross income, whereas non-residents are taxed only on their Hawaii-source income. A non-resident's taxable income does not include income from intangibles (interest, dividends, etc.) unless derived from a trade or business carried on in the state.

Allowable Deductions:

Deductions allowable under Hawaii law are similar to those allowable for federal income tax purposes.

State income taxes are deductible but federal income taxes are not. Non-residents must allocate their itemized deductions based on the ratio of Hawaii AGI to total AGI.

Rates for Married Filing Jointly:

From	To	Tax Rate
0	3,000	2.00%
3,001	5,000	4.00%
5,001	7,000	6.00%
7,001	11,000	7.25%
11,001	21,000	8.00%
21,001	31,000	8.75%
31,001	41,000	9.50%
41,001	Over	10.00%

Special rate tables are provided for other filing statuses. Credit is given only to residents for taxes paid to other states.

Source: CCH State Tax Handbook

Canadian Embassy
501 Pennsylvania Avenue N.W.
Washington, D.C. 20001
1-800-456-0000

**Atlanta - Consulate
General of Canada**
1 CNN Center
Suite 400, South Tower
Atlanta, Georgia 30303-2705
(404)577-6810 1-800-467-0000

**Boston - Consulate
General of Canada**
3 Copley Place, Suite 400
Boston, MA 02116
1-800-468-0000

Buffalo - Canadian Consulate
1 Marine Midland Centre
Suite 3550
Buffalo, New York 14203-2884
1-800-469-0000

**Chicago - Consulate
General of Canada**
310 South Michigan Avenue,
Suite 1200
Chicago, Illinois 60604-4295
1-800-470-0000

**Cleveland - Canadian
Consulate**
Illuminating Building
55 Public Square
Cleveland, Ohio 44113-1983
1-800-471-0000

**Dallas - Consulate
General of Canada**
St. Paul Place, Suite 1700
750 North St. Paul
Dallas, Texas 75201
1-800-472-0000

**Detroit - Consulate
General of Canada**
600 Renaissance Center,
Suite 1100
Detroit, Michigan 48243-1704
1-800-473-0000

**Los Angeles - Consulate
General of Canada**
300 S. Grand Avenue
10th Floor, Suite 1000
Los Angeles, CA 90071
(213)687-7432 1-800-476-0000

Minneapolis - Consulate General of Canada
701 - 4th Avenue South
Suite 900
Minneapolis, Minnesota
55415-1899
1-800-474-0000

New York - Consulate General of Canada
1251 Avenue of the Americas
16th Floor
New York, New York 10020-1175
1-800-457-0000

Seattle - Consulate General of Canada
412 Plaza 600
Sixth and Stewart Streets
Seattle, Washington 98101-1286
1-800-477-0000

U.S. Embassy & Consulates in Canada

United States Embassy
100 Wellington Street
Ottawa, Ontario K1P 5T1
(613)238-4470

Calgary
615 McLeod Trail South
Suite 1000
Calgary, Alberta T2G 4T8
(403)266-8962

Halifax
Suite 910, Cogswell Tower
Halifax, Nova Scotia B3M 4G9
(902)429-2480

Montreal
1155 St. Alexandre St.
Montreal, Quebec H2Z 1Z2
(514)398-9695

P.O. Box 65 Postal Station
Desjardins
Montreal, Quebec H5B 1G1

U.S. Consulate General
U.S. Mailing Address
Box 847
Champlain, New York 12919

Ottawa
100 Wellington Street
Ottawa, Ontario K1P 5T1
(613)238-5335 Ext. 301

APO/FPO U.S. Mailing Address
P.O. Box 5000
Ogdensburg, New York
13669-0430

Quebec City
2 Place Terrasse Dufferin C.P.
939
Quebec City, Quebec G1R 4T9
(418)692-2095

APO/FPO U.S. Mailing Address
P.O. Box 1545
Champlain, New York 12919-1547

Toronto
360 University Avenue
Toronto, Ontario M5G 1S4
(416)595-0228

APO/FPO U.S. Mailing Address
P.O. Box 135
Lewiston, New York 14092-0135

Vancouver
1095 W. Pender Street
Vancouver, British Columbia
V6E 2M6
(604)685-4311

APO/FPO U.S. Mailing Address
Box 5002
Pt. Roberts, Washington 98281

CANADIAN NEWSPAPERS

The Canada News
P.O. Box 1729
Auburndale, Florida 33823-1729
(813)967-6450
1-800-535-6788

The Sun Times Of Canada
515 West Bay Street
Tampa, Florida 33606
1-800-253-4323

Canada This Week
244 N. Country Club Drive, Suite 103
Mesa, Arizona 85201

CANADIAN FINANCIAL NEWSLETTERS IN THE U.S.

Sunbelt Canadian
4645 N. 32 Street, Suite A-125
Phoenix, Arizona 85018
1-800-678-5007

The Brunton U.S. Non-Resident Taxletter
4710 N.W. Boca Raton Blvd, #101
Boca Raton, Florida 33431
(407)241-9991

**Nomad 100, Travellink,
Travellink Economy**
(Offered through Ingle Health
Insurance)
800 Bay Street
Toronto, ON M5S 3A9
(416)961-0666
1-800-387-4770

Vancouver .... (604)684-0666
Calgary .... (403)236-1666
Winnipeg .... (204)694-0666
Ottawa .... (613)564-0666
London.................. (519)434-0666
Mississauga .... (416)275-0666
Oshawa .... (416)436-0666
Montreal .... (514)281-0666
Halifax .... (902)422-0666
Hamilton.............. (416)336-2666
All Canada 1-800-387-4770
B.C. & Alberta 1-800-663-9710
Manitoba............. 1-800-465-9742
Quebec................. 1-800-363-6710
Atl. Can. 1-800-665-0666
All USA 1-800-525-0666
Fort Lauderdale .... (305)561-8666

**The Canadian Automobile
Association (CAA)**

Travel insurance may be purchased through any Canadian Automobile Association (CAA) office in Canada. Individual Clubs offer a variety of Out of Canada medical insurance products including Lloyd's of London, Away From Home, and CAARE. For the location of your nearest office consult the white pages of your local directory. Out of province health insurance products are available to both CAA members and non-members.

**Bank of Montreal
Travel Protection Plan**
(Underwritten by North American
Life Assurance)
Bank of Montreal
1-800-661-9060

**Canada Trust
Travel Medical Insurance**
Canada Trust
1-800-263-4008

**Canadian Grey Panthers
Deluxe Travel Insurance**
(Underwritten by Desjardins Life)
Canadian Grey Panthers
1-800-668-4545

CARP Emergency Out-of-Country Medical Insurance
(Underwritten by London and Midland Insurance Inc.)
Canadian Association
of Retired Persons
1-800-561-7831

CIBC 65+
Travel Medical Insurance
(Underwritten by CIBC Life Insurance Co.)
Canadian Imperial Bank of Commerce
Available at any CIBC branch office.

Good Holiday Travel Insurance
(Underwritten by a group from Lloyd's of London)
Good Holiday Travel Inc.
1-800-561-3323

Healthpac,
Healthpac Super Preferred
(Underwritten by North American Life Assurance)
National Auto League
1-800-387-2298

Hong Kong Bank of Canada
Travel Insurance
Hong Kong Bank of Canada
1-800-387-5290

Journeyman Emergency Travel Health Insurance
(Underwritten by Liberty Mutual)
Journeyman Travel Protection Inc.
1-800-661-8785

Maritime Medical
Travel Health Plan
(Underwritten by Maritime Medical Care Inc.)
Maritime Medical Care Inc.
1-902-468-9700

Medicare International
1-800-461-2100

Medipac Medical Emergency Travel Insurance/CSA
(Underwritten by Crown Life)
Canadian Snowbird Association
1-800-563-5104

Medical Insurance for Long-Term Travel
(Underwritten by North American Life Assurance)
Travel Insurance Specialists
1-800-563-0314

Medi-Select Advantage
(Underwritten by ETFS Insurance Program Management)
1-800-267-8834

Montreal Trust Insurance Plan
Montreal Trust
1-800-263-0261

Municipal Trust
Travel Insurance
(Underwritten by The Citadel General Assurance Co.)
Municipal Trust
1-800-465-5077

Ontario Blue Cross Gold Healthplus, Silver Standard
(Underwritten by Ontario Blue Cross)
Ontario Blue Cross
1-800-268-3763

Protection +
(Underwritten by The Citadel General Assurance Co.)
Golden Age Insurance
1-800-387-0339

Pru-Tection Travel Insurance
(Underwritten by Prudential Insurance Co. of America)
Prudential Insurance Co.
1-800-267-8747

Royal Bank Travel Healthprotector
(Underwritten by North American Life Assurance Company)
Royal Bank
1-800-565-3129

Scotia Medical Insurance Plan
(Underwritten by Zurich Indemnity Co. of Canada)
Scotiabank
1-800-263-0997

TD Greenplan Travel Insurance
The Toronto Dominion Bank
Available at any TD branch or at
1-800-263-7769

The Relax Plan
(Underwritten by Mutual of Omaha)

TravelX
1-800-450-5201
TIC Bon Voyage
(The Snowbirder)
(Underwritten by Soverign General Insurance)
Travel Insurance Coordinators Agencies Ltd.
Available through any travel agent.

Travelcare
(Underwritten by Voyageur)
Voyageur Insurance Co.
Available through any travel agent.

Travelgold
(Underwritten by Canadian Group Underwriters)
Travel Underwriters
1-800-663-5389

Travellers Choice Out-of-Canada Medical Insurance
(Underwritten by The Prudential Insurance Co. of America)
First World Underwriters
1-800-665-8553

Travelrite Travel Insurance
(Underwritten by Zurich Indemnity Co. of Canada)
Travelrite Travel Insurance
Available through any travel agent.

Canadian Club of the Desert
P.O. Box 284
Cathedral City, California 92235

**Canadian Social Club
of Greater Phoenix**
4645 N. 32 Street
Suite A-125
Phoenix, Arizona 85018
1-800-678-5007

**Canadian Association
of Orange County**
7444 Calico Trail
Orange, California 92669

**Canadian Society
of Southern California**
908 Shenandoah Street
Suite 203
Los Angeles, California 90035

**Canadian American Society
of the Southeastern
United States, Inc.**
6472 E. Church Street
Douglasville, Georgia 30134
(404)920-0617

Canadian Women's Club
2581 Rock Point Lane
Lithonia, Georgia 30058
(404)979-7675

**The Canadian Society
of St. Petersburg**
370 N. 53rd Ave. #574
St. Petersburg, Florida 33703

The Canadian Club of Ocala
19125 SW Glenco Place
Dunnellon, Florida 32630

**The Canadian Club
of Springhills**
11038 Upton Street
Springhills, Florida 34608

**Royal Canadian Legion,
Post 144, Pinellas County**
3663 N. 58th Avenue, #354
St. Petersburg, Florida 33714

Braden-Sarasota Canadian Club
603 W. 63rd Avenue, #T24
Bradenton, Florida 34207
(941)756-4576

Canadian Snowbirds Pensioners
455 Trinidad Lane
Largo, Florida 34640

**Canadian Franco-American
Club of St. Petersburg**
6012 N. 68th Avenue
Pinellas Park, Florida 33565
(813)546-0601

Daytona Beach Canadian Club
c/o Mr. W. J. Connor
City Island Recreation Hall
Daytona Beach, Florida 32016
(904)252-0132

Canadian Club of America, Inc.
352 Davis Road
Palm Springs, Florida 33461
(407)967-3054

Canadian Club
304 Boca Ciega Point Blvd. South
Madeira Beach, Florida 33461
(813)392-8675

Canadian Society
211 S.E. 1st Avenue
Hallandale, Florida 33009

Clearwater Canadian Club
465 Ulmerton Road
Largo, FL 33541
(813)584-1975

**Canadian Club
of Charlotte County**
19505 Quesada Ave. # 3913
Port Charlotte, FL 23948
(941)624-2073

Canadian Club of Colony Cove
115 Pompano Drive
Ellenton, Florida 34222

Canadian Snow Bird Assoc.
P.O. Box 969
Lakeland, Florida 33802
1-800-265-3200

**Newfoundland Society of
Florida**
11809 Lakewood Drive
Hudson, Florida 34669

Snowbirds of Citrus County
6828 N. Birch Terrace
Hernando, Florida 34442
(904)726-5219

Department of State
Public Inquiries Division
2401 E Street, NW
Washington, DC 20522-0113
202-663-1254

**American Immigration
Lawyers Association**
1400 Eye Street, NW, Suite 1200
Washington, DC 20005
202-371-9377

INS REGIONAL OFFICES

EASTERN

Federal Building
70 Kimball Avenue
South Burlington, VT 05403-6813
802-660-5000
Fax: 802-660-5114

SOUTHERN
P.O. Box 568808
7701 Stemmons Freeway
Dallas, TX 75356-8808
214-767-7012

NORTHERN

**Bishop Henry Whipple
Federal Building**
Room 401; Fort Snelling
Twin Cities, Minesota 55111
612-725-4450/3850/3855/3470

Detroit District
Federal Building
333 Mt. Elliott St.
Detroit, Michigan 48207-4381
313-226-3250

Seattle District
Immigration Building
815 Airport Way, South
Seattle, Washington 98134
206-553-0070

Spokane Suboffice
691 Federal Courthouse Bldg.
W. 920 Riverside
Spokane, Washington 99201
509-353-2129

Buffalo District
68 Court Street, Room #113
Buffalo, New York 14202
716-846-4741

Albany Suboffice
James T. Foley Federal
Courthouse
445 Broadway, Room #227
Albany, New York 12207
518-472-7140

New York District
Jacob Javits Federal Building
26 Federal Plaza
New York, New York 10278
212-264-5942

Dallas District
7701 N. Stemmons Highway
Dallas, Texas 75247
214-655-5384

El Paso District
1545 Hawkins, Ste. 167
El Paso, Texas 79925
214-767-7011
Fax: 214-767-7477

Houston District
509 North Belt (Main Floor)
Houston, Texas 77060
713-229-2912

San Antonio District
U.S. Federal Building
8940 Four Winds Drive
San Antonio, Texas 78239
210-871-7000

Miami District
7880 Biscayne Road
Room #100
Miami, Florida 33138
305-530-7664

Jacksonville Suboffice
400 West Bay St., Room G-18
P.O. Box 35039
Jacksonville, Florida 32202
904-232-2624; 232-2625

Tampa Suboffice
5509 West Gray St., Suite #113
Tampa, Florida 33609
813-228-2138

Honolulu District
595 Ala Moana Boulevard
Honolulu, Hawaii 96813
808-541-1388; 541-1389

Phoenix District
2035 North Central Avenue
Phoenix, Arizona 85004
602-379-3122

Tucson Suboffice
Federal Building
300 West Congress, Room #1-T
Tucson, Arizona 85701
602-670-4624

Las Vegas Suboffice
3373 Pepper Lane
Las Vegas, Nevada 89120
702-451-3597

Reno Suboffice
1351 Corporate Bvld.
Reno, Nevada 89502-7102
702-784-5186

Index